Forgotten Soldiers

History of the 4th Tennessee Volunteer Infantry Regiment
(USA)
1863-1865

Eddie M. Nikazy

Illustrations by
Chad Nikazy

HERITAGE BOOKS
2006

HERITAGE BOOKS
AN IMPRINT OF HERITAGE BOOKS, INC.

Books, CDs, and more—Worldwide

For our listing of thousands of titles see our website
at
www.heritagebooks.com

Published 2006 by
HERITAGE BOOKS, INC.
Publishing Division
65 East Main Street
Westminster, Maryland 21157-5026

Copyright © 1995 Eddie M. Nikazy

Other books by the author:

Abstracts of Death Records for Johnson County, Tennessee, 1908 to 1941

Carter County, Tennessee Deaths, 1926-1934

Carter County, Tennessee Record Abstracts: Death Records, 1908-1925

Carter County, Tennessee Record Abstracts: Marriages, 1871-1920

Forgotten Soldiers: History of the 2nd Tennessee Volunteer Infantry Regiment (USA,) 1861-1865

Greene County, Tennessee Death Record Abstracts, Volume 1: 1908-1918

Sullivan County, Tennessee Death Records, 1908-1918, Volume 1

Sullivan County, Tennessee Death Records, 1919-1925, Volume 2

Unicoi County, Tennessee Death Record Abstracts, 1908-1936

Washington County, Tennessee Death Record Abstracts, 1908-1916

All rights reserved. No part of this book may be reproduced or transmitted in any form or by any means, electronic or mechanical, including photocopying, recording or by any information storage and retrieval system without written permission from the author, except for the inclusion of brief quotations in a review.

International Standard Book Number: 978-0-7884-0241-2

To the memory of the
officers and men
of the 4th Tennessee Volunteer Infantry Regiment
this volume is respectfully dedicated in
admiration and fraternity

the author

Table of Contents

FOREWORD... IV

INTRODUCTION.. V

    Indroduction by Mr. Charles Sherrill, Tennessee State Library and Archives

1. **BACKGROUND**

    Tennessee Divided: 1

    The attitude of the State concerning secession, in particular the strong Union sentiment in East Tennessee; the secession vote; the Greeneville and Knoxville conventions.

    The Vote in East Tennessee: 2

    Results of the June 8, 1861, popular vote to separate from the Union.

    Chaos in the Mountains: 5

    Rebellion over severing relations with the Union; torture, punishment and executions for taking a stand for the Union; fleeing to safety in Kentucky.

    East Tennessee's Loyalty to the Union: 8

    Patriotism; competition with slave labor; many descendents of Revolutionary War participants.

Events Leading to the Formation of the 4th
Infantry Regiment Tennessee Volunteer Infantry: **10**

> General Grant's capture of Fort Donelson in February 1862; appointment of Andrew Johnson as Governor.

2.   A BRIEF HISTORY OF THE REGIMENT........... **11**

> Recruitment of men; movement to Kentucky; appointment of Daniel Stover to form the 4th Regiment; surrender of the Regiment at McMinnville; rebuilding the Regiment; movement into East Tennessee.

3.   ORGANIZATION OF THE REGIMENT.............. **23**

> Authority to form the Regiment; officer authorizations and troop requirements; brief biography of field and company officers; Major Reeves letter to President Lincoln; promotion of officers; the companies; general site map of key locations in the State of Tennessee.

4.   SOLDIERS OF THE REGIMENT...................... **48**

> Abstracts of service records on each of the officers and men of the 4th Regiment.

NAME INDEX... **149**

Foreword

The 4th Tennessee Volunteer Infantry Regiment was one of many Southern units which fought for the preservation of the Union during the Civil War. The 4th Regiment was composed primarily of men from the eastern mountains of Tennessee. Men for the regiment came from Greene, Grainger, Carter, Johnson, Cocke, and Washington counties. The majority of men enrolled in Greene County.

Because of the strong Union sentiment in East Tennessee, in July 1861, President Lincoln directed the formation of five East Tennessee infantry regiments and one cavalry regiment. Colonel Daniel Stover, the son-in-law of Andrew Johnson, formed the 4th Regiment in the spring of 1863. Colonel Stover, a prominent resident of Carter County, Tennessee, had been active in the anti-secessionist movement in East Tennessee. The capture of the entire 4th Regiment by Confederate forces under Major General Joseph Wheeler in October 1863, lead to the regiment being virtually ineffective for the remainder of the War.

This history attempts to chronicle the events in the record of the 4th Regiment as well as identify the men and officers of the regiment. Service records of 1,040 soldiers who were assigned to the regiment are summarized in this work. Twelve percent of the soldiers died while in the service. Casualties are summarized as follows: 85 men died of disease; 21 men died in prison; 13 men were killed and three died soon after release from Confederate prison.

Very little has been written about Southerners who fought for the Union in the Civil War. This book is based almost entirely on primary sources mainly those in the *Official Records* of the war and muster rolls in the National Archives.

Eddie M. Nikazy, Lieutenant Colonel, U.S. Army (retired)
Hendersonville, Tennessee

Introduction

With interest in Civil War history spreading among more people every day, it is encouraging to see new works such as Eddie Nikazy's "History of the Fourth Tennessee Volunteer Infantry Regiment" being published.

As a career military man himself and the author of several genealogical works, Colonel Nikazy has applied careful scholarship as the story unfolds. He has also given particular attention to personal details in the abstracts of individual soldiers' records. Because of this combination, this work is of great interest to both the historian and the genealogist.

Since many people today are unaware of the important role played by Union soldiers from Tennessee during the Civil War, this regimental history is of particular significance. The reader will come to understand how the officers and men of the Fourth Tennessee risked their lives just to enlist in the Union army, not to mention the risks they endured as soldiers during their service.

This story of the Fourth Tennessee and its men is by turns both amusing and tragic, but always interests and informs the reader. It deserves an important place among the ranks of other Tennessee history works.

Charles A. Sherrill
Tennessee State Library and Archives

Chapter 1

Background

Tennessee Divided:

East Tennessee, a region with a relatively small slave population, had always felt shortchanged in its dealings with the slave holding areas of Middle and West Tennessee. This feeling was evident as early as 1841 when Andrew Johnson introduced a resolution in the Legislature calling for separation of East Tennessee from the rest of the State and, in 1842; proposed apportioning the Congressional districts in the State according to the "voting population", without regard to three-fifths of Negro population. In this endeavor, Andrew Johnson had tried to augment the political power of East Tennessee.[1]

It was evident, at the outset of the Civil War, that the leadership in Nashville favored withdrawing from the Union and joining the Confederacy.[2] Governor Isham G. Harris blamed the northern agitation of the slavery questions for the current national crisis. He described President-elect Lincoln as an abolitionist.[3] Moreover, he called for a special session of the State General Assembly to meet on January 7, 1861 to approve holding a convention to determine the attitude of the State toward the Federal Government. It was believed that this convention would lead to secession from the Union as other southern states had. Accordingly, the State held an election on the 9th of February 1861 and the result was 68,000 votes against holding the convention; or, convincingly 68,000 against secession.

In April 1861, Governor Harris, a West Tennesseean, was asked to furnish two regiments of militia to serve in the Federal Army. The governor replied: "Tennessee will not send a single man for the purposes of coercion, but 50,000, if needed to defend our rights and rights of our southern brothers."[4]

---

[1] George C. Rable, "Andrew Johnson in the Secession Crisis," Tennessee Historical Quarterly, Winter 1973, 346. Hereafter Cited, Rable, *Andrew Johnson*.
[2] Marlon D. Crow, Tennessee Blue Book, Kingsport Press, Inc., Kingsport, TN, 1983, 294
[3] Rable, *Andrew Johnson*, 346
[4] Jesse Burt, Your Tennessee, Steck-Vaughn Co., Austin, Texas, 1979, 180.

4th Tennessee Volunteer Infantry Regiment (USA)

The sentiment in the middle and western parts of the state was more closely identified with the cotton growing states, particularly that of engaging in cotton farming and owning large numbers of slaves.

Meanwhile, Tennessee went through the motions of aligning itself with the Confederacy. Troops were being organized and preparations for war were being made in great haste. Although, in May 1861, an act was passed calling for an election on 8 June to let the people decide on separation or no separation and representation or no representation in the Confederate Congress. Governor Harris, who was a staunch secessionist and not one to be stopped by legal technicalities, had begun negotiations with Confederate Secretary of War Leroy P. Walker to send three regiments of Tennessee troops to Virginia. In the spring of 1861, Confederate troops, from other southern states, were deployed in Tennessee with the enthusiastic support of state government.[5] To East Tennesseans it looked as if the decision had already been made to withdraw from the Union since an alliance appeared to have already been formed with the Confederacy. To East Tennesseans, The election appeared as simply a formality to give the appearance of legal withdrawal. This event made little difference to the firm stand already made by a convincing majority of the people of East Tennessee except to possibly strengthen their stand for the Union.

The County Vote in East Tennessee:

The result of the East Tennessee vote to separate from the Union was as follows:[6]

County:	% No	County:	% No
Johnson	88	Knox	72
Blount	81	Monroe	41
Carter	94	McMinn	56
Roane	78	Anderson	93
Campbell	94	Meigs	36
Hamilton	60	Scott	97
Morgan	94	Greene	78
Sullivan	28	Washington	59
Hawkins	62	Rhea	36
Hancock	69	Cocke	70
Sevier	96	Jefferson	77
Grainger	72	Claiborne	83
Polk	30	Bradley	73

---

[5] Rable, *Andrew Johnson*, 349.
[6] Anne H. Hopkins, Studies in Tennessee Politics, "Tennessee Votes 1799 - 1976", University of Tennessee, 1987, 43

Background

Graphically the vote in East Tennessee was as follows: *

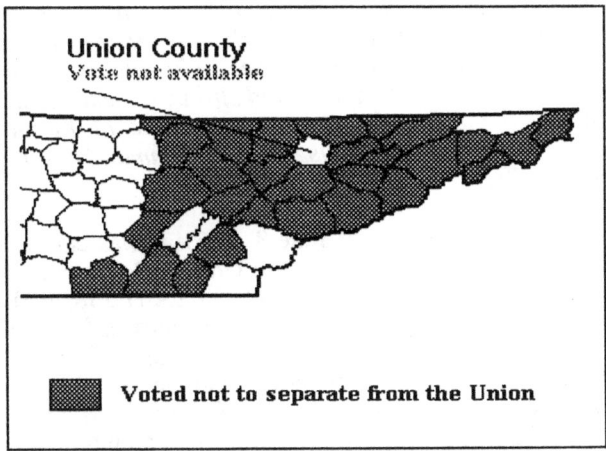

Union County
Vote not available

Voted not to separate from the Union

* Source: Tennessee Votes: 1799-1976, Anne H. Hopkins and William Lyons, Bureau of Public Administration, University of Tennessee, Knoxville, 1978

The leaders of the Union element in East Tennessee consisted of the very best talent. They had not been idle. It was clear however that they would not be able to influence remaining with the Union without aid from the Federal Government. They proceeded bravely and openly defied what was perceived as an unlawful procedure of the State Government. They even advocated severing from the state's middle and western divisions and forming a new state.[7]

An May 30, 1861, about 500 delegates, representing nearly every East Tennessee county, met in Knoxville to review resolutions of a committee representing each of the counties. Daniel Stover, who was later appointed to organize the Fourth Tennessee Volunteer Infantry Regiment (USA), was a delegate from Carter County. Some of the resolutions were as follows:

"The evil which afflict our beloved country, in our opinion, is the legitimate result of the ruinous and heretical doctrine of secession; that the people of East Tennessee have ever been, and we believe

---

[7]Samuel W. Scott and Samuel P. Angel, History of the Thirteenth Regiment, Tennessee Volunteer Cavalry, P.W. Zeigler & Co., Philadelphia, 1903, 35. Hereafter Cited, Scott, Thirteenth Regiment.

are still opposed to it by a very large majority ... That the Legislature of the State, without having first obtained the consent of the people, had no authority to enter into a "military league" with the Confederate States against the Federal Government, and by doing so put the State of Tennessee in hostile array against the government of which it then was, and still is, a member.... That, the position which the people of our sister State of Kentucky have assumed in this momentous crisis commands our highest admiration. Their interests are our interests."

Immediately after the election of June 8, 1861, it was claimed that the State had voted for separation from the Union. Records indicate that the separationists won by a vote of 108,511 to 47,238, with most of the Unionist votes coming from East Tennessee.[8] William G. Brownlow, a leading East Tennessee journalist, charged that the people of Middle and West Tennessee had been "tricked, cheated, duped, swindled, lied and betrayed out of their rights and liberties." The presence of 20,000 Confederate troops had an intimidating effect. Some of these soldiers from other southern states were even permitted to vote in the election.[9] Judge T.A.R. Nelson of Jonesboro, Tennessee, issued a call for the convention to meet in Greeneville on June 17, 1861. The convention remained in session several days and issued a declaration of grievances. The following grievances were later circulated in East Tennessee:

"The elections on the 8th of June were free, with few exceptions, but in Middle and West Tennessee, no speeches or discussion in favor of the Union were permitted; ballots were numbered in such a manner to permit exposing the Union voter; disunionists, in many places, had charge of the polls; before a detailed report of the voting was published and even before it was possible to ascertain the result, it was announced that separation had been carried from between 50,000 and 75,000 votes."

Further, the convention declared:

"No effort has been spared to deter the Union men of East Tennessee from the expression of their free thoughts; The penalties of treason have been threatened against them, and murder and assassination have been openly encouraged by leading secession journals; As secession has thus been intolerant and overbearing while in a minority in East Tennessee, nothing better can

---

[8]Ibid, 43.
[9]Rable, *Andrew Johnson*, 351-352.

Background

be expected of the pretended majority than wild, unconstitutional and oppressive legislation, an utter contempt and disregard of law, a determination to force every Union man in the State to swear to support the constitution he abhors, to yield his money and property to aid in a cause he detests, and to become the object of scorn and derision as well as the victim of intolerable and relentless oppression."

The convention then resolved:

"That we earnestly desire the restoration of peace to our whole country, and that our section of the State of Tennessee should not be involved in the civil war."

On June 24, 1861, Governor Harris issued a proclamation dissolving the relations of the State of Tennessee with the Federal Government. Technically, Tennessee did not secede from the Union; but declared independence, and joined the Confederacy. From May 7th through June 23, Tennessee had been a member of both the Confederate and Union governments. The Union leaders of East Tennessee ignored the proclamation of Governor Harris and proceeded to hold elections for representatives to the Congress of the United States. State authorities, enraged by the actions of the Union leaders, began to seek revenge. Judge Nelson, who had been elected to the Federal Congress, was sent to Richmond, Virginia as a political prisoner. W. G. Brownlow, who had wielded influence in his newspaper editorials, was threatened with indictment for treason.[10] He was thrown in jail in Knoxville where he remained for almost a month. Conditions in the jail were inhumane. Brownlow stated that at the time he was in jail, the prisoners numbered about one hundred and fifty; that on the lower floor where he was kept, there was not room for all to lie down at one time; prisoners had to stand on their feet and rest alternately; that the only article of furniture in the building was a dirty wooden bucket, from which they drank water with a tin cup.[11]

Chaos in the Mountains:

People who had taken a stand for either the Union or Confederacy were often treated violently by their neighbors or by lawless bands. The few adventurous Union people who assailed the new power

---

[10] Scott, Thirteenth Regiment, 57
[11] Humes, Thomas William, S.T.D., The Loyal Mountaineers of Tennessee, Reprint Company, Publishers, Spartainburg, S.C., 1974, 147-148

brought the wrath of the Confederate Government on the whole population. The sentiment of the new government toward Union sympathizers is evident in the following letter, dated November 20th, which Colonel Wood in Knoxville wrote to J. P. Benjamin, Confederate, Secretary of War:[12]

> "The rebellion in East Tennessee has been put down in some of the counties, and will be effectively suppressed in less than two weeks in all counties. Their camps in Sevier and Hamilton counties have been broken up and a large number of them made prisoners. Some are confined in this place and others sent to Nashville. In a former communication, I inquired of the Department what I should do. It is a mere farce to arrest them and turn them over to the courts. Instead of having the desired effect to intimidate them, it really gives encouragement and emboldens them in their traitorous conduct. Patterson, the son-in-law of Andrew Johnson, State Senator Pickens and several other members of the Legislature, besides others of influence and distinction in their counties, -- these men have encouraged the rebellion, but have so managed as not to be found in arms. Nevertheless all their actions and words have been unfriendly to the Government of the Confederate States. Their wrath and influence have been exerted in favor of the Lincoln Government and they are the parties most to blame.
>
> They really deserve the gallows, and if consistent with the laws, ought speedily to receive their deserts. But there is such a spirit of conciliation in the South, and especially here, that I have no idea that one of them will receive such a sentence at the hands of any jury. I have been here at this station for three months, half the time in command of this Post; and I have had a good opportunity of learning the feeling pervading this country. It is hostile to the Confederate Government. They will take the oath of allegiance with no intention to observe it. They are the slaves of Johnson and Maynard and never intend to be otherwise. When arrested, they suddenly become very submissive and declare they are for peace and not supporters of the Lincoln Government, but yet claim to be Union men. At one time while our forces were at Knoxville, they gave it out that a great change had taken place in East Tennessee and that the people were becoming loyal.
>
> At the withdrawal of the army from here to Cumberland Gap and the first intimation of the approach of the Lincoln army, they were in arms and scarcely a man but was ready to join it and make war

---

[12]Ibid, 139-140

Background 7

upon us. The prisoners we have, all tell us that they had every assurance that the enemy was already in the State and would join them in a few days. I have requested at least that the prisoners I have taken be held, if not as traitors, as prisoners of war. To convict them before a court is next to an impossibility. But if they are kept in prison for six months it will have a good effect. The bridge-burners and spies ought to be tried at once."

Secretary Benjamin issued the following instructions concerning the East Tennessee prisoners:[13]

War Department Richmond, November 25, 1861

Colonel Wood, your report on the 20th is received, and I now proceed to give your the desired instruction in relation to the prisoners of war taken by you among the traitors of East Tennessee.

First: All such as can be identified in having been engaged in bridge-burning are to be tried summarily by drum-head court-martial, and, if found guilty, executed on the spot by hanging. It would be well to leave their bodies hanging in the vicinity of the burned bridges.

Second: All such as have not been so engaged are to be treated as prisoners of war, and sent with an armed guard to Tuscaloosa, Alabama, there to be kept imprisoned at the depot selected by the Government for prisoners of war.

Whenever you can discover that arms are concentrated by these traitors, you will send out detachments, search for and seize the arms. In no case is one of the men, known to have been up in arms against the Government to be released on any pledge or oath of allegiance. The time for such measures is past. They are all to be held as prisoners of war, and held in jail until the end of the war. Such as come in voluntarily, take the oath of allegiance and surrender their arms, are alone to be treated with leniency.

Your vigilant execution of these orders is earnestly urged by the Government."

J.P Benjamin
Secretary of War

---

[13] Ibid, 140.

4th Tennessee Volunteer Infantry Regiment (USA)

P.S. "Judge Patterson, Andy Johnson's son-in-law, Colonel Pickens and other ring-leaders of the same class, must be sent at once to Tuscaloosa to jail as prisoners of war."

Arraignment of prisoners before judges sometimes rested on no foundation whatever. Reverend W. H. Duncan, a Methodist minister, of McMinn County, was charged in the indictment with having prayed for the United States Government. While still recovering from sickness with fever, the minister, a large man of two hundred and eighty pounds, was forced to walk nine miles, leading his horse, while being denounced, cursed and threatened with bayonets by his captors. With blistered feet, he gave out at seven miles. He was refused water or anything to eat from the time he was taken prisoner on Friday until Sunday. Evidence showed that he had done the praying before Tennessee had seceded from the Union.[14]

In the months to come, savagery and bloodshed prevailed in the mountains of East Tennessee. Homes and farms of secessionists were not safe from guerrilla forces which had been formed. Soldier's wives, children and property left behind were especially vulnerable. More often than not, it was the Unionists who were the victims. Johnson and Carter counties, on the North Carolina border, serve as an example of the extreme brutality in the mountain warfare and success of anti-Unionist gangs. During 1863 and 1864, four guerrilla bands were on the loose in these counties, killing almost without discrimination and ravaging Union lands. A man named Whicher led a gang into Carter County and killed nine alleged Unionists before leaving. One of the most extreme anti-Unionist guerrillas was Bill Parker who led a gang into Johnson County and killed eleven men, four over sixty years of age. He drove large numbers of women and children from the county, burned homes and barns and killed livestock. Other irregular Rebel leaders, B.H. Duvall and R.C. Bozen, brought a reign of terror to Carter and Johnson counties. Bozen was noted for torturing and killing Unionists he captured.[15]

All those who had taken an active part for the Union were compelled to seek safety in hiding out, or crossing the mountains to seek protection with the Federal Army which was forming in Kentucky.[16]

---

[14]Ibid, 144.
[15]Paludan, Philip Shaw, Victims: a True Story of the Civil War, University of Tennessee Press, Knoxville, TN, 1981, 78.
[16]Daniel Ellis, Thrilling Adventures of Daniel Ellis, Overmountain Press, Johnson City, TN., 1989, 36-44.

Background 9

East Tennessee's Loyalty to the Union:

Many reasons have been given for the loyalty of East Tennesseans to the Federal Government. One logical reason may be that the region is not suitable for growing cotton, rice, and tobacco as in other parts of the South, hence slave labor was not widely employed. The people of East Tennessee were poor and had to earn their living by their own labor. They also recognized that slave labor was competing with them and lessening their wages and their chances for employment. They could see that fighting for slavery was only insuring their own poverty. To them slavery was not an issue unless it was its abolishment. This is not meant to imply that East Tennessee favored abolition. Most believed that the institution of slavery was a principal ingredient of their political and social system. Many believed that the Negro slave was better off than the African at home. The people of mountainous East Tennessee were endowed with a spirit of patriotism and loyalty to country and have been shown to be the first to volunteer when threatened by foreign or domestic foes. History shows that this region of East Tennessee and the mountain sections of adjoining states, have always furnished more than their proportion of volunteers in all the wars which the country has been engaged.

The people of East Tennessee had a special reverence for the "Old Flag." They remembered that its was for the whole country that their fathers fought. Moreover, people of the region had a rich tradition of having had ancestors who had fought for the independence of the United States in the Revolutionary War. Even those who turned away from the old flag must have done so with feeling of sorrow and regret. It is estimated that East Tennessee furnished between 30,000 and 40,000 troops to the Federal army.[17] Much speculation has been offered about the effect the loyalty of East Tennessee had to the Union cause. More than 30,000 East Tennesseans fought for the Union. Also, 10,000 Confederate soldiers were needed to keep the Union people of East Tennessee in subjection and guard the mountain passes. In March 1862, Major General E. Kirby Smith, the Confederate Commander at Knoxville, reported that Confederate troops from East Tennessee could not be relied on and that even the officers were not free from suspicion of having more fidelity to the Federal than to the Confederate service. General Smith concluded that he could not defend East Tennessee effectively unless the East Tennessee Confederate soldiers were replaced. Had these people thrown their support to the Confederacy, we would have seen a vast improvement in the Confederate military capability.

---

[17] Scott, Thirteenth Regiment, 50.

4th Tennessee Volunteer Infantry Regiment (USA)

East Tennesseans turned the tide of battle at King's Mountain in the Revolutionary War. Descendants of these men again stepped into the ranks of the nation during the Civil War and gave it victory.

Events leading to the formation of the 4th Regiment Tennessee Volunteer Infantry:

General Grant broke the Confederate line in February 1862 when he captured Fort Donelson on the Cumberland River and declared martial law. The Confederate government of Tennessee was short lived, lasting only six months. It held its last session in Nashville on 15 February 1862, and on the following day, Governor Harris issued a call for the legislature to reconvene in Memphis.[18]

On March 3, 1862, President Lincoln appointed former governor Andrew Johnson as Military Governor of the State, with the rank of Brigadier-General. Johnson was convinced that most Tennesseeans had been led into secession by false persuasions of the leaders. Almost revengefully, he turned the tide in Tennessee by attempting to induce citizens to take the oath of allegiance to the Union. City and county offices were declared vacant when officeholders refused to take the oath; prominent citizens who refused to take the oath were imprisoned; and private property of secessionists was confiscated.[19] Before all of Governor Johnson's programs could be put in place, he departed for Washington, D. C. to assume duties of vice-president of the United States.

William G. Brownlow's vengeance then came. He became governor, succeeding Andrew Johnson. Following are some of Brownlow's harsh measures. He offered a $5,000 reward for the capture of former Governor Harris who had fled to Mexico. Discharged Union soldiers were permitted to carry firearms; former Confederate soldiers could not. Anyone who criticized the Brownlow regime or the federal government faced extreme punishment.[20]

---

[18] Crow, Tennessee Blue Book, 295.
[19] Ibid., 237.
[20] Burt, Your Tennessee, 191.

Chapter 2

A Brief History of the Regiment

The 4th Tennessee Volunteer Infantry Regiment, USA, was mentioned in Captain Daniel Ellis' book, *Thrilling Adventures of Daniel Ellis*. This book, written shortly after the Civil War, gave the writers account of his efforts to guide Union sympathizers from East Tennessee to safety in Kentucky. Daniel Ellis mentioned that on the night of November 14, 1862, he started on his first trip to Kentucky with Colonel James Grayson, of Johnson County, Tennessee, and a number of men from Carter and Johnson Counties. Captain Ellis specifically mentioned that Colonel James W. M. Grayson had recruited about one hundred men for the 4th Regiment of Tennessee Infantry which he was taking to Kentucky on the night of November 14th.[21] Captain Ellis felt so strongly for the Union cause that he served as a guide without compensation. Daniel Ellis later served as a captain in the 13th Tennessee Volunteer Cavalry (USA). Several years later, when he was almost in financial ruin, the government paid him $3050 for his three years of hazardous services as a guide.

The book, *Tennesseeans in the Civil War,* published in 1964 by the Tennessee Civil War Centennial Commission, states that the 4th Tennessee Regiment was recruited in East Tennessee in the spring of 1863 and that seven companies were mustered in at Nashville on June 15, 1863.

Tennesseans in the Civil War states that according to a report of the Tennessee Adjutant General, James P. Brownlow, Daniel Stover, the son-in-law of Andrew Johnson, was commissioned as colonel, on February 29, 1862, to command the 4th Tennessee Infantry Regiment. He recruited his regiment in the spring of 1863 from East Tennessee. Daniel Stover's service record file contains a letter from Edwin M. Stanton, Secretary of War, dated February 27th 1862. The content of the letter is quoted as follows:

---

[21]Ellis, Thrilling Adventures, 65.

4th Tennessee Volunteer Infantry Regiment (USA)

Colonel
Daniel Stover
Tennessee Volunteers

War Department
Washington, February 27th, 1862

Sir

You are hereby informed that the President of the United States has appointed you Colonel of the regiment of volunteers which you are authorized to raise in Tennessee, in the service of the United States, to rank as such from the 27th day of February, one thousand eight hundred and sixty two. Should the Senate at their next session, advise and consent thereto, you will be commissioned accordingly.

Immediately on receipt hereof, please communicate to this Department through the Adjutant General's Office, your acceptance or non-acceptance of said appointment; and with your letter of acceptance returned to the Adjutant General of the Army the oath herewith enclosed properly filled out, subscribed and attested, reporting at the same time your age, residence, when appointed, and the state in which you were born.

Should you accept, you will at once report, by letter, for your orders to

Edwin M. Stanton
Secretary of War

Men were brought out of the Confederate lines by guides or pilots who volunteered to lead men to Kentucky to join the Union army. These guides were residents of the area who usually knew the safest and easiest routes to take. They knew sympathetic residents along the way and were sometimes able to obtain emergency provisions. The marches to safety in Kentucky were made at night. The men usually hid in caves or forests during the day to avoid detection by Confederate conscript officers.

The 4th Tennessee Infantry Regiment was assembled in Louisville, Kentucky. On the 4th of May 1863, Colonel Stover reported that he had 505 men, in Kentucky, for the 4th Regiment. He reported that he would have had 519 but that 6 had died, 7 had deserted and 2 were

A Brief History of the Regiment

captured while on recruiting service in East Tennessee. On May 22, 1863, the unit was ordered to move to Lebanon, Tennessee. On 1 July 1863, Colonel Stover reported that his Regiment was located to the right of the penitentiary outside Nashville. On August 31, 1863 the unit, with seven companies, was reported at Camp Spears in Nashville.

Colonel Stover became seriously ill after reporting to Nashville and was never able to command the 4th Regiment in the field. He died in Nashville in 1864.

On September 9, 1863, the 4th Regiment left Nashville for McMinnville under the command of Major Michael. L. Patterson. It arrived at McMinnville on September 15th, 1863. On October 3, 1863, it was surrounded and captured by Confederate forces under Major General Joseph Wheeler.

Major Patterson prepared a detailed account of events leading up to the surrender of his command at McMinnville. The correspondence explaining his misfortune at McMinnville to his military superiors is quoted below:[22]

NASHVILLE, TENN
October 12, 1863

GENERAL: I have the honor to submit the following report relative to the surrender of the post at McMinnville, Tennessee: In compliance with an order issued by Major General G. Grainger, I moved my command from Nashville, Tennessee, on the 9th day of September and arrived at McMinnville on Tuesday, the 15th of September; reported to Major A.B. Brackett, Fifth Iowa Cavalry, then in command of the post. On Saturday, the 26th September, Major Brackett left the post under orders, as I understand, placing myself in command of the post.

Immediately upon assuming command of the post I made a thorough examination of the town and means of defense in case of an attack.

I found several long rifle-pits on the east and southwest sides of the town, at about the distance of half a mile from the center or

---

[22]Fred Ainsworth and Joseph Kirkley, The War of Rebellion, a Compilation of the Official Records of Union and Confederate Armies, Government Printing Office, Washington, D.C., 1900, Series I, Volume 30., 707. Hereafter Cited, Ainsworth, War of Rebellion.

courthouse. They undoubtedly had been prepared for a large force, brigade or division. I only having about 400 effective men - infantry - I could not see that they would be of any use to me, or that I could use them in any way to my advantage whatever, with so small a force, as I had seven different roads to picket, the quartermaster's and commissary stores to guard, as well as a provost guard, which, in all took 130 men daily on duty, also a railroad bridge with a guard of 1 commissioned officer, 1 sergeant, and 15 men.

Immediately upon assuming command of the post, I sent a telegram to Governor Johnson, asking him to send me the Third Tennessee Cavalry. He replied that he could not spare them from Nashville.

On the 28th instant, I telegraphed to the commander of the post at Murfreesboro to send me 200 cavalry. He replied he had no cavalry to send.

On the 30th September or October 1, I telegraphed Brigadier General R.S. Granger for cavalry, and he replied that he had no cavalry to send, and for me to impress horses and mount men for scouts, being all the time threatened by guerrillas.

On the 2d of October, I issued an order and impressed between 40 and 50 horses, mounted a like number of men, and sent out two scouting parties of 20 men each, one under Lieutenant Farnsworth, on the Sparta Road, to go 6 or 7 miles, and the other, under Lieutenant Allen, on the Pikeville road, to go the same distance. Both lieutenants reported to me at about 11 p.m. that they had executed their orders, and that there was no enemy in front.

However, in the meantime, a large number of citizens came into McMinnville, Tennessee, direct from Sequatchie Valley, among whom was Judge John C. Gaut, of Cleveland, Tennessee, who reported the enemy to have crossed the Tennessee River above Washington, from 5,000 to 10,000, and moving down the valley. Considering the reports of these citizens reliable, I concluded to burn the quartermaster's and commissary stores, and evacuate the place on the morning of the 3d.

About sundown on the same evening, Captain Blackburn, with Company A, Stokes' Cavalry, came in and reported he had just come off the road from Tracy City to McMinnville, and stated positively that there were no enemy in force this side of the

A Brief History of the Regiment   15

Tennessee River. Upon being interrogated, he stated the same again and again.

Again, at 8 o'clock in the evening, Judge Gaut came into my room and I sent for Captain Blackburn and Lieutenant Heath. Captain Blackburn could not come, but sent Lieutenant Heath. Judge Gaut on one side of the table stating that the rebels had crossed the Tennessee River in force, Lieutenant Heath on the other side stating most positively that there was no enemy in force this side of the Tennessee River, and offered to pledge his right arm that there was none.

Deeming it most proper to take the statement of a commissioned officer in preference to that of citizens, I came to the conclusion to not burn the stores, but remain quiet and await further information.

On the 29th or 30th instant, I ascertained how many men Surgeon St J.W. Mintzer, in charge of general hospital, had for duty. I had what old arms were at the post repaired and armed 50 of them and gave them ammunition, and on the morning of the fight sent a commissioned officer to take charge of them.

On the morning of the 3d, at 8 o'clock, I sent out a scout, under Lieutenant Farnsworth, of 24 men on the Pikeville Road, with orders to go 10 or 12 miles. Himself and command were cut off and failed to give me any information.

At 10:30 o'clock I ordered out Lieutenant Allen with 20 men on the same road; he had passed my pickets between one-fourth and one-half mile, and reported the enemy in force. I immediately drew up my command, consisting of about 270 men, together with 50 convalescents whom I had armed; this 50 men were ordered to guard two roads leading by the hospital to the center of the town. Companies B, D, and G were thrown to the immediate front in the suburbs of town, Company C ordered to go to the Sparta road, entering town. Companies E and A were placed so as to guard the Manchester and Woodbury roads, and also held in reserve, in case the enemy should succeed in making their way into the center of town, to hold them in check until the whole force could be rallied together, when it was my intention to put the men in houses and fight in that position.

While in this position we were attacked by their advance, and skirmished with them one and a quarter hours. While skirmishing they moved up a heavy force to the right and left of the town,

4th Tennessee Volunteer Infantry Regiment (USA)

surrounding us, and put their artillery in position (eight pieces). They then sent in a flag of truce, demanding verbally the immediate and unconditional surrender of the place, which I refused and sent the flag back, stating that I would not surrender until the demand was properly made, and not then until I was compelled to do so. In about half an hour the flag again returned borne by Colonel Hodge, commanding Kentucky brigade, with an order or demand in writing for the immediate and unconditional surrender of the post with the entire garrison. I herewith give a copy of the order.

HQTRS IN THE FIELD, OF MAJOR-GENERAL FORREST'S
FORCES OF CAVALRY AND ARTILLERY
October 3, 1863

*Maj. M.L. PATTERSON
Commanding at McMinnville*

MAJOR: I have the honor of stating to you that we are here in force with four divisions of cavalry and artillery, and demand the immediate and unconditional surrender of the post of McMinnville, with the entire garrison.
Respectfully, yours, &c.,

JOS. WHEELER
Major-General, C.S. Army

Seeing that I was surrounded by a greatly-superior force, and the enemy's artillery in position, after a conference with a portion of my officers, all deeming it useless to contend longer with so large a force, and in order to save life and the effusion of blood, I surrendered the post, asking the protection of my officers and men, both in person and private property. The same being granted, we made a formal surrender to Major-General Wheeler, C.S. Army. I lost 7 men killed and 31 wounded and missing. The enemy admit a loss of 23 killed and about twice that number wounded.

From a personal examination of the defenses around and about McMinnville, I could not see in what way the rifle-pits would be of any service to me with so small a force, neither could I see in what way I could improve the defenses of the place.

I have managed this thing the best of my ability, and have done what I believe to be the best under existing circumstances.

A Brief History of the Regiment 17

I am, general, very respectfully, your obedient servant.

M.L. PATTERSON
Major Fourth Tennessee Infantry

Major Patterson's response to Major-General Wheeler's demand for surrender was as follows:[23]

MCMINNVILLE, TENN., October 4, 1863

I hereby unconditionally surrender all the garrison at this post to Major-General Wheeler, C.S. Army.

It is agreed between us that the entire force shall be paraded and marched out of the garrison by our own officers, they being protected in their private property as they have about their persons, side-arms to be excepted.

M.L. PATTERSON
Major, Commanding Fourth Tennessee Infantry

To Major Patterson's request, General Wheeler's response was:

Approved:

JOS. WHEELER
Major-General, C.S. Army

A statement made by the commander and officers of the force which surrendered at McMinnville describes what then occurred:[24]

Agreeable to the terms of surrender, the arms [were] stacked and the garrison paraded, and everything [put] in readiness to be surrendered.

From 1 until 8 p.m. the men stood in line and were compelled to submit to the most brutal outrages on the part of the rebels ever known to any civilized war in America or elsewhere. The rebel troops or soldiers, and sometimes the officers, would call upon an officer or soldier standing in line, when surrendered, for his

---

[23]Ibid., 710.
[24]Ibid., 711.

overcoat, dress-coat, blouse, hat, shoes, boots, watch, pocket-book, money, and even finger-rings, or, in fact, anything that happened to please their fancy, and with a pistol cocked in one hand, in the attitude of shooting, demand the article they wanted. In this way the men of the Fourth Tennessee Infantry were stripped of their blankets, oil-cloths, overcoats, a large number of dress coats, blouses, boots and shoes, jewelry, hats, knapsacks, and haversacks.

Site map of McMinnville

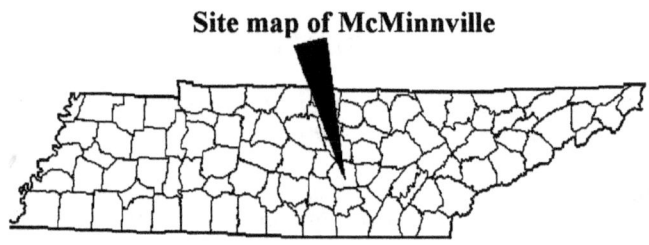

When the officers tried to save the records of their companies (the assistant quartermaster, acting commissary of subsistence, and commanding officers their records) the papers were pulled out of their pockets, torn to pieces, and thrown away. All, or about all, of the officer's clothing was taken - valises and contents. While all this was going on, Major-General Wheeler was sitting on his horse and around the streets of McMinnville, witnessing and, we think, encouraging the same infernal outrages, seeming to not want or desire to comply with his agreement. The attention of Major-General Wheeler, Major-General Wharton, General Martin, General Davidson, and General [Colonel] Gillespie, and Brigadier-General Hodge was called to the same several times by Major M.L. Patterson, to gain his officers and men protection according to promise and agreement, and they would send some subordinate officer, who had no control over the men, or would reply that he (Wheeler) could not control his men; that they would do as they pleased, &c. Several of the officers of the Fourth Tennessee Infantry called on General Wheeler for protection. He would pay no attention to them, saying that he had no control over his men, &c.

Major-General Wheeler then ordered the command outside of his immediate lines, on the Sparta road, a section of country infested with guerrillas, where there was robbing and plundering the

A Brief History of the Regiment 19

paroled prisoners all the way, even compelling captains to sit down in the middle of the road and pull off their boots.

Yours, respectfully,

        M.L. PATTERSON
            Major Fourth Tennessee Infantry
        R.C. CARTER
            Captain Company C
THOMAS H. REEVES
            Captain Company D
LEVI PICKERING
            Captain Company E
JOHN HAROLD
            Regimental Quartermaster

F.S. SINGLETARY
            Second Lieutenant Company B
ROBERT E. SWEENEY
            Second Lieutenant Company D
FRANK T.D. KETCHUM
            Acting Adjutant
S.M. NOXON
            Second Lt. 10th Wisconsin Vol Inf

Major Patterson's total force at McMinnville consisted of 270 men plus 50 convalescents who had been armed. He reported seven killed, 31 wounded and missing in the fighting prior to the surrender. The men were eventually paroled and started towards Sparta, Tennessee. Most of the men, figuring the war was over for them, went on to their homes in East Tennessee. On October 12, 1863, Governor Johnson reported that Major Patterson and about 50 of his men were at Nashville. The Governor also noted that Colonel Stover was sick in bed and that the Lieutenant Colonel was in East Tennessee raising men in order to fill out the regiment. The Governor inquired as to whether the paroles were to be considered valid. If they were to invalid, he proposed sending Major Patterson and his 50 men to East Tennessee to round up the parolees and reorganize the regiment. He was informed that the paroles were invalid and that the regiment was to be reorganized.[25]

Major Patterson proceeded to Camp Nelson, Kentucky, where the regiment was reorganized. On December 31st 1863, the regiment was

---

[25]Civil War Centenniel Commission, Tennesseeans in the Civil War, Nashville, TN., 1964, 383.

reported in General Fry's brigade in the District of North Central Kentucky with Major Patterson in command.

Neither Colonel Stover nor Lieutenant Colonel Grayson were ever reported with the regiment again. Lieutenant Colonel Grayson had joined the 13th Regiment Tennessee Volunteer Cavalry (USA) as a major on Oct 6, 1863, reportedly because of a disagreement with superior officers.[26]

It is interesting to note that a short time after the flag of the Fourth Regiment was captured by the rebels, it was recovered and returned to the regiment. The following correspondence was found in official records of the War of the Rebellion:[27]

HEADQUARTERS DEPARTMENT OF THE CUMBERLAND
Chattanooga, November 15, 1863

Brig. Gen. A. Johnson,
  Military Governor of Tennessee, Nashville:

GENERAL: I am directed by the general commanding to send you the colors of the Fourth Regiment Tennessee Volunteers captured from them by the rebel Wheeler at McMinnville. A bearer of dispatches from Wheeler to Bragg was captured in the vicinity of Trenton, Ga., by one of our scouting parties soon after Wheeler was driven from Middle Tennessee, and the flag taken from him among other things.
The general desires that it may be returned to the regiment, and trusts that it may never again fall into disloyal hands.
Very respectfully, your obedient servant.
                                            C. GODDARD
        Lieutenant Colonel and Assistant Adjutant General.

On February 8, 1864 the Regiment was assigned to 1st Brigade, 3rd Division, XXIII Corps with orders to report to Knoxville for instructions. On February 20, 1864, the Fourth Regiment was sent out 3 miles from Knoxville, on the Sevierville road, to support cavalry skirmishes with the enemy. Brigadier General Milo S. Hascall described what took place:

" *While I was visiting my command on the other side of the river, yesterday the enemy attacked my picket post and showed themselves rather prominently on all the roads. I thought it best to*

---

[26]Scott, Thirteenth Regiment, 272.
[27]Ainsworth, War of Rebellion, Part I, Volume 32, 165.

A Brief History of the Regiment

ascertain what was at our front, and accordingly took the Fourth Tennessee Infantry, under Major Patterson, about 150 to 175 men, and the left wing of the Third Indiana Cavalry, we started out on the road with the infantry in advance. About a mile out we encountered the enemy's outpost which was promptly driven away by the infantry .. the cavalry pushed them back about 2 or 3 miles .. we determined from prisoners that it was Martin's (rebel) cavalry that we were contending with, and deemed it prudent not to push any further. There were no casualties in the infantry force, the Cavalry lost 6 men wounded, 1 of whom will die."[28]

On February 28, 1864 the regiment was reported to be on the works south of the river, opposite Knoxville.

An inspection report dated February 27, 1864 stated: "The 1st Brigade in bad drill; has dirty or bad clothing; discipline not good. Some men were entirely without ammunition, others had 30 or 40 rounds." The report called specific attention to the Fourth and Eighth Tennessee Regiments as being in bad condition regarding appearance, discipline and drill.[29]

On April 10, 1864, the XXIII Corps was reorganized and the 4th Tennessee Volunteer Infantry assigned to the 3rd Brigade, 4th Division, District of East Tennessee. On the 12th of April 1864 the 4th was ordered to Loudon, Tennessee where it remained for some time. Major Patterson was promoted to lieutenant colonel and given command of the 3rd Brigade. Major Reeves, with three companies, was stationed at nearby Kingston. On August 19, 1864, Major Reeves reported that he had an almost solid line of scouts from Cumberland Mountain to Sweetwater Valley.

On October 30, 1864, Confederate Brigadier General John C. Vaughn, at Rheatown, Tennessee reported re-enforcement of Federal troops facing him by the 4th and 8th Tennessee Infantry Regiments.

The 4th Regiment remained at Loudon and Kingston until about the first of November 1864 when it moved to Knoxville.

On November 26, 1864 Major General George Stoneman, at Knoxville, making preparation for his expedition into East Tennessee and Virginia in December, reported the 4th Regiment with 400 men, would be ready by December 1, 1864.

---

[28]Ibid., 409.
[29]Ibid., 485.

4th Tennessee Volunteer Infantry Regiment (USA)

On December 7, 1864 General Tillson sent the 4th Tennessee and 3rd North Carolina regiments via Sevierville, to Paint Rock to hold the passes over the mountains into North Carolina until East Tennessee was evacuated by the Confederates. The 4th Tennessee was then instructed to move down the French Broad River to protect the government trains in collecting forage. Confederate Colonel John B. Palmer reported that he had driven the two regiments out of Paint Rock, almost captured the 3rd North Carolina Infantry, USA, and sent it back to Knoxville.

On February 5, 1865 the regiment was at Mosier's Mill, near Morristown. It marched to Greeneville on February 20, to conduct elections. On the way it had skirmishes with the enemy near Greeneville and Warrensburg. The regiment returned to Mosier's Mill on February 25, 1865.

On March 31, 1865 the 4th Regiment, with eight companies, under Major Reeves, was reported wint the 1st Brigade.

In preparation for Major General Stoneman's expedition into western Virginia and North Carolina, the 1st Brigade was concentrated at Morristown, Tennessee on March 22. The regiment proceeded to Roans Creek, in Johnson County, Tennessee, and arrived there on April 3, 1865. The 4th Tennessee, with 544 men, was stationed at Taylorsville, now Mountain City, Tennessee to hold the passes near there.

On April 20, 1865, the regiment was at Jonesborough. It was again reported to be located at Jonesborough on May 18, 1865. The regiment was ordered mustered out of service on July 20, 1865, and was mustered out at Nashville on August 2, 1865.

Chapter 3

Organization of the Regiment

The Fourth Tennessee Regiment was recruited in East Tennessee in the spring of 1863. On the 4th of May 1863, Colonel Stover had assembled 505 men in Kentucky for the 4th Regiment. He explained that he would have had 519 but that 6 had died, 7 had deserted and 2 were captured while on recruiting service in East Tennessee. On 5 May 1863, Colonel Stover reported that 12 more recruits had arrived. On 1 July 1863, Colonel Stover's Regiment had relocated to the right of the penitentiary outside of Nashville.

In a letter from the War Department, dated February 27, 1862, Colonel Daniel Stover was given authority to raise one regiment of Volunteer Infantry. This regiment was to be raised in the State of Tennessee and to serve for three years or the duration of the war. This regiment was to be organized as prescribed by Act of Congress, approved July 22, 1861, as follows:

Minimum		Maximum	
830 Company Officers and enlisted men		1010 Company Officers and enlisted men	
1	Colonel	1	Colonel
1	Lieutenant Colonel	1	Lieutenant Colonel
1	Major	1	Major
1	Adjutant (1st Lt)	1	Adjutant (1st Lt)
1	Quartermaster (1st Lt)	1	Quartermaster (1st Lt)
1	Surgeon	1	Surgeon
1	Assistant Surgeon	1	Assistant Surgeon
1	Sergeant Major	1	Sergeant Major
1	Quartermaster Sergeant	1	Quartermaster Sergeant
1	Commissary Sergeant	1	Commissary Sergeant
1	Hospital Steward	1	Hospital Steward
2	Principal Musicians	2	Principal Musicians

4th Tennessee Volunteer Infantry Regiment (USA)

Each company was to be organized by the same Act of Congress as follows:

Minimum		Maximum	
1	Captain	1	Captain
1	First Lieutenant	1	First Lieutenant
1	Second Lieutanant	1	Second Lieutenant
1	First Sergeant	1	First Sergeant
4	Sergeants	4	Sergeants
8	Corporals	8	Corporals
2	Musicians	2	Musicians
1	Wagoner	1	Wagoner
64	Privates	83	Privates
83	Aggregate	101	Aggregate

After the regiment was organized, it was authorized one Chaplain who was to be appointed by the Regimental Commander on the vote of the field officers and company commanders. The Chaplain had to be a regular ordained minister of a Christian denomination.

The enlisted members were to be mustered into the regiment as enrolled. The officers were to be appointed by the Regimental Commander, subject to approval of the War Department. The officers were authorized to be appointed and mustered into the service as follows:

Lieutenant Colonel	Upon completion of 4 minimum companies.
Major	Upon completion of 6 minimum companies.
Captains	Upon completon of the minimum of their companies.
Second Lieutenant	Upon completion of the minimum of their respective company.
First Lieutenant	Upon completion of half of the minimum of their respective companies.

Organization of the Regiment

The Fourth Tennessee Volunteer Infantry Regiment was staffed as follows:[31]

Field Officers:

Colonel Daniel Stover

Colonel Stover, age 35, enrolled at Cincinnati, Ohio on the 28th of February 1862. Colonel Stover, the son-in-law of Andrew Johnson, had been active in the anti-succession campaign. He had served as a delegate from Carter County in the East Tennessee Convention held at Knoxville and Greeneville. He came through the lines from East Tennessee on the 25th day of November 1862. In his effort to avoid capture by the Southern Confederates, he was forced to endure exposure to severe weather. Colonel Stover became seriously ill after reporting to Nashville and was never able to command the 4th Regiment in the field. He attributed the exposure, added to what he had had to endure while in the U.S. service, to the demise of "a once vigorous constitution." His health ruined, he resigned August 1st, 1864.

Lieutenant Colonel James W. M. Grayson

Lieutenant Colonel Grayson was active in the formation of the Fourth Tennessee Regiment, having recruited a number of men and escorting them to Camp Nelson, Kentucky. The Union guide, Daniel Ellis, made his first trip to Kentucky on the night of November 14, 1862, guiding Colonel James Grayson, of Johnson County, Tennessee, and a number of men from Carter and Johnson Counties. Colonel Grayson enrolled at Louisville, Kentucky on 1 May 1863. He was a prominent resident of Johnson County. He mustered out of the 4th Regiment on 9 September 1863 to accept a commission as a Major in the 12th Tennessee Cavalry (later 13th Tennessee Volunteer Cavalry) by order of Major General Burnside.

Lieutenant Colonel Michael L. Patterson

Lieutenant Colonel Patterson, age 35, enrolled at Louisville, Kentucky on 3 December 1862. He was commissioned quartermaster Lieutenant by the Governor of Tennessee on 3

---

[31] Civil War Centennial Commission, Tennesseans in Civil War, 383.

December 1862. He was promoted to Major on 9 September 1863 and placed in command of the Regiment. Less than a month later, his entire regiment was captured and paroled at McMinnville, Tennessee by a rebel force led by Confederate Major General Wheeler. Major Patterson was tried by a military court of inquiry for surrendering his command. After careful examination of facts the commanding general (General Thomas) was satisfied that Major Patterson had acted in the best judgment and he therefore was exonerated from all charges. He was promoted to Lieutenant Colonel to fill the vacancy of Lieutenant Colonel Grayson on 28 February 1864. He was placed in command of 3rd Brigade, 4th Division on 12 June 1864. During January and February 1864 he was reported sick in the officers hospital at Knoxville. On 4 Jan. 1864, a medical examiners board recommended he be placed on leave of absence. The medical board reported that Lieutenant Colonel Patterson has "one arm amputated, chronic ulcer of the other, chronic rheumatism, and recommends a 30 day leave of absence." He resigned on 12 March 1865 to accept a position as Clerk of the Supreme Court for the Eastern Division of the State of Tennessee.

Lieutenant Colonel Thomas H. Reeves

Lieutenant Colonel Reeves had previously served as a Captain commanding Company D, Fourth Regiment. He was promoted to Major on 12 Mar 1864 to fill Major Patterson's vacancy and placed in command of the Regiment. On 28 May 1865, Major Reeves requested a 20 day leave of absence to "attend to the wants of my mother and family, who have been neglected for nearly fout years by my absence in the Army". He listed his leave address as Fall Branch, Tennessee. Correspondence in his file indicates that he was questioned by General Ammen about his unauthorized sending Private W. T. L. Scott to East Tennessee on 6 July 1864 for the purpose of recruiting. General Ammen stated that the matter was a very serious offense and asked for the Major's explanation to preclude his being brought before a court martial. Moreover, his subsequent promotion to Lieutenant Colonel met with delay and concern when it was reported that Major Reeves was a deserter from the Second Regiment Tennessee Volunteer Infantry. The official responsible for controlling the enrollment and grades of officers in the units challenged the recommended promotion of Major Reeves when he discovered that he was reported as a deserter from the Second Tennessee Infantry

Organization of the Regiment

Regiment. Reeves had enrolled as a private in Company F of the Second Regiment on 6 December 1861. He was alleged to have deserted on 25 August 1862.

In an effort to resolve the dilemma, Major Reeves wrote a letter to the Secretary of War, E. M. Stanton, and also to President Lincoln. When forming these volunteer military units during the War, it appears that there may have been widespread deception and competition for soldiers. Following is the text of Major Reeves letter:

>Hd Qtrs 4th Tenn Vol Infy
>Kingston Tenn Oct 8, 1864

His Excellency
Abraham Lincoln
President of the U.S.

Sir

I have the honor to invoke your attention to my statement and at the same time to enlist your favour if your honor may think it for the good of the service.

On the 15th of November 1861, I organized a company of eighty-six (86) men for the U. S. A. at Chimney Top Mountain in Greene County, East Tennessee, with the intention of taking them to Kentucky and forming some of the East Tennessee regiments then in progress of organizing. But before I got started with my company, the Rebels came upon me and my men being unarmed had to disband and fled to the mountains for their safety, as at that time it was almost sure death if the Rebels caught anyone who espoused the Union cause. Finding myself thus situated, I concluded to make my escape to Kentucky, establish communication with the Federal Army which was then at Loudon, Kentucky and then return to E. Tennessee and take my company out and attach it to some of the Regiments. On arriving at Loudon, I found Colonel James Carter who was then organizing the 2nd Tennessee Volunteer Infantry. His regiment was not then full. He went to work after finding that I had a company in Tennessee to get me into his regiment. The Army was then expected to march into East Tennessee every day and I concluded not to return until the army went into the state. So Colonel Carter advised and persuaded me to enter the ranks of his regiment until we got

4th Tennessee Volunteer Infantry Regiment (USA)

there, and then he would release me and I might bring my company into his or any other regiment that I might desire. Having a desire to do all in my power for my country and not feeling myself above the task of shouldering a gun, as did many others, I consented to join his regiment if he would assure me that on reaching E. Tennessee, I would be released to bring into service my company - which assurance he gave in writing to the effect "that on reaching E. Tenn, I should be released for the purpose aforesaid", consequently, I joined his regiment, not with the intention of serving in it for three years as a private, but with the expectations and promise of being released at the time and place specified.

The Army did not enter Tennessee as soon as was expected by nearly twelve months, during which time I was in the ranks of said Regiment and performing all the duties of any soldier of the Army. At length the Army under General George Morgan took Cumberland Gap Tennessee and then our down trodden and oppressed brother Tennesseeans could be seen making their way to the Gap to join their friends for the redemptive of their honor. Several of my old company came in and would not go into the service because I told them that in a few days I would call them together and reorganize. Soon after this, I made application to Colonel Carter to comply with his promise which was evaded by saying that it was out of his power to do so. I did not stop but continued to ask and entreat him to let me go until he finally and peremptorily refused to grant what he had sacredly promised in writing and told me if I ever said any thing more to him about it that he would arrest me and put me in the guard house. Finding that he had deceived me into his regiment as well as the non compliance with his written promise and thinking thru his failing to comply with his promise released me entirely from my obligations to him or his Regiment, but not to the service for I intended to remain in the service where I thought I could do the most good. I came to the conclusion to leave his Regiment and get up my company and enter some other regiment with it - his having been filled - therefore I left his Regiment went into the interior of East Tennessee and after so long a time, succeeded in getting out with men enough to entitle me to a 1st lieutenancy. Meanwhile the U.S. troops had evacuated Cumberland Gap and the first Tennessee troops I found was Colonel Daniel Stover who was there organizing the 4th Tennessee Infantry, at Louisville. I made a statement of my case to him and he told me if I would raise or complete my

Organization of the Regiment 29

company for his regiment that the thing could be fixed up and he would make me a Captain of the company. So I went to work to complete my company and at Lexington, Kentucky, I got twenty-two (22) recruits and soon afterwards came across Colonel James Carter of the 2nd Tennessee Infantry, who had me arrested and tried to send my recruits on to his Regiment which was at Nashville. He also started me under guard to his regiment and when I got to Louisville, Kentucky, I wrote a note to Colonel Daniel Stover of the 4th Tennessee Infantry how I was situated. He went to General Boyle, made a full statement of the case to him and he ordered my release from prison and soon afterwards had Captain J. N. Knight his A.C.M. to muster me in as a 1st Lieutenant, Company D, 4th Tennessee Infantry - to date February 19, 1863. The thing passed away and no more was heard of it and I supposed all was right. I was again commissioned as Captain and mustered in to date, May 29, 1863 and continued to perform duties of a commissioned officer. Have passed and have been with Colonel Carter and his Regiment several times since and nothing more was said about the case. On the 12th of March, 1864, I was again commissioned by the Governor as a Major, 4th Tennessee Infantry, but the Regiment not being entitled to the compliment of field officers, I could not be mustered in as Major. On the 10th of August 1864, Colonel Daniel Stover's resignation was accepted which entitled me to muster. As soon thereafter as possible, I presented myself to the A.C.M. for muster-in as Major at which place I was informed that I had been dropped from the rolls of the 2nd Tennessee Infantry as a deserter and that I could not be mustered in until that charge was removed and I was discharged from that Regiment as a private. This was quite unexpected to me for I supposed that the thing was all right, but as it is the liabilities of the penalty of desertion and believing that I have done nothing intentional but what I thought was for the good of the service and having made a statement of facts that can be proven and believing that it is your pleasure to give justice to every one and to punish the guilty and being now guiltless of any thing that would be detrimental to the service, I appeal to you as the decisive judge and protector of the rights of the American people to grant me the following at the earliest moment it may be your pleasure to do so. <u>I have the honor to request that the charge of desertion as private, Company F, 2nd Tennessee Volunteer Infantry to date February 18, 1863 be dropped to accept a commission as 1st Lieutenant, Company D, 4th Tennessee Volunteer Infantry</u> and ever oblige one who has ever tried to do his duty. Allow me to beg your pardon for the length of my letter - and believe me sir.

> I am Very respectfully
> your obedient servant
> T. H. Reeves
> Major Commanding, 4th Tenn Inf

Concurrent with Major Reeves' letter to President Lincoln, concerning the desertion charge, Lieutenant Colonel Patterson, Commander of the 3rd Brigade, drafted a statement to Brigadier General Ammons in Reeves behalf. Colonel Patterson was not a witness to the incident but remembered discussing the matter with Colonel Stover. Commander of the 4th Division, 23rd Army of the Cumberland. Colonel Patterson's letter is quoted on the following page.

> Headquarters 3rd Brigade, 4th Division
> Army of the Cumberland
> Loudon, Tennessee October 8, 1864

General

I have the honor to make the following statement in regard to Major Thomas H. Reeves, 4th Tennessee Volunteer Infantry whose case is now being investigated. That on or about the 15th day of January 1863, Colonel Daniel Stover, then raising and organizing the 4th Regiment Tennessee Volunteer Infantry at Louisville, Kentucky made an agreement with the said Reeves that after he (Reeves) would raise or recruit a company of men for his (Stover) Regiment, he would appoint him Captain of the same. Said Reeves went to work to make up the company and had men enough to entitle him to be mustered in as 1st Lieutenant. He (Reeves) started out to get up some more men and went up from Louisville, Kentucky to Lexington, Kentucky at the later place it was reported that he recruited 72 men and here Colonel James Carter of the 2nd Tennessee Regiment had him (Reeves) arrested as a deserter and started him under guard to Nashville, Tennessee where the 2nd Tennessee was then stationed. When Reeves and the guard reached Louisville, Kentucky, Reeves was put in the military prison. Then Reeves wrote a little note stating his condition and situation to Colonel Daniel Stover asking him to

Organization of the Regiment 31

assist him and get him out of the prison. Colonel Stover and myself, at the request of Stover, went down to Brigadier General Boyle and then and there made a statement of the whole thing as we understood it at that time. As well as I recollect at the present, Colonel Stover told General Boyle that he, Carter, did not like him (Stover) very well and that he (Stover) believed that Colonel Carter arrested Reeves in order to keep him (Reeves) from recruiting for his (Stover's) regiment and also to get the 22 recruits that Reeves had at the time he was arrested - and not because he wished to keep Reeves in his Regiment or punish him as a deserter. Upon those statements being made to General Boyle, who was commanding at Louisville, Kentucky, had Reeves released from prison and under arrest and sent out the 4th Tennessee Volunteer Infantry. From a conversation I had with Colonel Stover after this, Colonel Stover held out the idea to me that he was satisfied that the whole matter was settled and adjusted and that Reeves could not be arrested again for the same offense.

Colonel Carter and Lieutenant Colonel Milton of the 2nd Tennessee has passed and repassed Reeves time and again since. Reeves has several times stated to me that he has been in the camp of the 2nd Tennessee and at the time the 2nd Tennessee came from Nashville to Louisville, I know Reeves was in their camp. Reeves has held correspondence with the officers and men of the 2nd Tennessee all the time upon some occasions showing me letters from that Regiment. Undoubtedly Colonel Carter and all the officers knew where Reeves was and knew they could have sent a communication to have him arrested at any time. Now over two years have elapsed before the complaint was made. And here I will close my statement.

I having been called upon for a statement by Brigadier General Ammen with all respects submitted the foregoing.

> *I am General Very Respectfully*
> *Your Obedient Servant*
> M.S. Patterson
> Lt Col Commanding 3rd Brigade

Major Reeves was promoted to Lieutenant Colonel on May 31, 1865 after resolving the desertion charge.

4th Tennessee Volunteer Infantry Regiment (USA)

Major Gaines Lawson

Major Lawson, age 21; enrolled as a private at Rogersville, 21 December 1862. He was promoted to sergeant on 15 April 1863. Along with the rest of the Regiment he was captured and paroled at McMinnville on 3 October 1863. He received a promotion to Captain to replace Captain Reeves, who was promoted to Major, on the 1st of April 1864. He was promoted to Major on 31 May 1865. He mustered out of service with the Regiment on 2 August 1865. Major Lawson received Medal of Honor for gallantry in action at McMinnville.

Major/Surgeon Robert J. Farguharson

Major/Surgeon Farguharson, age 38, joined at Nashville on 1 June 1863. He was detailed to hospital #12 at Nashville on 18 September 1863. He was ordered to rejoin the Regiment, which had moved to East Tennessee, on 1 March 1864. He resigned from service citing disability (deafness) and unfit for field duty on 21 March 1864.

Major/Surgeon Edward Norwood

Major/Surgeon Norwood, age 25, enrolled in Kingston on 12 June 1864. He was assigned to surgical hospital in Greeneville during March and April 1864. He requested a 30 day leave of absence on 7 January 1865 based on a medical examination board certificate that he "suffered hepatitis and conjunctivitis and needs a change of climate to prevent permanent disability." Later, on 20 June 1865, he requested a 20 day leave of absence to visit his family in Kentucky stating "family illness demanding his personal attention."

Assistant Surgeon Alexander B. Tadlock

Assistant Surgeon Tadlock, age 27, enrolled at Louisville on 26 March 1863. He was commissioned by Governor Andrew Johnson to fill the original vacancy. He was discharged for disability on 8 December 1863. His disability was "hemorrhage (?) of lungs." His file contains a leave of absence request to visit Indianapolis, Indiana on 20 July 1863 and a 20 day furlough to St. Anthony, Minnesota on 9 August 1863.

Organization of the Regiment

Assistant Surgeon William Cavener

Assistant Surgeon Cavener, age 48, enrolled on 1 May 1864 at Kingston where he was commissioned assistant surgeon on 1 April 1864. He resigned on 6 June 1865 citing bronchitis and infirmities of age, being 50 years old.

First Lieutenant John W. Hines

Lieutenant Hines was an Adjutant in the Fourth Regiment. He transferred from Company B, 59th Regiment, Ohio Volunteer Infantry on 17 June 1864 and enrolled at Kingston on 18 June 1864. He resigned on 24 April 1865 for disability. His resignation cited the surgeon's certificate claiming "hypertrophy of heart and general debility."

First Lieutenant John Murphy

Lieutenant Murphy was an Adjutant in the Fourth Regiment. He mustered in at Louisville on 1 May 1863. Along with the rest of the Regiment, he was captured and paroled at McMinnville on 3 October 1863. He requested a 5 day furlough to go to Louisville on 13 November 1863. In his furlough request he stated that all officers of the Regiment were under arrest in Nashville. He submitted his resignation request on 10 May 1864 citing physical disabilities. His discharge was based on the surgeons certificate of 23 April 1864, claiming "constitutional weakness of some time standing." He was discharged on 12 May 1864.

First Lieutenant Joseph A. February

Lieutenant February served in Companies B and G before being commissioned and assigned to the Field and Staff. He enrolled as a private at Jonesborough on 1 January 1863. He was captured and paroled at McMinnville on 3 October 1863. He received a promotion to commissary sergeant on December 1863 and promoted to 1st Lieutenant on 12 October 1864.

First Lieutenant Lewis F. Self

Lieutenant Self served as a private in Company A before being promoted and serving as quartermaster sergeant and later Regimental Quartermaster, Field and Staff. He enrolled at Greeneville on 25 July 1863 and mustered in at Strawberry

Plains on 31 March 1864. He was promoted to quartermaster sergeant on 3 December 1863 and promoted to First Lieutenant, Regimental Quartermaster on 5 Oct 1864. He resigned to accept an appointment as Postmaster at Greeneville on 21 May 1865. His resignation was approved by Major General Thomas, Commander at Nashville on 29 May 1865.

First Lieutanant Frederick S. Singletary

Prior to his military service, Lieutantant Singletary had been an activist for the Union cause. He enrolled as a private at Elizabethton on 16 July 1862. He mustered in as Second Lieutenant, Company B, on 11 May 1863 and where he served until he was appointed acting Regimental Adjutant on 8 March 1865. Additional information concerning Lieutenant Singletary's service in shown under the Company B listing.

Identified locations of the Regiment are as follows:

June-September 1863:	Nashville, Tennessee
September-October 1863:	McMinnville, Tennessee
February 1864:	Knoxville, Tennessee
March-April 1864:	Loudon, Tennessee
May-June 1864:	Knoxville, Tennessee
July-September 1864:	Kingston, Tennessee
November-December 1864:	8 miles Southwest of Dandridge, Tennesse
January-March 1865:	Mosier's Mill near Morristown, Tennessee

Company A:

Captain James L. Carter

Captain Carter joined at Greeneville, at age 40, on 23 November 1862. He was appointed 1st Lieutenant, 19 February 1863 and appointed Captain, Company A on 1 April 1863. Along with his company and the rest of the Regiment, he was captured and paroled at McMinnville on 3 October 1863. He was reported sick at Knoxville on 16 April 1864. He submitted his resignation request citing family hardships on 16 May 1864. He was court martialed for violation of an Act of War in "encouraging men to go home, stating that

Organization of the Regiment

authorities could not punish them for it in East Tennessee" during the June through July 1864 time frame. His resignation request was approved.

Captain William C. Allen

Captain Allen mustered in at Greeneville as First Lieutenant on the 27th of April 1863. He was captured and paroled at McMinnville on the 3rd of October 1863. He was appointed Regimental Quartermaster on the 17th of February 1864. He received a promoted to Captain on the 13th of July 1864. He mustered out with the Regiment on the 2nd of August 1865.

First Lieutenant Isaac A. Armitage

Lieutenant Armitage, age 32, enrolled on 6 April 1863 at Greeneville. He was promoted to sergeant from private on 24 March 1864. He was commissioned 1st Lieutenant, Company A, on 6 June 1865. He mustered out with the Regiment on 2 August 1865.

Second Lieutenant Gustavus A. Winslow

Second Lieutenant Winslow enlisted at Greeneville on 30 January 1863. He was appointed 4th sergeant on 10 April 1863 and promoted to 5th sergeant on 29 Aug 1863. He was captured and paroled at McMinnville on 3 October 1863. He was promoted to 1st sergeant on 1 April 1864. He received a commissioned to Second Lieutenant on 13 June 1864. On 29 December 1864, his record shows that he was under arrest for unspecified reasons. He resigned "for the good of the service" on 20 January 1865.

Company A consisted of men from East Tennessee, primarily Greene and Cocke Counties.

Company A, was shown to be in Nashville on 30 June 1863; from 30 June, 1863 through 29 February 1864, the records show it to be in Knoxville; in March and April 1864 the Company was shown to be at Loudon, Tennessee; during May and June 1864, Company A was again located at Knoxville; During July through September 1864 it was at Kingston, Tennessee; in November and December 1864, the company was located 8 miles South West of Dandridge, Tennessee; in January and February 1865, it was stationed at Mosier's Mill,

4th Tennessee Volunteer Infantry Regiment (USA)

Tennessee and in March and April 1865 at Jonesborough, Tennessee.

Company B:

Captain James I. R. Boyd

Captain Boyd enrolled at Elizabethton, Tennessee, at age 41, on 19 August 1861. He mustered in on 11 May 1863. His service record shows that he was sick in hospital at Knoxville on 18 April 1864. He resigned because of family concerns on 7 June 1864.

Captain John Harold

Captain Harold, age 24, enrolled at Greeneville on 12 August 1862 as a private. He he was commissioned a Lieutenant and detailed to brigade quartermaster on 9 September 1863. He was captured and paroled at McMinnville on 3 October 1863. He received a promotion to Captain of Company B on October 1864

First Lieutenant Tarlton A. Middleton

Lieutenant Middleton enrolled at Jonesborough as a private, in Company G, on 5 March 1863. He was promoted to First Lieutenant in Company B later resigning for the good of the service on 27 September 1864. His court martial record cited: "conduct unbecoming an officer and gentleman: drunk and disorderly, drinking and playing cards with enlisted men, calling Major Reeves a "damned fool."

First Lieutanant Frederick S. Singletary

Lieutantant Singletary, age 20; enrolled as a private at Elizabethton on 16 July 1862. He mustered in as Second Lieutenant, Company B, on 11 May 1863. He was captured and paroled at McMinnville on 3 October 1863. He was on detached service, 16 February 1864, with Major Kirk of the Second North Carolina Volunteers and 16 other officers and men to the upper counties of the State of Tennesse when on the 17th they were suddenly attacked by a cavalry force and forced to disburse in various directions. He was separated from the force and unable to rejoin the rest of the detail, so he proceeded to the Chilhowie Mountains and was compelled to

Organization of the Regiment 37

remain there for an unspecified time. He reported that he finally made it to Sevier County and subsequently rejoined the Regiment near Knoxville. He was reported under arrest on 11 April 1864 and requested permission to resign because of impending court martial charges on 9 May 1864. He received a general court martial, on 16 August 1864, for "conduct prejudice to good order and discipline; circulating a letter for signature criticizing Lieutenant Middleton; absent without leave, 4 Apr 1864 through 6 Apr 1864; conduct unbecoming an officer for writing a letter questioning authority of the Regimental Commander's order to move his company." As a result of the court martial he received a "written public reprimand in the form of a general order." Soon afterwards, on 27 October 1864, he was promoted to First Lieutenant, Company B. He was appointed acting Regimental Adjutant on 8 March 1865. He requested a 20 day furlough to attend to the needs of his family on 21 June 1865 and was discharged on 2 August 1865.

Second Lieutenant John P. Smith

Second Lieutenant Smith, age 18, enrolled at Taylorsville on 2 June. 1863. He was promoted to 4th corporal on 19 May 1864. He was promoted to sergeant on 10 September 1864. To fill Lieutenant Singletary's vacancy, who had moved to Regimental Adjutant, he was promoted to Second Lieutenant on 28 October 1864. He requested a 20 day furlough at Jonesborough on 25 June 1865 to attend to urgent personal business in Johnson County. He was discharged on 2 August 1865.

Company B consisted of men from East Tennessee

Company B, was shown to be in Nashville during 15 through 30 June 1863; the company was captured by the enemy on October 3, 1863 at McMinnville, Tennessee; from June through February the unit records show the unit located at Knoxville; in March and April 1864, the company was at Loudon, Tennessee; from May through August 1864, Company B was located at Kingston, Tennessee.

During November and December, the following is recorded in the company record: "Left Kingston November 18, 1864, arrived Loudon November 23, distance 18 miles. Left Loudon November 23, arrived Knoxville 24 November, distance 30

4th Tennessee Volunteer Infantry Regiment (USA)

Miles; left Knoxville on night of 4 December 1864, arrived Paint Rock on 13 December 1864, distance 90 miles; left Paint Rock 21 December, arrived 8 miles West of Dandridge on 29th of December 1864, distance 58 miles; had slight skirmish with the enemy on the 29th of December.

During January and February 1865 the Company was at Mosier's Mill, Tennessee.

During March and April 1865, the following was recorded in the company record: "Remained at Mosier's Mill, Jefferson County, Tennessee, until 16 March 1865; broke camp and with the balance of the Regiment, marched to Mossy Creek, distance of 16 miles. Brigaded with the 1st Brigade, 4th Division, Department of the Cumberland, Colonel Hawley, Commanding. With Brigade, broke camp March 20, 1865, passed Morristown, Russelville, Greeneville, Jonesborough, arrived at mouth of Roanes Creek, Johnson County, Tennessee, April 3, 1865. Had the pleasure of wading Watauga River, up to our middles and in good condition, made us remember that there is a North Pole. Distance marched 108 miles. April 4, 1865, detached from the Brigade and marched to Taylorsville, Tennessee, distance of 18 miles. Remained there until 19 April, 1865. Broke camp and marched to Jonesborough, distance 52 miles, arrived there April 21, 1865. We marched the entire round without the loss of a man or of anyone getting sick or giving out."

During May and June 1865 the company was located at Jonesborough, Tennessee.

Company C:

Captain Robert J. Carter

Captain Carter, at age 38, enrolled at Cincinnati, Ohio on 10 December 1862. He was captured and paroled at McMinnville on 3 October 1863. Records show that he was on detached service collecting parolees through April 1864. He was transferred to Company C as Captain and subsequently resigned on 30 April 1864 to "look after his family."

Organization of the Regiment

Captain Newton J. Hacker

Captain Hacker, age 31, enrolled at Greenevile on 26 January 1863. He mustered in as 1st Lieutenant on 25 April 1863. He was captured and paroled at McMinnville on 3 October 1863. He was promoted to Captain on 23 May 1864 and mustered out of service on 2 August 1865.

Second Lieutenant Theophilus Britton

Lieutenant Britton, age 29; enrolled at Staunton, Virginia on 6 April 1863. He was captured and paroled at McMinnville on 3 October 1863. He received a promotion to Sergeant on 1 July 1864. He was reported sick at Kingston 25 November 1864 through February 1865. He was commission as 2nd Lieutenant in Company C on 4 June 1865. He was discharged on 2 August 1865.

Second Lieutenant David Rush

Lieutenant Rush enrolled at Greeneville on 10 August 1862. He was promoted to First-Sergeant on 24 April 1863 and commissioned Second Lieutenant on 9 September 1863. He was captured and paroled at McMinnville on 3 October 1863 and never returned to duty with the 4th Regiment. Later muster rolls showed him as absent without leave. His file indicates that he made application in July 1864 for discharge to accept an appointment as Captain, 8th Tennessee Cavalry at Gallatin, Tennessee.

Company C enrolled at Greeneville

Company C, was shown to be in Nashville during 15 through 30 June 1863; from July 1865 through February 1864, the records show the Company to be located at Knoxville; in March and April 1864 the Company was shown to be at Loudon, Tennessee; during May through October 1864, during November and December 1864 the Company was located 8 miles South West of Dandridge, Tennessee; in January and February 1865, it was stationed at Mosier's Mill, Tennessee and in March and April 1865 at Jonesborough, Tennessee.

4th Tennessee Volunteer Infantry Regiment (USA)

Company D:

Captain Thomas H. Reeves

Captain Reeves had previously served as a private in the Second Regiment Tennessee Infantry. He had enrolled in Company F, 2nd Tennessee Volunteer Infantry on 6 Dec 1861 and served until August 1862. At age 21 he enrolled in the 4th Regiment at Louisville, Kentucky on 19 February 1863. Having recruited a number of men from Greene County, he was commissioned First Lieutenant by Governor Johnson. On 29 May 1863 he was promoted to Captain by Colonel Stover to command Company D. Along with his company, he was captured and paroled at McMinnville on 3 Oct 1863. Captain Reeves was promoted to Major on 12 March 1864 and placed in command of the Fourth Regiment.

Captain Gaines Lawson

Captain Lawson enrolled at age: 21 as a private at Rogersville on 21 December 1862. He was promoted to Sergeant on the 15th of April 1863. He was captured and paroled at McMinnville, Tennessee on the 3rd of October 1863. He was promoted to Captain to replace Captain Reeves, who was promoted to Major on the 1st of April 1864. He received a promoted to Major on the 31st of May 1865. He mustered out with the Regiment on the 2nd of August 1865. Captain Lawson received the Medal of Honor for gallantry in action at McMinnville.

Captain Richard S. Lane

Captain Lane, at age 26, enrolled at Louisville, Kentucky on the 29th of May 1863. He mustered in at Dandridge as a First Lieutenant in November 1862. He received a promotion to Captain on the 31st of May 1865. He mustered out with the Regiment on the 2nd of August 1865

First Lieutenant William P. Jones

Lieutenant Jones, age: 22; enrolled at Rutledge as a private on 14 April 1863. He was promoted to Sergeant on 17 April 1864. He was commissioned 1st Lieutenant on 5 June 1865 at Jonesborough. He mustered out with the Regiment on 2 August 1865.

Organization of the Regiment

Second Lieutenant Robert E. Sweeney

Lieutenant Sweeney at age 35, enrolled at Newport on 1 August 1862. He was commissioned by Governor Andrew Johnson, under Act of Congress on 29 May 1863. He was appointed to fill the original vacancy for 2nd Lieutenant, Company D. He was captured and paroled at McMinnville on 3 Oct 1863. He was mustered out on 2 August 1865. His file contains Special Order # 20, dated 27 Mar 1864, returning him to his company from a detail as Acting Surgeon.

Company D consisted of men from East Tennessee

Company D, was shown to be in Nashville during 15 through 30 June 1863; the company was captured by the enemy on October 3, 1863 at McMinnville, Tennessee; in March and April 1864, the unit was stationed at Dandridge, Tennessee; during May through October 1864, the Company was at Kingston, Tennessee; in November and December 1864, it was located 8 Miles southwest of Dandridge, Tennessee; during January and February 1865, the Company was located at Mosier's Mill, Tennessee and during March through June 1865 it was located at Jonesborough, Tennessee.

Company E:

Captain Levi Pickering

Captain Pickering, age 38, enrolled in the Fourth Regiment at Louisville, Kentucky on 9 April 1863. Records show that he was previously a private in Company K, First Tennessee Cavalry. Upon enrollment in the Fourth Regiment, he was commissioned a First Lieutenant by Governor Johnson. He was promoted to Captain by order of General Burnside on 29 April 1863. He was captured and paroled at McMinnville when the entire regiment was captured by Confederate General Wheeler's forces on the 3rd of October 1863. On 21 March 1864 he was shown on the muster roll as sick in the officers hospital at Knoxville. Captain Pickering was discharged on 2 August 1865. His file shows that he received a military pension.

4th Tennessee Volunteer Infantry Regiment (USA)

Second Lieutenant Abner J. Frazier

Lieutenant Frazier, age 23; enrolled as a private at Greeneville on 19 February 1863. He was appointed Sergeant Major on 1 May 1864 and promoted to 2nd Lieutenant at Kingston on 12 October 1864. His file contains prisoner of war record but place and date are not stated.

Second Lieutenant Green Click

Lieutenant Click enrolled at Greeneville on 1 April 1863 and mustered in at Louisville, Kentucky on 15 May 1863. Along with the rest of the Regiment, he was captured and paroled at McMinnville on 3 October 1863. He resigned, claiming incompetency, on 27 May 1864.

Company E enrolled at Greenville and consisted of men from East Tennessee.

Company E, was shown to be in Nashville during 15 through 30 June 1863. The company was captured by the enemy on October 3, 1863 at McMinnville, Tennessee; the Company reorganized in December 1863; in March through August 1864, the unit was stationed at Loudon, Tennessee; during September through October 1864, the Company was at Kingston, Tennessee; in November and December 1864, it was located 8 Miles Southwest of Dandridge, Tennessee; during January and February 1865, the Company was located at Mosier's Mill, Tennessee and during March through June 1865 it was located at Jonesborough, Tennessee.

Company F:

Captain Thomas Davis

Captain Davis enrolled at Louisville, Kentucky on 20 March 1863. He mustered in as 2nd Lieutenant. He was promoted to Captain on 15 June 1863. He was captured and paroled at McMinnville on 3 October 1863. He was reported on detached service during the period, 30 June 1863 through 29 February 1864. He had suffered a disabling gunshot wound in the left side on 21 March 1862. He resigned on 13 May 1864.

Organization of the Regiment

Captain George W. Holsinger

Captain Holsinger, at age 26, enrolled as a private at Greeneville on 26 January 1863. He appeared on Confederate prisoner of war rolls at Louisville, 15 April 1863 through 16 May 1863. He was appointed Sergeant by order of Colonel Stover on 16 August 1863. He was commissioned 1st Lieutenant to replace Lt. Farnsworth on 12 June 1864. He was reported sick at Kingston on 23 November 1864. He was promoted Captain to replace Captain Davis on 19 February 1865. He was reported sick at Greeneville on 5 March 1865. A physicians statement indicated that he "suffered typhoid fever and hepatitis." His date of discharge was not clear.

Captain Joseph Farnsworth

Captain Farnsworth, age 28, enrolled at Greeneville on 27 April 1863. He mustered in as 1st Lieutenant and was promoted to Captain on 12 June 1864. He requested release from service because of family concerns on 9 May 1864. He again, on 8 June 1864, asked approval of his resignation request, citing family and health concerns. On the 17th of July 1864, he requested a leave of absence. He was reported absent without leave on 1 August 1864. A court martial resulted in which he was charged by Major Reeves with being absent without leave and conduct unbecoming an officer, and desertion. He received a dishonorable discharged by War Department on 19 September 1864.

First Lieutenant Alexander B. Wilson

Lieutenant Wilson, age 25; enlisted as a private at Greeneville on 6 April 1863. He was promoted to 1st Sergeant on 26 April 1863. Along with his company, he was captured and paroled at McMinnville on 3 October 1863. He was promoted to Second Lieutenant on 5 October 1864 and commissioned First Lieutenant on 13 February 1865. He mustered out with the Regiment on 2 August 1865.

Second Lieutenant Robert M. Dobson

Lieutenant Dobson, at age 24, enrolled as a private at Greeneville on 28 April 1863. He was appointed Sergeant on 15 June 1863; He was captured and paroled, along with the

Majority of the Regiment at McMinnville on 3 October 1863. He was commissioned 2nd Lieutenant on 19 February 1865.

Company F enrolled at Greenville and consisted of men from East Tennessee

Company F, was shown to be in Nashville during 15 through 30 June 1863; the company was captured by the enemy on October 3, 1863 at McMinnville, Tennessee; the Company reorganized in December 1863, men were on parole; in March through April 1864, the unit was stationed at Loudon, Tennessee; during May and June 1864, the Company was located at (record illegible); in July through October 1864, it was located at Kingston, Tennessee; during November and December, 1864, it was located 8 Miles Southwest of Dandridge, Tennessee; during January and February 1865, the Company was located at Mosier's Mill, Tennessee and during March through June 1865 it was located at Jonesborough, Tennessee.

Company G:

Captain Samuel West

Captain West, age 24, mustered in as a First Lieutenant on 22 May 1863. He was commissioned Captain at Louisville to fill the original vacancy as Captain Company G, on 15 June 1863. He was captured and paroled at McMinnville on 3 October 1863. He was killed by the enemy in Washington County, Tennessee, while collecting his men who had been paroled at McMinnville.

Captain Joseph W. Chockley

Captain Chockley at age 37, mustered in at Cincinnati, Ohio, 2 December 1862. He appeared on a list of stragglers at Camp Chase, Ohio, 3 June 1863. He was promoted to Captain, 15 April 1864 to fill the vacancy caused by death of Captain Samuel West. His service record shows that he was sick in the hospital in Knoxville on 10 December 1864.

Organization of the Regiment

First Lieutenant William R. Munday

First Lieutenant Munday, at age 32, mustered in at Jonesborough as a private on 1 Jan. 1863. He was commissioned 1st Lieutenant, Company G, by Colonel Daniel Stover on 15 June 1863 to fill a vacancy created by the promotion of Captain West. He resigned for the "good of the service" on 30 June 1864. His resignation request cites his inability to write rendering him incompetent to perform the tasks required of him. He also cited family hardships in his resignation request.

First Lieutenant Charles W. Piper

Lieutenant Piper, age 19, enrolled in Company C at Greeneville on 6 April 1863. He was appointed 2nd Sergeant on 24 April 1863 and promoted to 1st Lieutenant, 9 September 1863 by order of Colonel Stover to fill the vacancy created by the promotion of Lieutenant Newton Hacker. He was captured and paroled at McMinnville, 3 October 1863. He was absent on detached service, 21 February 1864. On 14 August 1864, he was appointed commander Company G. He was appointed acting Regimental Quartermaster on 12 June 1865 and discharged from the service on 2 August 1865.

Second Lieutenant James H. Masoner

Lieutenant Masoner, at age 37, enrolled at Greeneville on 5 March 1863. He received his commissioned at Louisville on 22 May 1863. He was captured and paroled at McMinnville on 3 October 1863. He was reported on the muster roll as sick at Knoxville on 21 June 1863. He resigned for physical disability on 12 July 1864.

Company G consisted of men from East Tennessee

Company G, was shown to be in Nashville on 30 June 1863; the company was captured by the enemy on October 3, 1863 at McMinnville; in March through April 1864, the unit was stationed at Loudon, Tennessee; during May through October, 1864, the Company was located at Kingston, Tennessee; during November and December, 1864, it was located 8 Miles Southwest of Dandridge, Tennessee; during January and February 1865, the Company was located at Mosier's Mill,

4th Tennessee Volunteer Infantry Regiment (USA)

Tennessee and during March through June 1865 it was located at Jonesborough, Tennessee.

Company H:

Captain John A. Wagner

Captain Wagner, age 26, enrolled at Greeneville on 27 June 1863 as a private in Company A. He was appointed 3rd Sergeant on 1 April 1863. He was captured and paroled at McMinnville on 3 October 1863 and was absent on parole until February 1864. He was promoted to 2nd Sergeant on 1 August 1864 and promoted to Commissary Sergeant on 1 November 1864. He was commissioned Captain, Company H on 5 June 1865 to fill the original vacancy as commander of Company H. He was discharged on 2 August 1865.

First Lieutenant Landon H. P. Lusk

Lieutenant Lusk, served in Companies F and H. At age 25, he enrolled as a private at Carter County on 24 March 1863. He received a $25 enlistment bonus. He was promoted to hospital steward on 1 July 1863. He was reported to be on recruiting duty in May 1864. He received a promotion to First Lieutenant on 24 June 1865. Lieutenant Lusk's file shows that he was a prisoner of war, in a Confederate prison at Louisville, on 16 April 1863.

First Lieutanant John W. Tipton

Lieutenant Tipton, age 30, enrolled at Elizabethton, 9 Aug 1863. He was an enlisted man in the 13th Regiment Tennessee Volunteer Cavalry prior to mustering in to fill the original vacancy for First Lieutenant of Company H. He was commissioned by the Governor of Tennessee on 28 June 1864. He resigned for "the good of the service" on 5 June 1865.

Second Lieutenant John T. Pierce

Lieutenant Pierce, age: 32, was born in Carter County. He enrolled as a private in Company B at Strawberry Plains on 1 October 1863. From muster-in through October 1864, he was on recruiting duty in East Tennessee. He was promoted to 2nd Lieutenant, Company H, on 31 May 1865. He mustered in

Organization of the Regiment   47

Company H on 5 June 1865 and was discharged from the service on 2 August 1865.

Company H consisted of a detachment from the First Tennessee Congressional District who were mustered at Loudon, Tennessee on May 7, 1864, plus transfers from the 3rd Tennessee Volunteer Infantry in March.

Company H was not fully organized until 1865; the Company was located at Kingston in August 1865; during September and October it was located at Kingston, Tennessee; during November and December, 1864 the company was shown 8 miles Southwest of Dandridge, Tennessee; during January and February, 1865, the Company was at Mosier's Mill, Tennessee and during March through June 1865, the Company was at Jonesborough, Tennessee.

General site map of locations in the State of Tennessee:

State of Tennessee

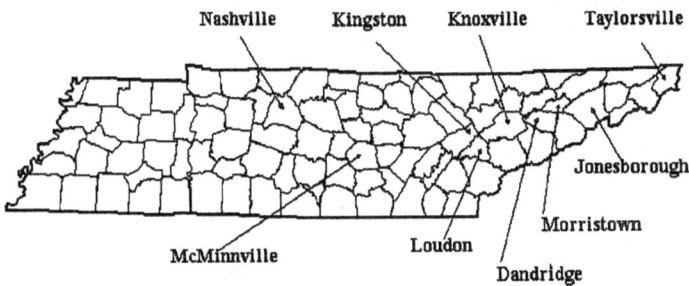

Additional places mentioned:

- Mossey Creek — Near Dandridge
- Mosier's Mill — Near Morristown
- Lebanon — Near Nashville
- Taylorsville — Now Mountain City
- Big Creek Gap — Now LaFollette
- Strawberry Plains — Near Knoxville

Chapter 4

Soldiers of the Regiment

(Soldiers who died in the service are identified in bold type.)

Adams, Abraham: private, Company H, age 41, home: Wilkes County, NC., mustered in on 10 Apr 1865 at Taylorsville, TN, mustered out 2 Aug 1865.

Adams, Gillespie: private, Company B, mustered in: 1 Apr 1863 at Robinson, Illinois, captured at McMinnville, mustered out 2 Aug 1865.

Adams, James C.: private, Company B, mustered in: 2 Jun 1863 at Taylorsville, TN, captured at McMinnville, absent on parole 3 Oct 1863 until 29 Feb 1864, mustered out 2 Aug 1865.

Adams, Wiley: private, Company A, mustered in: 1 Apr 1863 at Robinson, Illinois, captured at McMinnville and paroled on 3 Oct 1865, given a 20 day furlough on 30 Jun 1865 to go home to Blount County, TN, mustered out 2 Aug 1865.

Adkins, Caloway: private, Company D, mustered in at Newport, TN, on 18 Jun 1863 for 3 years, captured at McMinnville on 3 Oct 1863 and paroled, sick in camp during Sep - Oct 1864, absent without leave: 29 Nov 1864.

Adkins, Calvin: private, Company D, age: 23, mustered in at Newport, TN, 18 Jun 1863 for 3 years, discharged: 2 Aug 1865.

Adkins, Levi: private, Company D, age: 25, enlisted at Newport, TN, 18 Jan 1863 for 3 years, born: Campbell Co., TN, captured at McMinnville on 3 Oct 1863, reported at Knoxville on 24 Feb 1864 from missing in action, discharged: 2 Aug 1865.

Adkinson, William: private, Company E, no further record.

Alexander, Andrew J: corporal, enlisted at Greeneville, TN on 25 Mar 1863, appointed as corporal: 25 Mar 1863, captured and paroled at McMinnville on 3 Oct 1863, during period 30 Jun 1863 - 29 Feb 1864 reported in arrest, shown in Apr 1864 as private.

Alexander, Jeremiah: private, companies E & F, Age: 26, born: Greene Co., TN., enlisted 7 May 1864 at Lexington, KY., shown absent without leave 18 Apr - May 1864, sick in hospital in Kingston 1 Sep - Dec 1864, sick in hospital in Knoxville 18 Mar - May 1865, discharged 2 Aug 1865.

Allen, John M.:: sergeant, Company C, age: 21, enlisted at Greeneville 6 Apr 1863, appointed corporal 24 Apr 1863, sick in hospital 15-30 Jun 1863, captured and paroled at McMinnville 3 Oct 1863, promoted to sergeant 1 Aug 1864, mustered out 2 Aug 1865.

Soldiers of the Regiment   49

Allen, John W.:: private, company B, age: 18, enlisted at Taylorsville 6 Jan 1863, record indicates that he was a prisoner of war, shown sick in hospital at Knoxville during Nov - Dec 1864.
Allen, Samuel H.:, private, Company C, age: 18, enlisted at Jonesborough, transferred from 3 Infantry Regiment 1 Mar 1865, discharged 2 Aug 1865.
Allen, William C.:, captain, Company A, mustered in as 1st Lt on 27 Apr 1863 at Greeneville, captured and paroled at McMinnville on 3 Oct 1863, appointed regimental quartermaster 17 Feb 1864, promoted to captain 13 Jul 1864, discharged 2 Aug 1865.
Altum, Spencer: private, Company A, age: 25, born in Anderson Co., TN, transferred from 3 Infantry Regiment on 1 Mar 1865, in hospital in Knoxville Mar - Jul 1865, discharged 2 Aug 1865.
Ambers, James: private, Company G, age: 38, enrolled 15 Mar 1863 at Jonesborough, sick in hospital in Jun 1863, captured and paroled at McMinnville 3 Oct 1863.
Amitage, Isaac A.: see: Armitage, Isaac A.
Anderson, King D.: private, age: 19, transferred from 3 Infantry Regiment on 1 Mar 1865, discharged 2 Aug 1865.
Anderson, Thomas: private, Company F, enrolled 1 Oct 1863 at Dandridge, TN., reported absent without leave at Loudon, TN. 7 Apr 1864, dropped from rolls as deserter at Strawberry Plains, TN. on 31 Aug 1864.
Arowood, Samuel: private, Company D, age: 36. enrolled 2 Jan 1863 at Dandridge, TN., captured and paroled in McMinnville on 3 Oct 1863, requested a 10 day furlough in Jul 1865 to visit home in Jefferson County, TN.
Arington, Willis: musician, mustered in at Greeneville, TN 5 Apr 1863, appointed musician 1 May 1863, captured at McMinnville on 3 October, held prisoner at Camp Chase, Ohio, released at Aikens Landing, VA, 8 May 1864.
Armitage, Isaac A.: 1st Lieutenant, Age: 32, enrolled 6 Apr 1863 at Greeneville, TN, appointed as sergeant from private 24 Mar 1864, appointed 1st Lt Company A on 6 Jun 1865, discharged 2 Aug 1865.
Armstrong, Alexander: private, Company G, age: 37, enrolled 6 Apr 1863 at Greeneville, TN., died in the hospital at Louisville, KY. on 5 Jun 1863.
Arney, Alfred J.: private, Company B, age: 18, born: Johnson County, TN., enrolled at Loudon, TN. on 7 May 1864, contacted measles at Jonesborough in May 1864, suffered lung disease at time of discharge on 2 Aug 1865.
Arnold, Seth: private, Company A, age: 27, enrolled at Loudon, TN. on 7 May 1864, born: Hawkins County, TN., discharged on 2 Aug 1865.

Arrendell, William: private, Company B, age: 31, enrolled at Taylorsville, TN. on 22 Aug 1863, captured at McMinnville 3 Oct 1863, transferred to Company F on 29 Apr 1864, dropped as missing in action on 1 Apr 1865.
Ashley, Benjamin H.: private, Company A, enrolled at Elizabethton, TN. on 24 Apr 1864, deserted at Kingston, TN. in 1864, restored to duty 1 Mar 1865, deserted 25 Apr 1865, discharged 2 Aug 1865.
Aston, James M.: private, Company C, age: 23, enrolled at Jonesborough, TN. 5 Jan 1863, died on 8 Oct 1863 in general hospital in McMinnville, TN.
Atkinson, William E.: private, Company B, age: 25, enrolled 11 Jul 1863 in Nashville, born: Washington County, TN., captured at McMinnville on 3 Oct 1863, on duty with provost marshall, 4th Division, Dept of Cumberland in March and April 1865, discharged 2 Aug 1864.
Ausborn, Daniel: private, Company H, age: 18, enrolled 29 Apr 1864 in Elizabethton, TN., died in general hospital in Knoxville on 22 Feb 1865.
Babb, Abner: private, Company G, age: 18, enrolled 18 Mar 1863 at Greeneville, TN., captured and paroled at McMinnville on 3 Oct 1863, discharged 2 Aug 1865.
Babb, Barnet: private, Company C, age: 38, enrolled at Nashville on 10 Jul 1863, captured and paroled at McMinnville 3 Oct 1863, on parole or missing until Mar - Apr 1865, discharged 2 Aug 1865.
Babb, Charles: corporal, Company E, age: 18, enrolled at Greeneville, TN. 11 Aug 1862, captured and paroled at McMinnville 3 Oct 1863, appointed corporal 1 Aug 1864, sick in hospital at Kingston 25 Nov 1864 - Jan 1865, discharged 2 Aug 1865.
Babb, James W.: private, Company B, age: 24, enlisted at Blountville, TN. 13 Aug 1863, died in hospital at Louisville, KY. 2 Dec 1863.
Babb, Martin V.: private, Company F, age: 21, enlisted at Greeneville, TN. 15 Apr 1863, died in hospital at Louisville, KY. 2 Jun 1863 of pneumonia.
Babb, Samuel H.: private, Company E, age: 34, enlisted at Greeneville, TN. 15 Mar 1863, sick in hospital at Nashville, discharged 2 Aug 1865.
Bagwell, Hiram: private, Company G, age: 30, enlisted at Taylorsville, TN. 15 Aug 1862, captured and paroled at McMinnville 3 Oct 1863, no additional information.
Baker, James A.: private, Company D, age: 31, enlisted 1 Mar 1863 at Greeneville, TN., captured and paroled at McMinnville 3 Oct 1863, deserted 30 Jul 1864, dropped from rolls as a deserter on 31 Aug 1864 at Kingston, returned to duty 22 Dec 1864, discharged 2 Aug 1865.

Soldiers of the Regiment 51

Baker, Robert N.: 1st Sergeant, Company H, transferred from 3 Regiment Tennessee Infantry on 1 Mar 1865, had been promoted to 1st Sgt 1 Jul 1864, discharged 2 Aug 1865.
Baldwin, Drewry P: private, Company C, no additional information.
Bales, Abner C.: private, Company G, age: 37, entered service 5 Sep 1862 at Jonesborough, TN., captured and paroled at McMinnville 3 Oct 1863, absent until Mar 1865, discharged 2 Aug 1865.
Bales, Lewis R.: private, Company H, age: 18, transferred from 3 Regiment Tennessee Infantry on 1 Mar 1865, deserted at Knoxville 25 Mar 1865, nothing further.
Bales, Henry H.: private, Company E, age: 19, entered service on 15 Mar 1863 at Greeneville, TN., captured and paroled at McMinnville 3 Oct 1863, discharged 2 Aug 1865.
Balinger, William H.: private, Company D, age: 18, entered service at Dandridge, TN. on 1 Feb 1863, born: Jefferson County, TN., captured and paroled at McMinnville 3 Oct 1865, sick in hospital in Knoxville 29 May 1865, mustered out with disability on 21 Jun 1865.
Bandy, James P.: private, Company B, age: 19, entered service at Lexington, KY., deserted at Louisville on 27 Aug 1863.
Banner, William D.: 1st Sergeant, Company B, age: 24, joined at Boone, NC., 10 Jul 1862, promoted to sergeant 11 May 1863, sick in hospital at Nashville 28 Aug 1863 through 11 May 1865 when he was discharged.
Barnes, Allen R.: private, Company B, age: 37, joined at Jonesborough, TN., 24 Nov 1862, captured and paroled at McMinnville on 3 Oct 1863, discharged 2 Aug 1865.
Barnes, Isaac N.: **private, Company B, age: 20, joined at Jonesborough, TN., 24 Nov 1862, died in the hospital at Louisville, KY., of measles on 20 Jan 1863.**
Barnes, James H.: private, Company H, age: 22, entered service in Jonesborough, TN., on 12 Sep 1863, discharged 2 Aug 1865.
Barnes, John L.: corporal, Company B, age: 20, enlisted at Jonesborough, TN., on 24 Nov 1862, promoted to corporal 19 Feb 1863, captured and paroled at McMinnville on 3 Oct 1863, promoted to sergeant on 11 Mar 1865, reduced in rank to private on 30 May 1865, discharged on 2 Aug 1865.
Barnes, Madison M.: private, Company B, age: 37, enlisted 24 Nov 1862 at Jonesborough, TN., captured and paroled at McMinnville 3 Oct 1865, discharged 2 Aug 1865.
Barnett, Maridy: private, age: 28, enlisted 1 Jan 1864 at Strawberry Plains, TN., born at Newport, TN., absent without leave 3 May 1864, dropped from rolls as deserter on 31 Aug 1864, returned to duty and restored 21 Jan 1865, discharged 2 Aug 1865.
Barnes, Allen R.: private, Company B, no additional information.

Basket, Burton S.: private, Company C, age: 29, enlisted at Greeneville, TN., 6 Apr 1863, reported deserted 27 Apr 1863 at Louisville, KY., absent on leave 15-30 Jun 1863, no additional information.
Bates, Adam: private, Company D, age: 24, enlisted 1 Feb 1863 at Rutledge, TN., reported as a prisoner at McMinnville 3 Oct 1863, deserted 2 Aug 1864 at Kingston, restored to duty 3 Sep 1864, discharged 2 Aug 1865.
Bates, John: corporal, Company D, age: 28, enlisted 1 Feb 1863 at Rutledge, TN., promoted to corporal 2 Jun 1863, captured and paroled at McMinnville 3 Oct 1863, reduced to private 7 Mar 1864, in arrest Sep - Oct 1864, discharged, 2 Aug 1865.
Baxter, Levi W.: private, Company C, age: 23, enlisted at Greeneville, TN on 6 Apr 1863, captured and paroled at McMinnville on 3 Oct 1865, absent on parole until Sep 1864, discharged 2 Aug 1865.
Baxter, Samuel H.: 2nd Lieutenant, Company C, age: 39, mustered in as 2nd Lt., absent on recruiting duty in East Tennessee Jun 1863, reported 18 Aug 1863 as absent without leave, dropped as deserter 31 Aug 1863, honorable discharged 9 Sep 1863 to permit filling his vacancy.
Baxter, Thomas: private, Company C, age: 31, enlisted at Greeneville, TN., on 15 Mar 1863, sick in hospital 15-30 Jun 1863, captured and paroled at McMinnville 3 Oct 1863, absent on parole until Mar 1864, deserted 23 Jul 1864 at Kingston, dropped from rolls 31 Aug 1864, restored to duty 10 Mar 1865.
Bayles, Abner B.: private, Company G, no additional information.
Beals, Henry H.: private, Company E, see Bales, Henry H.
Bell, Elbert: private, Company C, age: 23, enlisted 5 Apr 1863 at Jonesborough, TN., captured at McMinnville 3 Oct 1863, shown missing in action Mar - Apr 1865, died in prison in Andersonville, GA., 10 Apr 1865.
Bellomy, Hiram P.: private, Company A, joined 26 Mar 1862 at Eastonville, VA., deserted at Nashville on 20 Aug 1863.
Belt, Robert C.: private, Company B, age: 34, joined at Nashville on 7 May 1863, Jun 1863 through Aug 1864 shown as sick at home in Blount County, TN., Sep - Oct 1864 present for duty, sick in hospital in Knoxville 29 Apr 1865, discharged 2 Aug 1865.
Benner, John: private, Company C, age: 23, enlisted at Newport, TN., 13 Dec 1863, no further record.
Benner, William: corporal, Company A, age: 21, enrolled at Newport, TN., 13 Dec 1862, appointed corporal 1 May 1863, captured and paroled at McMinnville on 3 Oct 1863, reported killed by the enemy while on parole in Cocke County, TN on 24 Dec 1863.

Soldiers of the Regiment   53

Berry, John D: private, Company H, age: 33, enrolled 13 Apr 1865 at Taylorsville, TN., resided in Hancock County, TN., discharged 2 Aug 1865.
Bibens, John: private, Company D, age: 19, joined 20 Feb 1863 at Rutledge, TN., resided in Grainger County, TN., mustered in 31 Mar 1864, in arrest 28 Aug 1864, absent without leave 8 Dec 1864, discharged 2 Aug 1865.
Bible, Christian: private, Company F, age: 43, joined at Greeneville, TN on 20 Feb 1863, prisoner of war record (particulars not stated, assume captured at McMinnville), absent without leave 3 May 1864, deserted 30 May 1864, dropped from rolls 31 Aug 1864, restored to duty 28 Oct 1864, sick in hospital at Knoxville 27 May 1865, discharged 2 Aug 1865.
Bible, John: private, Company D, age: 38, joined at Greeneville on 30 Jan 1863, captured and paroled at McMinnville 3 Oct 1863, sick in hospital at Knoxville 29 May 1865, mustered out 17 Jun 1865 because of disability.
Bible, Noah: private, Company F, age: 18, entered service from Greeneville 28 Jan 1863, died in the hospital in Nashville 22 Jul 1863 of chronic diarrhea.
Bible, Phillip: corporal, Company D, age: 19, enlisted at Greeneville 1 Jan 1864, promoted to corporal 14 Jul 1865, discharged 2 Aug 1865.
Bibons, John: private, Company D, no additional information.
Bird, David F.: private, Company E, age: 19, enrolled in Loudon, Tennessee, on 7 May 1864, born in Greene County, discharged: 2 Aug 1865.
Bird, Jacob N.: corporal, Company D, age: 20, enrolled 7 Feb 1863 at Rutledge, TN., promoted to corporal on 7 Jun 1865, captured and paroled at McMinnville, 3 Oct 1863, discharged: 2 Aug 1865.
Bird, James: **private, Company E, age: 19, enrolled in Greeneville on 16 Jan 1863, died in the Hospital in Nashville on 23 Apr 1864 of fever, father: William Bird, Greeneville, TN.**
Bird, James: private, Company D, age: 19, enrolled at Rutledge, TN., on 6 Jan 1863, shown as sick during 15 Jun - 30 Jun 1863, shown in arrest in Knoxville during May and Jun 1865 by sentence of a General Courts Martial for insubordinate conduct, serving a 1 year sentence at hard labor, discharged: 29 Aug 1865.
Bishop, Richard M.: private, Company A, age: 45, enlisted at Strawberry Plains on 6 Jan 1864, born: Hawkins County, absent without leave on 28 Aug 1864, dropped as a deserter, returned to duty on 16 Nov 1864, stated that while on pass, he was captured by rebels and after 8 days he escaped and returned to the Regiment to learn that he had been dropped as a deserter, sick: 31 Mar 1865.

4th Tennessee Volunteer Infantry Regiment (USA)

Black, John W.: private, Companies D & F, age: 19, enrolled at Newport on 20 Feb 1862, shown sick in Hospital 15-30 Jun 1863, sick in Hospital 5 Sep 1863, transferred to Company F on 30 Apr 1864, shown sick in Hospital at Nashville on 1 Jan 1864 through Jul 1865 when he was transferred to Company B, 17th Regiment.

Blackburn, Richard W.: sergeant, Company H, age: 22, joined at Taylorsville on 1 Jan 1865, born: Johnson County, school teacher, promoted to sergeant 28 Apr 1865, discharged 2 Aug 1865.

Blackburn, W.P.: private, Company H, joined 1 Jun 1864 at Elizabethton, Tennessee, deserted at Strawberry Plains on 28 Jun 1864.

Blaser, Christian: private, Company A, age: 22, enlisted at Newport, TN., 13 Dec 1862, captured and paroled at McMinnville on 3 Oct 1863, absent on parole until Feb 1864, absent without leave 27 May 1864, dropped as a deserter on 31 Aug 1864, restored to duty 20 Dec 1864, discharged on 2 Aug 1865.

Blazer, Daniel: private, Company A, age: 20, enlisted at Newport on 13 Dec 1862, captured and paroled at McMinnville 3 Oct 1863, on parole until Feb 1864, discharged on 2 Aug 1865.

Blazer, Eranens: private, Company A, age: 27, enrolled at Newport on 13 Dec 1862, absent without leave 29 May 1864, dropped as deserter on 31 Aug 1864, restored to duty 14 May 1865 at Jonesborough, requested desertion charges be dropped on 5 Oct 1886, request was denied.

Blazer, Peter: private, Company A, age: 22, enrolled at Newport, TN., on 13 Dec 1862, died in hospital at McMinnville on 20 Sep 1863 of typhoid and pneumonia.

Blazer, Phillip: private, Company A, age: 23, enrolled at Greeneville, TN., on 20 Apr 1863, captured and paroled at McMinnville on 3 Oct 1863, on parole until Feb 1864, discharged 2 Aug 1865.

Blazer, Samuel: private, Company A, age: 29, enrolled at Newport, TN., 13 Dec 1862, captured and paroled at McMinnville 3 Oct 1863, absent on parole until Feb 1864, discharged 2 Aug 1865.

Blazer, Soloman: private, Company A, age: 39, enrolled at Newport, TN., 13 Dec 1862, captured and paroled at McMinnville 3 Oct 1863, absent without leave 29 May 1864, dropped as deserter 31 Aug 1864, returned to duty 25 Apr 1865, sick in Hospital in Knoxville 27 May 1865 till 14 Jul 1865.

Blazor, Jacob: private, Company G, age: 22, enlisted 5 May 1863 at Greeneville, TN., captured and paroled at McMinnville 3 Oct 1863, absent on parole until Feb 1864, absent without leave 25 Dec 1864 until 22 Jan 1865.

Blevins, Allen: private, Company B, enrolled at Elizabethton, TN, 30 May 1864; detailed as cook for the Captain, 1 Dec 1864; discharged: 2 Aug 1865.

Soldiers of the Regiment 55

Blevins, Dillens: corporal, Company A, transferred from 3 Infantry Regiment Apr 1865 from sick in hospital, joined from desertion 10 Mar 1865 at Jonesborough, discharged 2 Aug 1865.
Blevins, Henry: private, Company A, transferred from 3 Infantry Regiment which he deserted 25 Mar 1865, record was corrected in 1887, he had rejoined his unit from hospitalization during 25 Mar 1865 through 7 May 1865.
Blevins, James C.: private, Company B, age: 18, enrolled 20 May 1863 at Elizabethton, TN., captured and paroled at McMinnville 3 Oct 1863, absent on parole until 29 Feb 1864, Transferred to Company H, 30 Jun 1864; absent without leave, 30 Jun 1865; mustered out, 2 Aug 1865.
Blevins, Lune B.: private, Company H, age: 44; enrolled at Strawberry Plains, 5 Apr 1863, mustered in, 7 May 1864 at Loudon, TN.; discharged 2 Aug 1865.
Blevins, Thomas: private, Company H, age: 19, enlisted 27 Apr 1864 at Elizabethton, TN.; mustered in 7 May 1864 at Loudon, TN., died in hospital at Loudon, TN of fever on 14 Jul 1864.
Blevins, William H.: private, Company H, age: 21, enrolled 29 Apr 1864 at Elizabethton, TN., discharged: 2 Aug 1865.
Boatman, Nathan A.: private, Company C, transferred from 3 Infantry 1 May 1865; sick in hospital at Knoxville May - Jun 1865; discharged: 23 Jun 1865.
Bobb, Abner: private, Company G, age: 27, enrolled at Greeneville, 6 Apr 1863; sick in hospital 30 Jun 1863; captured and paroled at McMinnville 3 Oct 1863; absent until Feb 1865, discharged: 2 Aug 1865.
Bogart, William: sergeant, Company G, age: 27, enrolled at Jonesborough 25 Nov 1862; promoted to sergeant 22 May 1862; captured and paroled at McMinnville 3 Oct 1863; on parole through Feb 1864; discharged, 2 Aug 1865.
Bohanon, John: corporal, Company A, enrolled at Greeneville, 27 Jan 1863; promoted to corporal in Apr 1864; sick in hospital in Kingston 23 Nov 1864; discharged: 2 Aug 1865.
Bolian, James: private, Company D, age: 18, enrolled at Greeneville, 17 Apr 1862; captured and paroled at McMinnville 3 Oct 1863; absent without leave, 12 May 1864; deserted at Loudon, TN., 12 May 1864; dropped as a deserter, 31 Aug 1864.
Boring, John W: 2nd Lt., age: 20, enrolled at Jonesborough, 5 Sep 1862; captured and paroled at McMinnville 3 Oct 1863; commissioned 2 Lt, 12 Oct 1864; held prisoner at Camp Chase, Ohio until 27 Mar 1864; discharged 2 Aug 1865.
Boring, Thomas: private, Company B, age: 22, enlisted at Jonesborough, 24 Nov 1862; died in hospital in Nashville 21 Jul 1863 of malaria.

Bowers, Henry N.: private, Company B, age: 21, born: Washington County; enrolled at Nashville on 11 Jul 1863; captured and paroled at McMinnville, 3 Oct 1863; sick in hospital at Camp Nelson 7 Dec 1863; died in hospital at Camp Nelson of syphilis on 30 Dec 1863.
Bowler, William A.: private, Company G, age: 20, enrolled at Greeneville, 31 May 1863; captured and paroled at McMinnville, 3 Oct 1863; discharged, 2 Aug 1865.
Bowlin, Asa: private, Company C, age: 34, enrolled at Greeneville, 26 May 1863; captured and paroled at McMinnville, 3 Oct 1863; absent on parole until Feb 1864; discharged: 2 Aug 1865.
Bowman, Andrew: private, Company E, age: 18; enrolled at Greeneville, 22 Jul 1863; captured and paroled at McMinnville, 3 Oct 1863; absent without leave, 22 Dec 1864; no additional records.
Bowman, Isaac J.: private, Company G, age: 27; enrolled at Greeneville, 31 Dec 1862; absent without leave, 13 Apr 1864; deserted, 19 Apr 1864 at Strawberry Plains, TN.; no additional records.
Bowman, John: private, Company G, age: 24; enlisted at Jonesborough, 27 Feb 1863; absent without leave, 13 Apr 1864; deserted, 19 Apr 1864.
Bowman, Joseph: private, Company E, age: 21, enrolled at Greeneville, 15 Nov 1861; captured and paroled at McMinnville, 3 Oct 1863; mustered out 8 Jul 1865.
Bowman, Martin: private, Company E, age: 22, enrolled at Greenville, 15 Nov 1861; died in hospital at Nashville, 21 Aug 1863 of typhoid fever.
Bowman, Sparling: private, Company E, age: 36, enrolled at Greeneville, 18 Nov 1861; sick in hospital 15 - 30 Jun 1863; captured and paroled at McMinnville, 3 Oct 1863; mustered out, 8 Jul 1865.
Bowman, Thomas J.: private, Company E, age: 18, enrolled at Greeneville, 22 Jul 1863; captured and paroled at McMinnville, 3 Oct 1863, no additional records.
Bowman, William: private, Company E, age: 31, enrolled at Greeneville, 15 Mar 1863; captured and paroled at McMinnville, 3 Oct 1863; died in the hospital at Loudon, TN., 18 May 1864.
Boyd, James J.: captain, Company B, age: 41; enrolled at Elizabethton, TN., 19 Aug 1861; mustered in 11 May 1863; absent, sick in hospital at Knoxville 18 Apr 1864; resigned because of family concerns, 7 Jun 1864.
Bradshaw, George: private, Company H, age: 24, transferred from Company E, 3rd Infantry, sick in hospital in Nashville, mustered out 23 Jul 1865.
Bradshaw, John: private, Company H, age: 45, transferred from 3rd Infantry, 30 Apr 1865; dropped from rolls 30 Apr 1865 as a deserter.

Soldiers of the Regiment 57

Bradshaw, John E.: private, Company H, age: 23, transferred from 3rd Infantry: discharged at Knoxville, 17 Jul 1865 with disabling wound of ankle.
Bradshaw, William E.: private, Company H, transferred from 3rd Infantry, 1 Mar 1865; dropped as a deserter, 30 Apr 1865 at Knoxville, deserted at Barboursville, KY on 10 Jun 1862; mustered out 2 Aug 1865.
Brandon, Craigue: private, Company E and F, age: 31, enrolled at Greeneville on 9 Oct 1862; captured and paroled at McMinnville, 3 Oct 1863; reported on parole until Feb 1865; transferred to Company F, 30 Apr 1864; status changed to missing in action, Apr 1865; died as a prisoner of war at Andersonville, GA, 4 Apr 1864.
Broyles, William: private, Company E, age: 18, enrolled at Strawberry Plains on 6 Apr 1864; born: Greene County, record includes enlistment papers; discharged, 2 Aug 1865.
Breiden, Augustus H.: private, Companies E and H, age: 24; enrolled 9 March 1863 at Knoxville; sick in hospital in Nashville, 30 Jun 1863; captured and paroled at McMinnville, 3 Oct 1863; in hospital in Louisville, KY., 1 Aug 1864; discharged on 1 Jun 1865.
Brimer, Robert: private, Company F, age: 38, enrolled 28 Jan 1863; received $25.00 bounty; sick in hospital in Knoxville, 17 Apr 18 Jan 1863 through June 1863, discharged, 2 Aug 1865.
Brisandine, Thomas J.: private, Company H, age: 34; enrolled at Newport on 18 Jan 1863; received $25.00 bounty; captured and paroled at McMinnville, 3 Oct 1863, absent and carried in hospital in Knoxville 17 Apr 1864 through June 1865; letter in file indicating individual was absent without leave several months; discharged 30 Jun 1865.
Britt, Wilson: private, Companies B and F; age: 27; born: Grayson County, VA., enrolled at Elizabethton, TN., 15 Jul 1863; captured and paroled at McMinnville, 3 Oct 1863, absent on parole until March 1864; transferred to Company F, 29 Apr 1864; sick in hospital at Knoxville, 8 Dec 1864; absent without leave on 24 Feb 1865; record includes enlistment papers.
Britton, George E.: private, Company C, age: 33; enlisted at Greeneville on 6 Apr 1863; captured and paroled at McMinnville, 3 Oct 1863; absent on parole until Feb 1865; reported missing in action Mar and Apr 1865; returned to duty 6 May 1865; discharged on 2 Aug 1865.
Britton, Theophilus: sergeant, Company C; age: 29; enrolled at Staunton, VA., on 6 Apr 1863; captured and paroled at McMinnville, 3 Oct 1863; promoted to sergeant on 1 Jul 1864, sick at Kingston 25 Nov 1864 through Feb 1865; discharged 4 Jun 1865 to accept

commission as 2nd Lt in same company; discharged, 2 Aug 1865; records include promotion orders.

Britton, Valentine S.: sergeant, Company G, age: 26; enrolled at Nashville, 5 May 1863; promoted to sergeant, 1 Jun 1863; captured and paroled at McMinnville, 3 Oct 1863; absent on parole until Feb 1864; mustered out 7 Jul 1865.

Britton, William A.: private, Company G; age: 18; enrolled at Nashville, 15 Jul 1863; born: Greene County; captured and paroled at McMinnville, 3 Oct 1863; record includes enlistment papers.

Britton, William H.: private, Company C; age: 28; enrolled at Greeneville, 17 Mar 1863; captured and paroled at McMinnville, 3 Oct 1863; absent on parole until Feb 1864; deserted at Kingston, 23 Jul 1864; dropped as a deserter on 31 Aug 1864.

Brock, John: private, Company H: age: 18; enrolled at Kingston, 11 Jul 1864; discharged on 2 Aug 1865.

Broglin, Tilman: private, Company C, age: 18; born: Greene County; enrolled at Loudon, 7 May 1864; reported sick near Dandridge, TN, 6 Jan 1863; discharged, 2 Aug 1865; record includes enlistment papers.

Brooks, David J.: private, Company H, age: 19; enrolled at Elizabethton, TN, 18 May 1864; born: Jefferson, NC; captured at Cumberland Gap, TN; prisoner of war; paroled at Aikens Landing, VA, 6 Oct 1862; deserted at Loudon, TN, 1 Jun 1864.

Brooks, Marion W.: private, Company F; enrolled 31 Jan 1863; received $25.00 bounty; captured and paroled at McMinnville, 3 Oct 1863, absent until Feb 1864, discharged on 2 Aug 1865.

Brooks, Stephen P.: **Company F, did not muster in, admitted to hospital in Lousiville, KY, 6 Jun 1863; died, 2 Jul 1863 of diarrhea.**

Brooks, Thomas: private, Company H, age: 40; enrolled at Elizabethton, TN, 1 May 1864; deserted at Loudon on 1 Jun 1864.

Brookshire, Joel: private, Company B; age: 27; enrolled at Taylorsville, TN, 1 Jul 1863; resided in Wilkes Co., NC; a record dated 29 Oct 1889 shows that he was captured by enemy on 25 Jul 1864 and held as a prisoner until Aug 1864, he escaped and reached Union lines on 20 Mar 1865, record contains enlistment papers; discharged on 2 Aug 1865.

Brown, Bird W.: **1st Lieutenant, age: 31; Joined at Jonesborough on 12 Apr 1863, sick at Knoxville 18 Mar 1864 through June 1864; died in hospital in Lexington, KY of diarrhea on 24 Jun 1864; miscellaneous correspondence in file.**
through June 1864; died in hospital in Lexington, KY of diarrhea on 24 Jun 1864; miscellaneous correspondence in file.

Brown, Elijah K.: 1st Lieutenant; age: 19; joined at Greeneville on 15 Mar 1863, promoted to sergeant, 15 Mar 1863; captured and

Soldiers of the Regiment 59

paroled at McMinnville, 3 Oct 1863; promoted to 2 Lt, 1 Jun 1864; promoted to 1 Lt, 5 Oct 1864; sick in hospital at Knoxville, Nov - Dec 1864; on detached service, Jan - Feb 1865; file contains numerous papers.
Brown, Felix: private, Company A; age: 27; enlisted at Greeneville, 26 Jan 1863; absent without leave, 10 Jun 1864; changed to deserted on 10 Jun 1864 at Loudon, TN.; dropped from rolls as deserter, 31 Aug 1864; restored to duty, 13 Feb 1865; discharged, 2 Aug 1865; charge of desertion removed by War Department, 22 Sep 1885.
Brown, Foster: private, Company G; age: 19; transferred from 3rd Tennessee Infantry Regiment, 1 Mar 1865; discharged on 2 Aug 1865: transfer record in file.
Brown, Henry: corporal, Company D; age: 18; joined at Louisville, KY, 10 Apr 1863; promoted to corporal, 3 Jun 1863; discharged, 2 Aug 1865.
Brown, Isaac W.: private, Company G; age: 17; born at Spring Place, GA.; joined at McMinnville, 1 Jun 1863, May - June reported sick; captured and paroled at McMinnville, 3 Oct 1863; no additional information.
Brown, James D: private, age: 30; joined at Greeneville on 26 Jan 1863; captured and paroled at McMinnville, 3 Oct 1863; absent on parole through Feb 1864; deserted at Kingston, 23 Jul 1864; dropped from rolls as deserted, 31 Aug 1864; restored to duty, 13 Feb 1865; desertion charges reversed by War Department, 29 Apr 1886.
Brown, Newton D.: **private, Company C; age: 34; enrolled at Jonesborough, 6 Apr 1863; captured at McMinnville, 3 Oct 1863; absent on parole through Feb 1865, presumed dead; prisoner of war record shows imprisonment at a Southern prison (Castle Thunder); file contains miscellaneous records including a casualty sheet.**
Brown, Robert: private, Company G; age: 18; enrolled at Jonesborough, 22 Jul 1863; captured and paroled at McMinnville, 3 Oct 1863; deserted at Knoxville, 6 Mar 1864; in arrest in Kingston, 30 Jun 1864; restored to duty, 30 Jun 1864; escaped from arrest, 12 Aug 1864 absent until 20 May 1865; returned to duty at Jonesborough, TN.; court martial charges dropped because he entered the Army under age (age 16) and at the time of charges was not 18 years old; discharged, 2 Aug 1865; numerous papers in file.
Brown, Theiphilus: private, Company F; age: 18; enrolled at Louisville, KY, 14 Jul 1863; received $25.00 bounty; discharged, 2 Aug 1865; no additional records.
Browning, Robert A.: 1st Sergeant, Company G; age: 39; enrolled at Greeneville, 12 Mar 1863; promoted to sergeant, 22 May 1863; captured and paroled at McMinnville, 3 Oct 1863; absent on parole

until Feb 1864; reduced to private, 29 May 1864 by Lt Col Patterson; discharged, 2 Aug 1865.
Broyles, Adam F.: Sergeant Major, Company C and Field & Staff; age: 19, enrolled at Greeneville, 6 Apr 1863; appointed to corporal, 24 Apr 1863 and sergeant, 9 Sep 1863; captured and paroled at McMinnville, 3 Oct 1863; promoted to Sergeant Major, 1 Nov 1864 vice A.J. Frazier.
Boyles, Anderson S.: private, Company E; age: 24; enrolled at Greeneville, 25 Mar 1863; captured and paroled at McMinnville, 3 Oct 1863, on parole until Feb 1864; discharged, 2 Aug 1865.
Broyles, Archibold: private, Company E; age: 30; enrolled at Greeneville, 18 Nov 1862; captured and paroled at McMinnville, 3 Oct 1863; absent without leave, 17 Jul 1864; deserted, 1 Sep 1864; restored to duty from deserter per Presidents Proclamation, 10 Mar 1865; discharged, 2 Aug 1865.
Broyles, George F.: private, Company G; age: 24; enrolled at Jonesborough, 12 Nov 1862; sick in hospital at Nashville, 30 Jun 1863; died in hospital at Nashville, 18 Aug 1863 of dysentery; file contains miscellaneous records.
Broyles, Isaac W.: private, Company E; age: 19; enrolled at Greeneville, 15 Nov 1861; discharged, 8 Jul 1865 at Knoxville.
Broyles, King H.: private, Company E; age: 26; enrolled at Greeneville, 15 Apr 1863; captured and paroled at McMinnville, 3 Oct 1863; discharged, 2 Aug 1865.
Broyles, Simeon: private, Company G; age: 35; enrolled at Greeneville, 15 Mar 1863; captured at McMinnville, 3 Oct 1863; absent on parole until Feb 1865; dropped from rolls an missing in action in Mar 1865; confined at rebel prison in Richmond, VA., 3 Oct 1863 until 9 Feb 1864; sent to Andersonville, GA., 12 Mar 1864; died of smallpox; file contains miscellaneous papers.
Broyles, Thomas: private, Company A; age: 18; enrolled at Greeneville, 26 Mar 1863; sick in hospital 30 Jun 1863; captured and paroled at McMinnville, 3 Oct 1863; absent on parole until Feb 1864; discharged, 2 Aug 1865.
Broyles, Thomas N.: private, Company E; age: 32; enrolled at Greeneville, 1 Apr 1863; captured and paroled at McMinnville, 3 Oct 1863; discharged, 2 Aug 1865.
Brumly, David: private, Company F; age: 18; enrolled at Greeneville, 18 Feb 1865; discharged, 2 Aug 1865, file contains enlistment papers.
Buck, Osborn D.: private, Company B; enrolled at Elizabethton, TN, 24 Nov 1862; captured and paroled at McMinnville, 3 Oct 1863; absent on parole until Feb 1864; deserted at Kingston, 19 Jul 1864; returned to duty 24 Oct 1864; desertion charge removed from record, 5 Dec 1874; file contains enlistment papers.

Soldiers of the Regiment 61

Buckner, Joseph/Jasper: private, Company F; age: 22; enrolled at Newport, TN, 1 Jan 1864; absent without leave, 8 Apr 1864; in arrest in Kingston, 25 Jun 1864; discharged, 2 Aug 1865; file contains enlistment papers
Buckner, Robert H.: private, Company H; age: 18; enlisted at Dandridge, TN, 11 Dec 1864; discharged, 2 Aug 1865; file contains enlistment papers.
Buckner, Samuel: private, Company D; age: 18; enlisted at Newport, TN, 1 Oct 1863; deserted, 20 Jul 1864 at Kingston; dropped as a deserter, 31 Aug 1864 at Kingston; file contains enlistment papers.
Bulden, Drewrey P.: private, Company C; transferred from 3rd Tennessee Infantry Regiment, 1 Mar 1865; sick in hospital at Knoxville; discharged, 2 Aug 1865.
Burgner, Joseph: private, Company F; age: 21: enlisted at Greeneville, 24 Mar 1863, captured and paroled at McMinnville, 3 Oct 1863; absent on parole through Feb 1865; changed to missing in action, Mar 1865; present for duty, May 1865; discharged, 2 Aug 1865.
Burlison, Benjamin: private, Company B & H; age: 29; enlisted at Greeneville, 25 Nov 1862; captured and paroled at McMinnville, 3 Oct 1863; absent on parole until Apr 1864; transferred to Company H at Jonesborough, 30 Jun 1864; deserted at Kingston, 16 Aug 1864; file contains miscellaneous papers.
Burrell, William: private, Company F; age: 27; enrolled at Strawberry Plains, TN, 1 Apr 1863; born: Greeneville; deserted at Jonesborough, 19 May 1864; dropped as deserter, 31 Aug 1864; restored to duty, 25 Jan 1865; deserted at Jonesborough, May 1865; file contains enlistment papers, etc.
Butler, West S.: private, Company H; age: 18; gained from transfer from 3rd Infantry Regiment; reported sick in hospital at Knoxville since 6 Jun 1865; mustered out of service, 23 Jun 1865 when term of service ended.
Campbell, John H.: private, Companies B and G; enrolled at Elizabethton, TN., 3 Jun 1863; transferred to Company B, 1 Jul 1863; captured and paroled at McMinnville, 3 Oct 1863; absent on parole until Feb 1864; sick at home in Carter County, 2 Apr 1865; discharged, 2 Aug 1865.
Campbell, James M.: sergeant, Company C; age: 21; enrolled at Greeneville, 15 Nov 1861; mustered in at Nashville, 15 Jun 1863; appointed sergeant, 24 Apr 1863; deserted, 27 Apr 1863 at Louisville, KY.; again deserted 25 Feb 1864; application in file shows that the War Department denied his request to have the desertion charge removed from the record, 15 Mar 1889.

Campbell, Meredith Y: private, Company B; age: 16; enrolled at Elizabethton, TN., 1 Mar 1864; mustered in at Loudon, 7 May 1864; discharged, 2 Aug 1865; file contains enlistment papers.
Campbell, Rankins: private, Company H; enrolled at Elizabethton, TN., 29 Apr 1864; reported as a deserter at Elizabethton, TN., 29 Apr 1864.
Campbell, Smith: private, Company C; age: 45; transferred from 3rd Tennessee Volunteer Infantry, 1 Mar 1865; reported sick in hospital at Knoxville during Mar - Apr 1865; present for duty, May - Jun 1865; discharged, 2 Aug 1865.
Cannon, Joseph: private, Company E and F; age: 24; enrolled at Jonesborough, 25 Nov 1862; captured and paroled at McMinnville, 3 Oct 1863; transferred to Company F, 29 Apr 1864, reported sick in hospital in Knoxville during 2 Mar 1864 through Aug 1864; reported sick in hospital at Kingston, 12 Oct 1864 through Dec 1864; reported sick in hospital at Knoxville 10 Jan 1865 through Apr 1865; discharged for disability, 26 May 1865.
Canon, Joseph: private, Company E; age: 19; joined at Greeneville, 1 Sep 1863; mustered in at Knoxville, 8 Feb 1864; sick in hospital at Knoxville, 30 Jun 1863 through Feb 1864; returned to duty, 13 Mar 1864; discharged, 2 Aug 1865.
Canter, William: private, Company G; enrolled at Jonesborough, 25 Nov 1862; mustered in at Nashville, 15 Jun 1863; absent without leave, 1 Dec 1863; deserted at Camp Nelson, KY., 20 Dec 1863.
Carriger, Nicholas: private, Company B; age: 22; enrolled at Elizabethton, TN., 19 Jan 1863, captured and paroled at McMinnville, 3 Oct 1863; deserted at Kingston, 7 Sep 1864; returned to duty, 18 Oct 1864; discharged, 2 Aug 1865; desertion charge removed by War Department, 13 Jan 1886.
Carroll, Charles N.: private, Company H; age: 18; enrolled at Kingston, 20 Jul 1864; resident of Thomasville, GA.; absent without leave, 22 Dec 1864; present for duty, Jan 1865; discharged, 2 Aug 1865.
Carroll, William C.: private, Company B; age: 25; enrolled at Elizabethton, TN, 25 Dec 1862; mustered in at Nashville, 15 Jun 1863; captured and paroled at McMinnville, 3 Oct 1863; sick in hospital at Knoxville, Mar - Apr 1864; discharged, 2 Aug 1865.
Carson, Tipton: private, Company D; age: 20; enrolled at Dandridge, TN., 18 Jan 1863; captured and paroled at McMinnville, 3 Oct 1863; sick in hospital in Knoxville, 29 Dec 1863; sick in hospital at Knoxville, 17 Apr 1864 through Aug 1864; sick in hospital at Kingston, Sep 1864 through Jan 1865; mustered out with disability, 23 Jun 1865; file contains miscellaneous correspondence.
Carter, James L.: captain, Company A; age: 40; joined at Greeneville, 23 Nov 1862; appointed 1st Lieutenant, 19 Feb 1863;

Soldiers of the Regiment 63

appointed captain, Company A, 1 Apr 1863; captured and paroled at McMinnville, 3 Oct 1863; sick at Knoxville, 16 Apr 1864; court martialed for violation of an Act of War in "encouraging men to go home, that authorities could not punish them for it in East Tennessee", Jun - Jul 1864; submitted resignation request citing family hardships, 16 May 1864; resignation approved; miscellaneous correspondence in file.

Carter, Joseph F.: private, Company A; age: 31; enrolled at Greeneville, 27 Jan 1863; sick in hospital, Jun 1863; captured and paroled at McMinnville, 3 Oct 1863; absent on parole until Feb 1864; deserted at Kingston, 23 Jul 1864; dropped as deserter, 31 Aug 1864; rejoined at Jonesborough, 1 May 1865; discharged, 2 Aug 1865.

Carter, Landon: 1st Lieutenant, Company B; age: 36; enrolled at Elizabethton, TN., 27 Jan 1863; mustered in as 1st Lieutenant by Colonel Stover, 19 Feb 1863; absent without authority, 15 - 30 Jun 1863; on recruiting duty in East Tennessee, Jul - Aug 1863; mustered out to accept an appointment as Captain in the 13th Tennessee Volunteer Cavalry, 27 Feb 1864; letter in file from Colonel John K. Miller, appointing him captain in 13th Cavalry.

Carter, Robert C.: captain, Companies A and C; age: 38; enrolled at Cincinnati, Ohio, 10 Dec 1862; captured and paroled at McMinnville, 3 Oct 1863; on detached service collection parolees through Apr 1864; transferred to Company C as captain; resigned to "look after his family", 30 Apr 1864; resignation papers in file.

Carter, Russell B.: 1st Lieutenant, Company A; age: 21; enrolled at Greeneville, 11 Aug 1862; promoted to sergeant, 1 Mar 1863; promoted to 2nd Lieutenant, 29 Aug 1863; promoted to 1st Lieutenant, 13 Jan 1864; in arrest, 18 Sep 1864; court martialed for being absent from his unit, 27 - 29 Nov 1864, and other charges including disrespect to superiors; resigned, 28 Dec 1864 for the good of the service; miscellaneous correspondence in file.

Carter, William: private, Company F; age: 30; transferred from 3rd Regiment, Tennessee Infantry at Jonesborough, 28 Aug 1865; file shows he was charged with desertion, 1 Nov 1862 and returned on 15 Jan 1864.

Carter, Young: private, Company A; age: 23; enrolled at Greeneville, 1 Feb 1863; captured and paroled at McMinnville, 3 Oct 1863; absent on parole until Feb 1864; sick in hospital in Knoxville, 7 May 1864 through Apr 1865; War Department note dated, 6 Dec 1886, shows he was admitted to asylum in Knoxville 20 May 1864, was in convalescent camp at Knoxville and deserted in Aug 1864; application for removal of desertion charge was denied by War Department

Casteel, Jeremiah: private, Company A; age: 32; enrolled at Greeneville, 27 Jan 1863; died in hospital at Nashville of

64   4th Tennessee Volunteer Infantry Regiment (USA)

"erysilipus", 6 Jul 1863; interment at City Cemetery (Nashville) # 4839; miscellaneous records in file.

Cate, Elijah: private, Company C, age: 18; transferred from 3rd Tennessee Infantry Regiment , 1 Mar 1865; sick in hospital in Knoxville, sick at time of muster out.

Cavener, William:, assistant surgeon, F&S; age: 48; enrolled 1 May 1864 at Kingston, commissioned assistant surgeon, 1 Apr 1864; resigned, 6 Jun 1865; reason given for resignation: suffering from bronchitis and infirmities of age, being 50 years old; resignation papers in file.

Cozart, John M.: private, Company C; age: 36; enrolled at Greeneville, 15 Apr 1863; captured and paroled at McMinnville, 3 Oct 1863; sick in hospital in Knoxville, 4 Apr 1864 through Jun 1864; sick in hospital in Knoxville, 8 Dec 1864 through Apr 1865; discharged, 2 Aug 1865.

Chedester, Ezra B: private, Company E; age: 20; enrolled at Greeneville, 1 Apr 1863, captured and paroled at McMinnville, 3 Oct 1863; discharged, 2 Aug 1865.

Chedester, George: private, Company G; age: 18; enrolled at Strawberry Plains, 20 Apr 1864; born: Greene County; died in hospital in Knoxville of diarrhea, 24 Sep 1864.

Chedester, James H.: private, Company E; age: 29; enrolled at Greeneville, 15 Jan 1865; captured and paroled at McMinnville, 3 Oct 1863; absent without leave, 23 Dec 1864; discharged for disability at Knoxville, 13 Jun 1865.

Chockley, Joseph W.: captain, Company G; age: 37; mustered in at Cincinnati, Ohio, 2 Dec 1862; appeared on a list of stragglers at Camp Chase, Ohio, 3 Jun 1863; promoted to captain, 15 Apr 1864 to fill vacancy caused by death of Captain Samuel West; sick in hospital in Knoxville, 10 Dec 1864; miscellaneous papers in file.

Christmas, William W.: private, Company D; age: 23; enrolled at Rutledge, TN., 20 Feb 1863; born: Grainger County, TN.; in arrest, 28 Aug 1864; discharged, 2 Aug 1865; file contains enlistment papers.

Clay, John H.: private, Company A; age: 18; transferred from 3rd Tennessee Infantry Regiment, 1 Mar 1865; discharged, 2 Aug 1865.

Clawson, George W.: private, Company H; age: enrolled at Elizabethton, TN., 1 Feb 1865; resided at Watauga County, NC., sick in hospital in Knoxville, 21 Mar 1865 through Aug 1865; discharged, 2 Aug 1865; file contains enlistment papers.

Clem, John: private, Company A; age: 38; enrolled at Greeneville, 27 Jan 1863, promoted to wagoner, 1 May 1863; captured and paroled at McMinnville, 3 Oct 1863; discharged, 2 Aug 1865.

Click, Green: 2nd Lieutenant, Company E; enrolled at Greeneville, 1 Apr 1863; mustered in at Louisville, KY, 15 May 1863; captured and

Soldiers of the Regiment 65

paroled at McMinnville, 3 Oct 1863; resigned, stating incompetency, 27 May 1864; miscellaneous papers in file.

Click, Harvey D.: private, Company E; age: 37; enrolled at Greeneville, 15 May 1863; captured and paroled at McMinnville, 3 Oct 1863; sick in hosptial, 8 Dec 1864; discharged, 2 Aug 1865.

Click, James R.: private, Company E; age: 21; enrolled at Greeneville, 1 Aug 1863; captured and paroled at McMinnville, 3 Oct 1863; discharged, 8 Jul 1865.

Click, John L.: private Company E; age: 31; enrolled at Greeneville, 15 Nov 1861; mustered in at Nashville, 15 Jun 1863; captured and paroled at McMinnville, 3 Oct 1863; discharged, 8 Jul 1865.

Click, Levi D.: private, Company E; age: 36; enrolled at Greeneville, 6 Apr 1863; captured and paroled at McMinnville, 3 Oct 1863; sick in hospital at Kingston, 30 Oct 1864 through Jun 1865; discharged, 20 Jun 1865.

Click, Marion F.: private, Company E; age: 18; enrolled at Greeneville, 1 Sep 1863; mustered in at Knoxville, 8 Feb 1864; absent without leave, 22 Dec 1864; discharged, 2 Aug 1865; enlistment papers in file.

Click, Washington: corporal, Company E; age: 37; enrolled at Greeneville, 1 Sep 1862; appointed corporal, 15 Mar 1863; captured and paroled at McMinnville, 3 Oct 1863; sick in hospital at Kingston, 4 Sep 1864; died in hospital in Knoxville of diarrhea, 11 Jan 1865; file contains miscellaneous papers.

Cline, Alfred J.: private, Company D; age: 34; enrolled in Dandridge, 9 Dec 1862; captured and paroled at McMinnville, 3 Oct 1863; sick in hospital in Knoxville, 8 Dec 1864 through Apr 1865; discharged, 2 Aug 1865.

Cline, Charles C.: private, Company G; age: 31; enrolled at Dandridge, 9 Dec 1862; promoted to wagoner, 1 May 1862; discharged at Nashville for unspecified disability, 18 Aug 1863.

Cline, Peter: private, Company C; age: 37; enrolled at Dandridge, 19 Dec 1862; discharged at Nashville for unspecified disability, 1 Jul 1863.

Cloyd, David: private, Company G; age: 19; enrolled at Jonesborough, 31 May 1863; killed in battle at McMinnville, 3 Oct 1863.

Colbock, Peter: private; enrolled at Elizabethton, TN., 30 Jun 1864; deserted at Elizabethton, TN., 1 Jul 1864.

Cole, Anderson L.: private, Company B; age: 18; enrolled at Elizabethton, TN., 30 May 1863; captured and paroled at McMinnville, 3 Oct 1863; absent on parole through Apr 1864; discharged, 2 Aug 1865.

Collet, James M.: private, Company A; age: 24; enrolled at Jonesborough, 10 Sep 1862; captured and paroled at McMinnville, 3 Oct 1863; discharged, 8 Jul 1865.
Combs, William: private; enrolled at Kingston, 1 Jun 1864; deserted at Kingston, 18 Jul 1864.
Cook, Augustus S.: private, Company H; enrolled at Jonesborrough, 1 Apr 1865; deserted at Jonesborough, 5 May 1865.
Cook, John T.: corporal, enrolled at Jonesborough, 1 Apr 1865; promoted to corporal, 28 Apr 1865; deserted at Jonesborough, 5 May 1865.
Cook, Thomas J.: private, Company F; age: 27; enrolled at Strawberry Plains, 1 Apr 1863; born: Spartainburg, SC.; resided at Newport, TN., absent without leave, 30 May 1864; reported as deserter at Strawberry Plains, 30 May 1864; restored from desertion, 25 Apr 1865; discharged, 2 Aug 1865; miscellaneous papers in file, including record of courts martial.
Cooke, James M.: private, Company G; age: 20; enrolled at Jonesborough, 5 May 1863; captured and paroled at McMinnville, 3 Oct 1863; reported absent in Confederate prison in Knoxville, 2 May 1864; no discharge, died near Knoxville after escaping from prison.
Cook, John L.: corporal, Company H; enlisted at Greeneville, 31 Jan 1863; captured and paroled at McMinnville, 3 Oct 1863; on parole until Feb 1863; discharged, 2 Aug 1865.
Cooter, Phillip: sergeant, Company F; age: 25; enrolled at Greeneville, 31 Jan 1863; received $25.00 enlistment bonus; appointed sergeant, 15 Jun 1863; discharged, 2 Aug 1865.
Corcoran, Edward: private, Company B; age: 29; enrolled at Knoxville, 8 Mar 1863; captured and paroled at McMinnville, 3 Oct 1863; discharged, 2 Aug 1865.
Cotter, Mervin E.: private, Company C; age: 21; enlisted at Greenville, 17 Mar 1863; sick in hospital 15 - 30 Jun 1863; captured and paroled at McMinnville, 3 Oct 1863; sent to hospital in Knoxville, 28 Apr 1864; died in asylum in Knoxville, 1 May 1864; file contains numerous papers.
Cotter, William: private, Company C; age: 27; enlisted at Greeneville, 20 Jan 1863; discharged, 2 Aug 1865.
Cotter, William H.: corporal, Company C; enrolled at Greeneville, 20 Jan 1863; promoted to corporal, 1 Aug 1864, sick in hospital during Nov - Dec 1864; discharged, 2 Aug 1865.
Courtney, James: private, Company D; age: 33; enlisted at Greeneville, 1 Mar 1863; captured and paroled at McMinnville, 3 Oct 1863; on parole until Feb 1864; sick in Knoxville, 16 May 1865; discharged with disability, 29 May 1865; file contains miscellaneous papers.

Crabtree, Alexander B.: corporal, Company C; age: 25; enlisted at Greeneville, 15 Jan 1863; appointed corporal, 24 Apr 1863; sick in hospital 15 - 30 Jun 1863; captured and paroled at McMinnville, 3 Oct 1863; absent on parole Mar - Apr 1865; gained from missing in action; discharged 2 Aug 1865.
Crabtree, Jacob: private, Company C, age: 28; enlisted at Greeneville, 6 Apr 1863; sick in hospital, 15 - Jun 63 through Feb 1864; sent to hospital in Unionville, TN, 10 Mar 1864; Sep - Oct 1864 on furlough from hospital; Nov - Dec 1864 through Feb 1865 sick in hospital at Kingston; discharged, 2 Aug 1865.
Crawford, John H.: private, Company F; age: 18; enrolled at Strawberry Plains, 20 Feb 1864; born: Greene County; mustered in at Loudon, 7 May 1864; discharged, 2 Aug 1865, file contains enlistment papers.
Crawford, Martin: private, Company F; enrolled at Blountville, 11 Sep 1862; sick in hospital, 15 - 30 Jun 1863; died at Louisville, KY, records captured, date unknown; file contains death record.
Crawford, Thomas: private, Company D; enrolled at Blountville, 11 Sep 1862; sick in hospital, 15 - 30 Jun 1863; captured and paroled at McMinnville, 3 Oct 1863; on parole until Feb 1864; discharged, 8 Jul 1865.
Creswell, John E.: private, Company C; transferred from 3rd Tennessee Infantry Regiment, 1 Mar 1865; discharged, 2 Aug 1865.
Cross, Joseph: private, Company F; age: 18; enrolled at Strawberry Plains, 1 May 1864; resident of Madison County, NC; mustered at Loudon, 7 May 1864; deserted, 15 Jun 1864; file contains enlistment papers.
Crosswhite, Alfred C.: private, Company B; age: 29; enrolled at Taylorsville, 22 Aug 1862; captured and paroled at McMinnville, 3 Oct 1863; absent on parole until Mar - Apr 1864; admitted to hospital at Kingston with fever, 17 Jun 1864; deserted at Kingston, 6 Aug 1864 through 19 Feb 1865; restored to duty Apr 1865; desertion charged removed by War Department, 1885; file contains enlistment papers.
Crosswhite, John M.: private, Company B; age: 24; enlisted at Taylorsville, 22 Aug 1862; captured and paroled at McMinnville, 3 Oct 1863; absent on parole until Feb 1864; mustered out at Knoxville, 7 Jul 1865; file contains enlistment papers.
Crosswhite, Thomas J.: corporal, Company B; enlisted at Taylorsville, 22 Aug 1862; captured and paroled at McMinnville, 3 Oct 1863; absent on parole until Feb 1864; promoted to corporal, 2 May 1865; mustered out at Knoxville, 7 Jul 1865; file contains enlistment papers.

Crosswhite, William C.: private, Company B; enlisted at Taylorsville, 30 May 1863; captured and paroled at McMinnville, discharged, 2 Aug 1865.

Crudgeion, George: private, Companies B and F; enrolled at Blountville, 30 Nov 1862; captured at McMinnville, 3 Oct 1863; carried on rolls as on parole until Feb 1865; carried on rolls as missing in action, Apr 1865; reported, died at Andersonville Prison, GA, date unknown.

Crum, Andrew: private, Company F; age: 39; enlisted at Greeneville, 16 Mar 1861; captured and paroled at McMinnville, 3 Oct 1863; captured at Madisonville, TN., 8 Feb 1864; reported missing in action Mar 1865; sent to Richmond Prison 14 Feb 1864, transferred to Andersonville Prison, Feb 1864; died at Andersonville, 17 Sep 1864.

Crum, Emanuel: private, Company F; age: 26; enrolled at Greeneville, 30 Jun 1863; captured and paroled at McMinnville, 3 Oct 1863; died in hospital at McMinnville of consumption, 26 Nov 1863.

Crum, Michael L.: private, Company F; age: 18; enrolled at Greeneville, 1 Jul 1863; discharged, 7 Jul 1865; file contains enlistment papers.

Crumley, Frederick: private, Company H; age: 18; enlisted at Elizabethton, 29 Apr 1864; mustered at Loudon, 7 May 1864; discharged, 2 Aug 1865; file contains enlistment papers.

Crumley, John: private, Company F; age: 18; enrolled at Newport, TN., 26 Jan 1865; born: Cocke County; deserted, 17 Apr 1864; present for duty, Jan - Feb 1865; discharged, 2 Aug 1865; file contains enlistment papers.

Crumley, Rufus: private, Company F; age: 18; enrolled at Newport, TN., 21 Jan 1865; born, Cocke, County; discharged, 2 Aug 1865; file contains enlistment papers.

Crye, Hugh: private, Company H; age: 23; enrolled at Kingston, 4 Jul 1864; resided at Roane County; discharged, 2 Aug 1865.

Curtis, Archibald: private, Company B; enrolled at Jonesboro, 24 Nov 1862; captured and paroled at McMinnville, 3 Oct 1863; absent on parole until Feb 1864; discharged, 2 Aug 1865.

Curtis, Bowling: private, Company B; age: 44; enrolled at Bulls Gap, TN., 1 Aug 1863; resided in Carter County; sick in hospital at Knoxville, 10 May 1865; discharged from hospital and service, 8 Jun 1865.

Curtis, John: private, Company B, age: 21; enlisted at Jonesboro, 24 Nov 1862; captured and paroled at McMinnville, 3 Oct 1863; absent on parole until Feb 1864; deserted at Kingston, 19 Jun 1864; restored to duty, 8 Oct 1864; discharged, 2 Aug 1865.

Soldiers of the Regiment 69

Cutshall, James G.: private, enrolled at Greeneville, 1 Mar 1865; deserted at Greeneville, 25 Mar 1865.
Daniel, Isaac: private, Company D; age: 27; enrolled at Rutledge, TN., 15 Apr 1862; captured and paroled at McMinnville, 3 Oct 1863; absent on paroled until Feb 1864; absent without leave, 20 Jul 1865 through 14 Aug 1864; in arrest, 19 Aug 1864; absent without leave, 8 Dec 1864; mustered out, 8 Jul 1865.
Daniel, John: corporal, Company D and F; age: 24; enrolled at Rutledge, TN., 1 May 1863; promoted to corporal, 3 Jun 1863; captured and paroled at McMinnville, 3 Oct 1863; on parole through Feb 1864; reduced in rank and transferred to Company F, 30 Apr 1864; absent without leave, 1 Dec 1863 through May - Jun 1864; appointed corporal, 1 Apr 1865; discharged, 2 Aug 1865; numerous papers in file.
Daniel, Levi N.: private, Company D; age: 36; enrolled at Newport, TN., 18 Jan 1863; born in Jefferson County; captured and paroled at McMinnville, 3 Oct 1863; arrested as straggler 17 Mar 1864 at Morristown, TN., sent ot New Market, TN., 19 Mar 1864; absent until 19 Mar 1864; discharged, 2 Aug 1865.
Daniel, Marcus: private, Company D; age: 18; enrolled at Rutledge, TN., 15 Aug 1863; born: Grainger County; absent without leave, 24 Dec 1864; discharged, 2 Aug 1865; file contains enlistment papers.
Dave, John: private, Company H; enlisted at Elizabethton, 16 Jun 1864; deserted at Knoxville, 28 Jun 1864.
Davenport, Silas B.: corporal, Company A; age: 32; enrolled at Greeneville, 31 Jan 1863; promoted to corporal, 1 Aug 1864; captured at McMinnville, 3 Oct 1864; sent to prison in Richmond, VA; suffered in prison hospital from rheumatism and ulcerated foot; paroled at Camp Parole, MD, 2 May 1864; admitted to hospital at Knoxville for ulcerated foot, 21 Jun 1865; returned to duty, 21 Jun 1865; file contains miscellaneous prisoner of war records.
Davis, James: private, Company E; file contains only prisoner of war record; he was captured at Taswell, TN., 1 Feb 1864 and sent to Savannah, GA., 19 Nov 1864; he was paroled, 26 Nov 1864; nothing additional.
Davis, James A.: private, Company G; age: 37; enlisted at Greeneville, 5 May 1863; sick in hospital, 30 Jun 1863; discharged with disability at Nashville, 1 Jul 1863; file contains discharge papers.
Davis, John M.: private, Company C; age: 29; enrolled at Greeneville, 5 Apr 1863; captured and paroled at McMinnville, 3 Oct 1863; on parole until Feb 1864; discharged, 2 Aug 1865.
Davis, Phillip: private, Company C; age: 19; enlisted at Greeneville, 6 Apr 1863; sick in hospital 15 - 30 Jun 1863; captured and paroled at McMinnville, 3 Oct 1863; on parole until Feb 1864; discharged, 2 Aug 1865.

Davis, Samuel B: private, Company C; enlisted at Greeneville, 5 Apr 1863; sick in hospital 15 - 30 Jun 1863; captured and paroled at McMinnville, 3 Oct 1863; on parole until Feb 1864; discharged, 2 Aug 1865.
Davis, Thomas: captain, Company F; enrolled at Louisville, KY., 20 Mar 1863; mustered in as 2nd Lieutenant; promoted to Captain, 15 Jun 1863; captured and paroled at McMinnville, 3 Oct 1863; on detached service during the period, 30 Jun 1863 through 29 Feb 1864; had suffered a disabling gunshot wound in the left side, 21 Mar 1862; resigned, 13 May 1864.
Davis, Travis D.: private, Company D; age: 18; joined at Kingston, 1 May 1864; residence: Clinton, TN.; discharged, 2 Aug 1865.
Davis, William J.: private, Company E; age: 25; mustered in at Loudon, 7 May 1864; resident of Carter County; absent without leave, 8 Dec 1864; discharged, 2 Aug 1865; file contains enlistment papers.
Day, James R.: private, Company F; age: 20; enrolled at Greeneville, 1 Mar 1863; absent without leave, 15 -13 Jun 1863; reported as a deserter at Nashville, 12 Jul 1863.
Dearstone, Christopher: corporal, Company F; age: 28; enrolled at Greeneville, 6 Apr 1863; received $25.00 bonus; appointed corporal, 15 Jun 1863; absent without leave, 13 Apr 1864; sick in hospital at Kingston, 23 Nov 1864; detached as clerk in Knoxville, 7 Feb 1865; discharged at Knoxville, 16 May 1865 with disability.
Debus/Debusk, Elisha K.: private, Company G; age: 19; mustered in at Knoxville, 2 Mar 1865; born: Greene County; discharged, 2 Aug 1865; file contains enlistment papers.
Deerstone, Isaac: private, Company F; age: 21; enrolled at Greeneville, 6 Apr 1863; captured and paroled at McMinnville, 3 Oct 1863; discharged, 2 Aug 1865.
Deerstone, Jacob: private, Company F; age: 27; enrolled at Greeneville, 6 Apr 1863; discharged at Nashville, 11 Sep 1863 with "phitisis pulmonalis"; file contains discharge papers.
Deerstone, Robert: private, Company F; age: 20; enrolled at Greeneville, 6 Apr 1865; sick in hospital, 15 Jun 1863 through Feb 1864; discharged, 2 Aug 1865; file contains enlistment papers.
Dempsey, James: private, Company B; age: 30; enrolled at Nashville, 1 May 1863; born at Spartainburg, SC.; resided in Nashville; discharged 2 Aug 1865; file contains enlistment papers.
Dobson, James H.: corporal, Company F; age: 18; enlisted at Greeneville, 6 Apr 1863; received $25.00 enlistment bounty; appointed corporal, 26 Apr 1863; discharged for unspecified disability, 18 Aug 1863.
Dobson, Joseph W.: private, Company G; age: 23; enrolled at Greeneville, 1 Jan 1863; died in the hospital at Nashville of an unknown disease, 11 Jul 1863; file contains numerous documents.

Soldiers of the Regiment 71

Dobson, Robert M.: 2nd Lieutenant, Company F; age: 24; enrolled at Greeneville, 28 Apr 1863; received $25.00 bonus; appointed sergeant, 15 Jun 1863; captured and paroled at McMinnville, 3 Oct 1863; commissioned 2nd Lieutenant, 19 Feb 1865; file contains numerous documents.
Dodd, Andrew J.: corporal, Company A; age: 20; enrolled at Greeneville, 27 Jan 1863; captured and paroled at McMinnville, 3 Oct 1863; absent on parole until Feb 1864; promoted to corporal, 1 Aug 1864, discharged, 2 Aug 1865.
Dodd, Joseph: private, Company A; age: 41; enrolled at Greeneville, 27 Jan 1863; captured and paroled at McMinnville, 3 Oct 1863; absent until Feb 1864; discharged, 2 Aug 1865.
Dogget, William A.: private, Company F; age: 38; enrolled at Dandridge, TN., 16 Jan 1863; died in hospital at Louisville, KY., 18 Mar 1863; casualty sheet in file.
Donally, James C.: corporal, Company B; age: 23; enrolled at Taylorsville, 1 Oct 1862; sick in hospital, 15 - 30 Jun 1863; captured and paroled at McMinnville, 3 Oct 1863; sick in hospital in Knoxville, 7 Apr 1864; promoted to corporal, 11 Mar 1865; discharged at Knoxville, 7 Jul 1865.
Donnelly, John M.: private, Company B; age: 26; enrolled at Taylorsville, 5 Sep 1862; captured and paroled at McMinnville, 3 Oct 1863; discharged at Knoxville, 7 Jul 1865; file contains enlistment papers.
Doston, Samuel A.: private, Company A; age: 23; enrolled at Greeneville, 4 Nov 1862; sick in hospital, 30 Jun 1863; captured and paroled at McMinnville, 3 Oct 1864; sick in hospital at Knoxville, Feb 1864; nothing additional in file.
Driskell, James: private, Company F; age: 8; enrolled at Newport, 1 Oct 1863; absent without leave, 4 Apr 1864; dropped from rolls as deserter at Strawberry Plains, TN., 31 Aug 1864; file contains enlistment papers.
Dryman, John: private, Company F; age: 18; enrolled at Greeneville, 15 Apr 1863; received $25.00 enlistment bonus; sick in hospital at Louisville, 30 Jun 1863; captured and paroled at McMinnville, 4 Oct 1863; discharged, 2 Aug 1865.
Dunbar, George: private, Company G; age: 18; enrolled at Strawberry Plains, 12 Nov 1862; born: Washington County, TN.; sick in hospital in Kingston, 9 Jul 1864; died in hospital in Knoxville, 27 Jan 1865.
Dunbar, George W.: private, Company G; age: 18; enrolled at Greeneville, 7 Apr 1864; born: Greene County; discharged 2 Aug 1865; file contains enlistment papers.
Dunbar, William A.: private, Company G; Age: 21; enlisted at Jonesborough, 25 Nov 1862; sick in hospital, 13 - 30 Jun 1863;

4th Tennessee Volunteer Infantry Regiment (USA)

captured and paroled at McMinnville, 3 Oct 1863; absent until Feb 1864; discharged, 2 Aug 1865.

Duncan, Pharo: private, Company H; age: 24; gained from transfer from 3rd Tennessee Infantry Regiment, 1 Mar 1865; sick in hospital in Knoxville until April 1865; discharged, 2 Jun 1865.

Dunkin, John: private, Company C; age: 18 years; enlisted at Kingston, 1 May 1864; born: Anderson County; Resident of Taylorsville, Johnson County; discharged, 2 Aug 1865.

Dunkins, Joseph: private, Company E; age: 18; enrolled at Loudon, 20 Apr 1864; born: Greene County; sick in hospital in Knoxville, 11 Jan 1865; discharged, 2 Aug 1865; file contains enlistment papers.

Dyer, Taylor: corporal, Company D; age: 18; enrolled at Rut ledge, 1 Nov 1863; promoted to corporal, 14 Jul 1865; discharged: 2 Aug 1865; note in file "deserted Company B, 8th Tenn. Cavalry"

Dyer, Thomas L.: wagoner, Company F; age: 44; enrolled at Rutledge, 15 Apr 1862; appointed wagoner, 1 May 1863; captured and paroled at McMinnville, 3 Oct 1863; absent on parole until Feb 1864; absent without leave, 15 Jun 1864: deserted at Kingston, 1 Sep 1864.

Dykes, Abraham: private, Company D; enrolled at Rogersville, 10 Nov 1862; sick in hospital, 15 - 30 Jun 1863; discharged 15 Jul 1863 with disability.

Dykes, Jasper: private, Company D; age: 37; enrolled at Greeneville, 1 Dec 1862; captured and paroled at McMinnville, 3 Oct 1863; sick in hospital at Kingston, 8 Mar 1864 through Dec 1864; nothing else; file contains enlistment papers.

Dykes, Jesse R.: private, Company D; age: 20; enrolled at Rogersville, 11 Sep 1862; captured and paroled at McMinnville, 3 Oct 1863; absent on parole until Feb 1864; discharged, 8 Jul 1865.

Dykes, Joseph: private, Company D; age: 30; enrolled at Greeneville, 11 Nov 1862; captured and paroled at McMinnville, 3 Oct 1862; discharged, 2 Aug 1865.

Eakin, Hugh M.: corporal, Company B; age: 24; enlisted at Robinson, Illinois, 1 Apr 1863; captured and paroled at McMinnville, 3 Oct 1863; promoted to corporal, 11 Mar 1865; submitted furlough request to go home to Blount County, TN., for 20 days; furlough request in file.

Eakin, John W.: private, Company B; enrolled at Robinson, Illinois, 1 Apr 1863; captured and paroled at McMinnville, 3 Oct 1863; mustered out, 10 Jun 1865 at Knoxville.

Earnest, Oliver P.: private, Company C; age: 36; enlisted at Greeneville, 6 Apr 1863; captured and paroled at McMinnville, sent to general hospital at Knoxville, 3 Mar 1864; died in asylum in Knoxville, 4 may 1864.

Soldiers of the Regiment 73

Estep, Henry C.: private, company H; age: 18; enrolled at Elizabethton, 29 Apr 1864; mustered in at Loudon, 7 May 1864; sick in hospital at Knoxville with measles, 18 Mar 1865; discharged, 6 Jun 1865; file contains enlistment papers.
Estep, Ransom: private, Company H; age: 20; enrolled at Elizabethton, 15 Apr 1863; mustered in at Loudon, 7 May 1864; discharged, 2 Aug 1865; file contains enlistment papers.
Estep, William: private, Company H; age: 18; enrolled at Elizabethton, 15 Jun 1864; mustered in at Kingston, 23 Jul 1864; discharged, 2 Aug 1865.
Easterly, Abraham H.: private, Company A; age: 20; enrolled at Greeneville, 13 Dec 1862; captured and paroled at McMinnville, 3 Oct 1863: discharged, 2 Aug 1865.
Easterly, Rufus: sergeant, Company A; enrolled at Greeneville, 13 Dec 1862; promoted to corporal, 23 Feb 1863; prisoner of war record - but blank; promoted to sergeant, 1 Apr 1864; discharged, 2 Aug 1865.
Eastridge, Joel: private, Company G; age: 23; enlisted at Taylorsville, 11 Jan 1863; captured and paroled, 3 Oct 1863; discharged, 2 Aug 1865.
Edington, John H.: private, Company D; age: 22; enrolled at Greeneville, 6 Jun 1863; killed in battle at McMinnville, 3 Oct 1863; file contains enlistment papers.
Edington, William: private, Company D; age: 22; enrolled at Greeneville, 6 Jun 1863; captured and paroled at McMinnville, 3 Oct 1863; arrested by military in Knox County, Kentucky as straggler, 1 Dec 1863; gained from missing in action, 2 Feb 1864; discharged, 2 Aug 1865; file contains enlistment papers.
Edmonds, Elmore: private, Company H; age: 36; transferred from 3rd Tennessee Infantry Regiment, 1 Mar 1865; discharged, 2 Aug 1865.
Eggers, Joel: private, Company B; age: 21; enrolled at Boone, NC., 1 Aug 1862; died in hospital in Nashville of diarrhea, 21 Aug 1863; file contains enlistment papers and casualty sheet.
Eisenhour, Martin: corporal, Company C; age: 23; enlisted at Newport, 10 Jan 1863; captured and paroled at McMinnville, 3 Oct 1863; promoted to corporal, 1 Aug 1864; died of fever at Mosier's Mill, TN., 16 Mar 1865; file contains numerous papers.
Eisenhour, Powell: private, Company C; age: 19; enlisted at Newport, 14 Feb 1863; captured and paroled at McMinnville, 3 Oct 1863; discharged, 2 Aug 1865.
Elder, Casper: private, Company F; age: 30; enrolled at Greeneville, 10 Nov 1861; received $25.00 bounty; mustered in at Nashville, 15 Jun 1863; captured and paroled at McMinnville, 3 Oct 1863; absent without leave, 30 May 1864; charged with desertion, 31 Aug 1864;

voluntarily returned to unit, 21 Dec 1864; restored to duty from desertion, 5 Jan 1865; discharged, 8 Jul 1865; file contains numerous papers.
Elder, William R.: private, Company C; age: 24; joined at Spartainburg, SC., 5 Nov 1861; mustered in at Nashville, 15 Jun 1863; died in hospital at Nashville of diarrhea, 28 Sep 1863; miscellaneous papers in file.
Ellenburge, William: private, Company G; age: 36; enlisted at Greeneville, 15 Mar 1863; captured and paroled at McMinnville, 3 Oct 1863; sick in hospital in Kingston, 7 Sep 1864 through Jun 1865; discharged, 23 Jun 1865.
Ellis, Benjamin: private, Company E; age: 21; enrolled at Greeneville, 23 Apr 1863; reported sick in hospital in Nashville, 15 - 30 Jun 1863; captured and paroled at McMinnville, 3 Oct 1863; discharged, 2 Aug 1865.
Ellis, Isaac: corporal, Company B; age: 18; enrolled at Greeneville, 12 Apr 1863; received $25.00 bounty; sick in hospital in Nashville, 15-30 Jun 1863; captured and paroled at McMinnville, 3 Oct 1863; promoted to corporal, 19 May 1864.
Ellison, Benjamin: private, Company H; age: 19; transferred from 3rd Tennessee Infantry, 1 Mar 1865; on 10 day leave to visit home in Jefferson County, 5 Feb 1864; discharged, 2 Aug 1865.
Elrod, Joseph: private, Company B; age: 18; joined at Taylorsville, 1 Mar 1865; resided at Ashe County, NC., discharged, 2 Aug 1865; file contains enlistment papers.
Emeret, William: private, Company H; enrolled at Elizabethton, 24 Apr 1864; reported as a deserter at Elizabethton, 31 Aug 1864.
Emmert, George W.: sergeant; age: 32; enrolled at Greeneville, 15 Nov 1861; received $25.00 bounty; appointed corporal, 26 Apr 1863; sick in hospital in Kingston, 1 Jul 1864 - Feb 1865; promoted to sergeant, 1 Apr 1865; discharged, 8 Jul 1865.
Emmert, James C.: sergeant, Company G; enrolled at Elizabethton, 12 Jan 1863; promoted to sergeant, 22 May 1863; captured and paroled at McMinnville, 3 Oct 1863; prisoner of war record shows he was captured at Marysville, TN., 24 Nov 1863 and again captured in Washington County, TN., 26 Dec 1863; confined at Richmond, VA., 20 Jan 1864 sent to Andersonville, GA; died of pneumonia.
Ervin, Joseph: private, Company C; age: 18; enrolled at Flat Creek, Greene County, 10 Mar 1864; born: Hawkins County; mustered in at Loudon, 7 May 1864; discharged, 2 Aug 1865; file contains enlistment papers.
Fair, George W.: private, Company H; age: 18; enrolled at Elizabethton, 24 Apr 1864; mustered in at Loudon, 7 May 1864; absent without leave, 20 May 1864; reported as deserter at Bulls Gap,

Soldiers of the Regiment   75

TN., 19 Jul 1865; charges of absent without leave and desertion removed by War Department, 6 Sep 1913; file contains enlistment papers.
Fanning, William: corporal, Company G; age: 19; enrolled at Greeneville, 5 Nov 1862; promoted to corporal, 22 May 1863; wounded and captured at McMinnville, 3 Oct 1863; hospitalized at McMinnville until 3 Mar 1864; discharged, 7 Jul 1865.
Fannon, William: private, Company E; age: 19; enlisted at Greeneville, 31 Jan 1863; absent without leave, 22 Dec 1864; discharged, 2 Aug 1865; file contains enlistment papers.
Farnsworth, Joseph: 1st Lieutenant, Company F; age: 28; enrolled at Greeneville, 27 Apr 1863; mustered in as 1st Lt.; promoted to Captain, 12 Jun 1864; requested release from service because of family concerns, 9 May 1864; again asked approval of resignation request, citing family and health concerns, 8 Jun 1864; requested leave of absence, 17 Jul 1864; reported absent without leave, 1 Aug 1864; charged with absent without leave and conduct unbecoming an officer, and desertion by Major Reeves, received dishonorable discharged by War Department 19 Sep 1864; file contains numerous papers.
Farguharson, Robert J.: major/surgeon; age: 38; joined at Nashville, 1 Jun 1863; detailed to hospital #12 and Nashville, 18 Sep 1863; ordered to rejoin the regiment, 1 Mar 1864; resigned from service citing disability (deafness) and unfit for field duty, 21 Mar 1864; file contains numerous papers.
Farris, John: private, Company H; age: 18; joined at Taylorsville, 6 Apr 1865; born: Johnson County; discharged, 2 Aug 1865; file contains enlistment papers.
Farrow, John W.: private, Company D; age: 21; enrolled at Knoxville, 1 Feb 1863; captured and paroled at McMinnville, 3 Oct 1863; captured at Cumberland Gap, near Knoxville, 17 Feb 1864; sent to confederate prison at Richmond, VA., 17 Feb 1864; transferred to prison at City Point, VA., 21 Mar 1864; sent to a prison in Ohio and paroled; died of diarrhea in military hospital at Annapolis, MD., 18 Apr 1864; file contains numerous papers.
Faun, Adam: private, Company F, age: 45; enrolled at Newport, 25 Mar 1863; sick in hospital, 15 - 30 Jun 1863; transferred to invalid corps, date unknown (records captured).
Fauver, Isaac: private, Company D; age: 18; enrolled at Dandridge, 25 Jun 1863; mustered in at Strawberry Plains, 31 Mar 1864; discharged, 2 Aug 1865.
Fawver, John A.: private, company D; age: 20; enlisted at Dandridge, 16 Jan 1863; discharged, 2 Aug 1865.
Feathers, John C.: private, Company B; age: 21; enrolled at Jonesborough, 24 Nov 1862; absent without leave, 15 - 30 Jun 1863; reported deserter at Nashville, 27 Aug 1863.

4th Tennessee Volunteer Infantry Regiment (USA)

February, Joseph A.: 1st Lieutenant, Company B, G and F&S; enrolled as a private at Jonesborough, 1 Jan 1863; captured ant paroled at McMinnville, 3 Oct 1863; promoted to commissary sergeant; Dec 1863; promoted to 1st Lieutenant., 12 Oct 1864; file contains numerous records.

Fellers, Jackson G.: private, Company G; age: 24; enrolled at Greeneville, 6 Apr 1863; sick in hospital, 30 Jun 1863; transferred to Madison Indiana, 19 Dec 1863; assigned to invalid corps, 15 Feb 1864.

Fields, John H.: private, Company H; age: 22; enlisted at Taylorsville, 11 Apr 1865; resident of Smith County, VA., discharged, 2 Aug 1865; file contains enlistment papers.

Fincher, Samuel, M.: private; age: 18; enrolled at Greene County, 1 Mar 1865; name not borne on the rolls of the 4th Regiment.

Fletcher, Andrew J.: private, Company G; age: 23, enrolled at Elizabethtown (?), 3 Jun 1863; sick in hospital in Louisville, Jan - Apr 1864; transferred to Cumberland Hospital Nashville, 30 Apr 1864; transferred to invalid corps, date not known.

Fletcher, John: private, Company G; age: 25; enrolled at Taylorsville, 25 Aug 1862; captured and paroled at McMinnville, 3 Oct 1863; absent on parole until Apr 1864; mustered out, 7 Jul 1865; file contains enlistment papers.

Fondren, James E.: **private, Company A; age: 18; enrolled at Knoxville, 1 Nov 1864; resided in Cocke, County; died in hospital at Greeneville, 9 May 1865.**

Fondren, Andrew C.: private, Companies B & F; age: 23; enrolled at Elizabethtown, Ill (?), 1 Aug 1863; absent on leave, 15 - 30 Jun 1863; absent on recruiting service, 30 Jun 1863 through 29 Feb 1864; transferred to Company F, 29 Apr 1864; absent on detached service, 7 Mar 1864 through Jun 1864; discharged to accept promotion to 2nd lieutenant and transfer to Company M, 13th Tennessee Cavalry, 18 Apr 1864; file contains numerous papers.

Ford, Alexander : **private, Company C; age: 18; enrolled at Strawberry Plains, 6 Sep 1863; resided in Greene County; mustered in at Loudon, 7 May 1864; died at hospital at Kingston of fever. 7 Jun 1864; file contains enlistment papers.**

Ford, John S.: private, Company G; age: 18; enrolled at Jonesborough, 31 May 1863; captured and paroled at McMinnville, 3 Oct 1863; dropped as "missing in action", Mar 1865; prisoner of war record shows: "captured and paroled at McMinnville, went home where he was again captured, admitted to hospital at Andersonville, GA., 11 Oct 1864 with "scorbutus", was receipted as exchange of prisoners at Vicksburg, MS., 29 Apr 1865, was reported at Benton Barracks, MO., and was mustered out of service on 29 Jul 1865 at St. Louis, MO."; file contains numerous prisoner of war records.

Soldiers of the Regiment 77

Forrester, John H.: private, Company F; age: 22; enrolled at Taylorsville, 25 Aug 1862; captured and paroled at McMinnville, 3 Oct 1863; sick in hospital at Camp Nelson, KY., 26 Dec 1863 through Jun 1865; file contains enlistment papers.
Forster, James: private, Company H; enrolled at Knoxville, 2 May 1864; deserted at Knoxville, 10 May 1864.
Forster, William: private, Company H; enrolled at Knoxville, 2 May 1864; deserted at Knoxville, 10 May 1864.
Fortner, Jacob L.: private, Company E; age: 25; enrolled at Greeneville, 15 Mar 1863; appointed corporal, 15 Mar 1863; captured and paroled at McMinnville, 3 Oct 1863; on parole until Oct 1864; charged with desertion, Nov 1864; restored to duty, 10 Mar 1865; discharged, 2 Aug 1865; desertion charge removed by War Department, 5 Aug 1885.
Fortner, John: private, Company E; age: 22; enrolled at Greeneville, 5 May 1863; captured and paroled at McMinnville, 3 Oct 1863; absent on parole until Oct 1864; charged with desertion, 1 Nov 1864; restored to duty, 10 Mar 1865; discharged, 2 Aug 1865; desertion charge removed by War Department, 4 Jun 1885.
Fortner, Pleasant: private, Company E; age: 28; enrolled at Greeneville, 5 May 1863; captured and paroled at McMinnville, 3 Oct 1863; absent on parole until Oct 1864; charged with desertion, 1 Nov 1864; restored to duty, 10 Mar 1865; discharged, 2 Aug 1865; desertion charge removed by War Department, 4 Aug 1885, stating that he was sick from Oct 1863 through Feb 1865.
Foster, Joseph A.: private, Company A; age: 43; enrolled at Greeneville, 1 Aug 1863; captured and paroled at McMinnville, 3 Oct 1863; absent without leave, 16 Apr 1864; charged with deserting at Strawberry Plains on 16 Apr 1864; discharged, 2 Aug 1865; desertion charge removed by War Department, 1 Sep 1886.
Foster, Samuel: private, Company H; enrolled at Knoxville, 2 May 1864; deserted at Knoxville, 10 May 1864.
Foust, Daniel: private, Company B; age: 24; enrolled at Elizabethton, 2 May 1862; captured in Wise County, VA., 31 Dec 1862, confined at Castle Thunder, VA., 12 Feb 1863; paroled at City Point, VA., 18 Mar 1863; sick in hospital, 15 Jul - Aug 1863; captured and paroled at McMinnville, 3 Oct 1863; present for duty, Mar 1864; deserted at Kingston, 19 Jul 1864; returned to duty, 1 Oct 1864; discharged, 2 Aug 1865; desertion charge removed by War Department, 15 Jun 1886; file contains numerous papers.
Foust, James: private, Company B; age: 32; enrolled at Elizabethton, 1 Sep 1863; resided in Johnson County; deserted at Kingston, 17 Aug 1864.
Fowler, John: private, Company A; age: 20; enrolled in Newport, 25 Jan 1863; sick in hospital, 30 Jun 1863; ; captured and paroled

at McMinnville, 3 Oct 1863; absent on parole through Feb 1864; [editorial note: there appears to be a conflict in the following:]; captured at Dandridge, 1 Jan 1864, sent to prison at Richmond, VA., 25 Feb 1864; died at Richmond of diarrhea, 22 Mar 1864; captured in Cocke County, 3 Jan 1864; sent to Richmond, VA., 31 Jan 1864; sent to Andersonville, GA., 12 Mar 1864; admitted to hospital at Andersonville, 3 Jul 1864; file contains numerous papers.
Fowler, William C.: private, Company A; age: 22; enrolled at Newport, 25 Jan 1863; captured and paroled at McMinnville, 3 Oct 1863; reported absent on parole through Feb 1865; reported missing in action, Mar 1865; died in rebel hospital at Richmond, VA., 22 Mar 1864.
Fowler, Richard M.: private, Company E; age: 23; enrolled at Greeneville, 15 Nov 1861; captured and paroled at McMinnville, 3 Oct 1863; died in hospital at Knoxville of consumption, 8 Apr 1865; file contains numerous papers.
Fox, John W.: private, Company F; age: 19; enrolled at Newport, 17 Jan 1865; resided in Cocke County; discharged, 2 Aug 1865; file contains enlistment papers.
Fox, Robert M.: private, Company M; age: 23; enrolled at Newport, 29 Jan 1865; resided in Cocke County; enlisted under Article 22 of War as being a deserter on 22 Apr 1864 from the 8th Tennessee Infantry; discharged, 2 Aug 1865; file contains enlistment papers.
Francis, Andrew J.: private, Company E; age: 25; enrolled at Greeneville, 6 Apr 1863; captured and paroled at McMinnville, 3 Oct 1863; discharged, 2 Aug 1865.
Frazier, Abner J.: 2nd Lieutenant, Company E; age: 23; enrolled as a private at Greeneville, 19 Feb 1863; appointed sergeant major, 1 May 1864; promoted to 2nd lieutenant at Kingston; 12 Oct 1864; file contains prisoner of war record but place and date not stated; file contains numerous records.
French, Henry C.: sergeant, Company E; age: 23; enrolled at Greeneville, 18 Dec 1862; appointed sergeant, 26 May 1863; captured and paroled at McMinnville, 3 Oct 1863; sick in hospital at Knoxville, 11 May 1864; died in general hospital at Knoxville, 8 Aug 1864, cause not stated.
French, Oliver T.: private, Company G; age: 20; enrolled at Greeneville, 20 Nov 1862; sick in hospital, Jun 1863; captured and paroled at McMinnville, 3 Oct 1863; absent on parole until Mar 1864; discharged, 2 Aug 1865.
Fritz, Thomas: private, Company B; age: 21; enrolled at Taylorsville, 1 Sep 1862; died in general hospital at Louisville of measles, 20 Jan 1863; file contains casualty sheet.

Fugatt, Andrew J.: private, company A; enrolled at Loudon, 29 Apr 1864; resided in Greene County; discharged, 2 Aug 1865; file contains enlistment papers.
Gaby, Henry H.: private, Company C; enrolled at Greeneville, 5 Mar 1862; captured and paroled at McMinnville, 3 Oct 1863; on parole through Feb 1864; discharged, 8 Jul 1865.
Galyon, Jasper, R.: private, Company D; age: 18; enrolled at Rutledge, 1 Feb 1863; born: Grainger County; sick, 15 - 30 Jun 1863; captured and paroled at McMinnville, 3 Oct 1863; on detached service as an orderly at Kingston, Nov 1864 through Feb 1865; on duty as a musician, Jun 1865; discharged, 2 Aug 1865.
Garland, James D.: private, Company H; enrolled at Taylorsville, 1 Apr 1865; deserted at Jonesborough, 2 May 1865.
Garland, Mordica: private, Company H; age: 38; enrolled at Elizabethton, 28 Apr 1864; mustered at Loudon, 7 May 1864; deserted at Kingston, 19 Jul 1864; returned to duty, 23 Apr 1865; absent without leave, 30 Jun 1865; desertion charge upheld by War Department, 8 Jul 1887; file contains enlistment papers.
Garland, Prior L.: private, Company H; age: 26; enrolled at Elizabethton, 29 Apr 1864; mustered in at Loudon, 27 May 1864; discharged, 2 Aug 1865; file contains enlistment papers.
Garner, James C.: private, Company G; age: 25; transferred from 3rd Regiment, Tennessee Infantry, 21 Mar 1865; mustered out at hospital at Knoxville, 10 Jun 1865.
Garner, John G.: private, Company G; gained from transfer from 3rd Regiment, Tennessee Infantry, 1 Mar 1865; sick in hospital at Loudon since 27 Apr 1865; sick in hospital at Knoxville since Apr 1864; discharged, 2 Aug 1865.
Gass, Charles: private, Company E; age: 25; enrolled at Greeneville, 15 Mar 1863; captured and paroled at McMinnville, 3 Oct 1863; discharged, 2 Aug 1865.
Gass, David A.: private, Company A; age: 18; enrolled at Loudon, 1 Sep 1863; resident of Greene County; discharged, 2 Aug 1865; file contains enlistment papers.
Gass, George: private, Company A; age: 32; enrolled at Greeneville, 16 Apr 1863; captured and paroled at McMinnville, 3 Oct 1863; absent on parole through Feb 1865; absent without leave, 26 May 1864; charged with desertion, Aug 1864; gained from desertion, returned, 1 May 1865; discharge, 2 Aug 1865; application to remove desertion charged denied by War Department, 7 Oct 1885.
Gentry, James: private, Company H; enrolled at Loudon, 1 Jun 1864; born: Carter County; died in field hospital at Jefferson County, TN., 5 Jan 1865; cause of death not stated.
George, William H.: private, Company G; age: 27; enrolled at Greeneville, 15 Nov 1861; captured and paroled at McMinnville, 3 Oct

1863; absent on parole through Feb 1864; discharged, 8 Jul 1865; file contains enlistment papers.
Gfellers, Henry: corporal, Company E; age: 22; enrolled at Greeneville, 6 Apr 1863; captured and paroled at McMinnville, 3 Oct 1863; promoted to corporal, 8 Apr 1865; discharged, 2 Aug 1865.
Gfellers, Joseph: private, Company E; age: 18; enrolled at Greeneville, 22 Jul 1863; discharged, 2 Aug 1865; file contains enlistment papers.
Gfellers, Madison: private, Company E; age: 26; enrolled at Greeneville, 5 Apr 1863; captured and paroled at McMinnville, 3 Oct 1863; sick in hospital in Knoxville, 29 Oct 1864 through Feb 1865; discharged, 2 Aug 1865; file contains enlistment papers.
Gfellers, Thomas: private, Company E; age: 27; enrolled at Greeneville, 6 Apr 1863; captured and paroled at McMinnville, 3 Oct 1863; sick in hospital at Kingston, 20 Jul 1864 through May 1865; discharged, 26 May 1865 at Knoxville with disability.
Gfellers, Washington: private, Company E; age: 20; enrolled at Greeneville, 6 Apr 1863; discharged, 2 Aug 1865.
Gibson, Pleasant: private, Company B; age: 45; enrolled at Jonesborough, Ill (?), 24 Nov 1862; captured and paroled at McMinnville, 3 Oct 1863; discharged, 2 Aug 1865.
Gibson, Thomas: private, Company B; age: 21; enrolled at Jonesboro, Ill (?), 24 Nov 1862; captured and paroled at McMinnville, 3 Oct 1863; sick in hospital at Kingston, 22 Oct 1864; sick in hospital at Kingston, 27 Nov 1864 through Feb 1865; deserted at Kingston, 10 Mar 1865; application to have desertion charge dropped, denied by War Department, 9 Apr 1892.
Gibson, William: private, Company B; age: 19; enrolled at Jonesboro, Ill (?), 24 Nov 1862; captured and paroled at McMinnville, 3 Oct 1863; discharged, 2 Aug 1865.
Gilmore, Samuel: corporal, Company D; enrolled at Rutledge, 1 Feb 1863; born: Grainger County; promoted to corporal, 19 Feb 1863; died in Nashville, 2 Jul 1863 of typhoid.
Gleason, John: private, Company F; age: 18; transferred from 3rd Regiment, Tennessee Infantry, Mar 1865; discharged, 2 Aug 1865.
Glover, Daniel: private, Company C; age: 33; enrolled at Elizabethton, 3 Aug 1863; mustered in at Strawberry Plains, 31 Mar 1864; discharged, 2 Aug 1865.
Goan, William M.: private, Company M; age: 32; enrolled at Dandridge, 3 Jan 1863; sick in hospital, 30 Jun 1863; sick in hospital at Knoxville, 28 Apr 1864; absent without leave, 26 Dec 1864; discharged, 2 Aug 1865.
Good, Hartsell: private, Company A; age: 31; enrolled at Greeneville, 27 Jan 1863; died in general hospital at Nashville, 14

Soldiers of the Regiment

Jul 1863 with "febris intermitten"; file contains numerous documents.

Good, Nathan: 1st sergeant, Company F; age: 20; enrolled at Greeneville, 1 Jan 1863; appointed 1st sergeant, 14 Apr 1863; promoted to 2nd lieutenant, 15 Aug 1863; resigned for "good of service", reason not stated, 30 Jul 1864.

Gosnell, Rufus: private, Company F; age: 30; enrolled at Greeneville, 15 Apr 1863; sick in hospital at Kingston, 10 Aug 1864 through Feb 1865; sick in hospital at Knoxville, 28 May 1865; discharged, 16 Jun 1865.

Gourley, William M.: private: Company B and F; age: 33; enrolled at Elizabethton, 14 Apr 1863; captured and paroled at McMinnville, 3 Oct 1863; reported absent on parole through Feb 1865; transferred to Company F, 28 Apr 1864; reported missing in action, 7 Apr 1865; pension office record (11 Mar 1889) shows he was discharged, 17 Mar 1864 to accept appointment as a Captain in the 13th Tennessee Volunteer Cavalry.

Grace, David L.: private, Company G; age: 24; enrolled at Taylorsville, 22 Aug 1863; captured and paroled at McMinnville, 3 Oct 1863; deserted at Kingston, 9 Aug 1864; restored to duty, 6 Apr 1865 by Presidential proclamation; file contains enlistment papers.

Graham, Alexander: private, Company C; age: 21; enrolled at Loudon, 1 May 1864; born: Greene County; sick in hospital at Greeneville, 27 Mar 1865; discharged, 2 Aug 1865; file contains enlistment papers.

Graham, Emanuel: private, Company C; age: 26; enrolled at Greeneville, 26 Feb 1863; mustered in at Strawberry Plains, 31 Mar 1864; died at post hospital in Kingston, 6 Jun 1864; file contains casualty sheet.

Graham, George J.: private, Company A; age: 28; enrolled at Greeneville, 6 Apr 1863; died in hospital in Nashville, 14 Jul 1863 of measles and diarrhea; file contains numerous papers.

Graham, William: private, Company A; age: 18; enrolled at Greeneville, 1 Jan 1863; mustered in at Strawberry Plains, 31 Mar 1864; died in regimental hospital at Mosier's Mill of typhoid fever, 15 Feb 1865; file contains casualty sheet.

Graham, William A.: private, Company; A; age: 24; enrolled at Greeneville, 6 Apr 1863; sick in hospital, 30 Jun 1863; captured and paroled at McMinnville, 3 Oct 1863; absent on parole through Jan 1865; reported missing in action, Apr 1865; gained from missing in action at Jonesborough, 2 May 1865; discharged, 2 Aug 1865.

Gray, Andrew C.: private, Company E; age: 33; enrolled at Greeneville, 12 Nov 1862; mustered in at Knoxville, 8 Feb 1864; sick in hospital at Knoxville, 14 Feb 1864; discharged with disability (unspecified), 21 May 1865.

Gray, Isaac B.: corporal, Company C; age: 19; enrolled at Greeneville, 6 Apr 1863; sick in hospital 15 - 30 Jun 1863; captured and paroled at McMinnville, 3 Oct 1863; absent on parole through Feb 1864; discharged, 2 Aug 1865.

Gray, John: private, Company D; enrolled at Rogersville, 1 Nov 1863; mustered at Strawberry Plains, 31 May 1864; sick at Kingston, 25 Nov 1864 through Feb 1864; prisoner of war record, blank; discharged, 2 Aug 1865.

Grayson, Benjamin C.: private, Company G; age: 37; enrolled at Taylorsville, 25 Aug 1862; sick in hospital at Camp Nelson, 15 Jun 1863 through Aug 1864; sick in hospital in Kingston, 24 Nov 1864 through May 1865; mustered out of service from hospital, 23 May 1865.

Grayson, James W.M.: Lieutenant Colonel; enrolled at Louisville, 1 May 1863; resident of Johnson County; mustered out of regiment, 9 Sep 1863 to accept commission as Major in the 12th Tennessee Cavalry by order of Major General Burnside.

Green, Enoch: private, Company F; age: 30; enrolled at Bulls Gap, 1 Dec 1864; resided: Greene County; mustered at Loudon, 7 May 1864; sick in hospital at Knoxville, 8 Jun 1864; absent without leave, 22 Dec 1864; discharged, 2 Aug 1865; file contains enlistment papers.

Greenlee, James L., Sr.: wagoner, Company D; enrolled at Greeneville, 30 Nov 1862; promoted to wagoner, 3 Jun 1863; captured and paroled at McMinnville, 3 Oct 1863; reduced in ranks, 1 Jul 1864; nothing further.

Greenlee, James L., Jr.: private, Company D; age: 26; enrolled at Rutledge, 30 Nov 1862; captured and paroled at McMinnville, 3 Oct 1863; promoted to corporal, Apr 1864; absent without leave, 19 Jun 1864; reduced to ranks, 1 Jul 1864; discharged, 2 Aug 1865.

Greenlee, Mamon: private, Companies D and F; age: 18; enrolled at Greeneville, 30 Jan 1863; sick, 15 - 30 Jun 1863; captured and paroled at McMinnville, 3 Oct 1863; reported absent on parole through Feb 1865; transferred to Company F, 30 Apr 1864; reported missing in action, Mar 1865; prisoner of war record shows that he was captured at McMinnville and sent to Richmond, 23 Oct 1863 and to Andersonville, GA., 11 Mar 1864; file contains numerous records.

Greenway, John H.: corporal, Company G; age: 18; enrolled at Greeneville, 20 Nov 1862; promoted to corporal, 22 May 1863; captured at McMinnville, 3 Oct 1863; paroled at City Point, VA., 8 May 1864; War Department record shows that he was sent from Columbus, OH., to Louisville, 13 Oct 1864 and from Louisville to Nashville, 2 Nov 1863, he was charged for transportation from Ohio; discharged, 2 Aug 1865.

Soldiers of the Regiment

Greer, Thomas: private, Company B; age: 19; enrolled at Jefferson, NC., 27 Nov 1862; captured and paroled at McMinnville, 3 Oct 1863; discharged, 2 Aug 1865.
Gregg, Benjamin: private, Company C; age: 25; enrolled at Newport, 6 Apr 1863; captured and paroled at McMinnville, 3 Oct 1863; absent on parole through Feb 1865; gained from missing in action at Knoxville and placed under arrest, 6 Mar 1865; sentenced to 3 years at hard labor; escaped confinement, 9 Jun 1865; War Department voided charges of desertion, 31 May 1910.
Gregg, Henry: private, Company F; age: 18; enrolled at Parrotsville, TN., 10 Mar 1865; record indicates he deserted from Company K, 8th Tennessee Infantry; mustered out with the 4th Regiment, 2 Aug 1865; file contains enlistment papers.
Gregg, Samuel: private, Company C; age: 36; enrolled at Greeneville, 6 Apr 1863; captured and paroled at McMinnville, 3 Oct 1863; reported missing in action, Mar 1865; note in file from War Department (24 Nov 1900) dishonorable discharge is voided.
Grider, Sidney E.: corporal, Company A; age: 18; enrolled at Rogersville, 2 Jan 1863; sick from enrollment through 30 Jun 1863; captured and paroled at McMinnville, 3 Oct 1863; promoted to corporal, 1 Aug 1864; discharged, 24 May 1865; furlough papers in file.
Grider, William M.: private, Company D; age: 29; enrolled at Rogersville, 5 Jan 1863; discharged; 2 Aug 1864; file contains furlough papers.
Griffin, Jacob M.: private: Company B; age: 23; enrolled at Dandridge, 14 Apr 1863; absent without leave, 15 -30 Jun 1863; reported as a deserter at Nashville, 12 Jul 1863.
Griffin, James F.: private, Company H; transferred from 3rd Tennessee Infantry, 1 May 1865; sick in hospital at Knoxville, discharged, 2 Aug 1865; resided in Jefferson County.
Grubbs, Alexander or Andrew: private, Company C; age: 18; enrolled at Bulls Gap, 1 Feb 1864; resided at Greene County; discharged, 2 Aug 1865; file contains enlistment papers.
Guin, Paine E.: private, Company D; age: 22; enrolled at Greeneville, 1 Mar 1863; captured and paroled at McMinnville, 3 Oct 1863; absent on parole through Mar - Apr 1865; reported as missing in action; Mar - Apr 1865; file contains casualty sheet.
Guinn, David: private, Company F; age: 19; enrolled at Greeneville, 13 Apr 1863; received $25.00 bounty; captured and paroled at McMinnville, 3 Oct 1863; discharged, 2 Aug 1865.
Guinn, McDonald: private, Company F; age: 35; enrolled at Greeneville, 15 Apr 1863; died in the hospital at Louisville, KY., 30 Oct 1863; file contains numerous papers.

4th Tennessee Volunteer Infantry Regiment (USA)

Hacker, Newton: Captain, Company C; age: 31; enrolled at Greeneville, 26 Jan 1863; mustered in as 1st Lieutenant, 25 Apr 1863; captured and paroled at McMinnville, 3 Oct 1863; promoted to Captain, 23 May 1864; mustered out, 2 Aug 1865; file contains numerous documents.

Hardin, Oliver: private, Company A; enrolled at Greeneville, 5 Apr 1863, sick from enrollment through 30 Jun 1863; captured and paroled at McMinnville, 3 Oct 1863; sick at Kingston, 23 Nov 1864 through Feb 1865; discharged, 2 Aug 1865.

Hair, George S.: private, Company C; age: 37; enrolled at Greeneville, 6 Apr 1863; captured and paroled at McMinnville, 3 Oct 1863; died in the hospital at Camp Nelson, KY., of diarrhea, 13 Jan 1864; file contains miscellaneous papers.

Hale, Andrew: private, Company G; age: 26; enrolled at Louisville, 1 Apr 1863; deserted at Nashville, in Jul 1863.

Hale, George: private, Company A; age: 19; enrolled at Mosier's Mill, TN., 1 Feb 1865; resided in Greene County; sick in hospital at Greeneville, 30 May 1854; discharged, 2 Aug 1865; file contains enlistment papers.

Hale, James M.: 1st Sergeant, Company D, age: 21; enrolled at Newport, 24 Jan 1863; captured and paroled at McMinnville, 3 Oct 1863; promoted to sergeant, 3 Feb 1864; promoted to 1Sgt, 11 Jun 1865; discharged, 2 Aug 1865.

Hale, John C.: private, Companies B and F; transferred from 3rd Tennessee Volunteer Infantry, 29 Jan 1863; enrolled at Maryville, TN., 8 Nov 1862; absent on recruiting duty, 1 Aug 1863 through Jun 1864; transferred to Company F, 29 Apr 1864; discharged to accept a commission as in a Tennessee Cavalry unit; file contains numerous papers.

Hall, Daniel: private, Company H; age: 18; enrolled at Kingston, 5 Jul 1864; resided in Kingston; born: Morgan County; mustered in at Kingston, 23 Jul 1864; deserted at Kingston, 24 Sep 1864.

Hall, John T.: private; age: 20; enrolled at Kingston, 2 Jun 1864; resided in Elizabethton, TN., name did not appear on any muster rolls of the Regiment.

Hall, William: private, Company F; transferred from 3rd Regiment Tennessee Volunteer Infantry, Mar 1865; discharged, 2 Aug 1865.

Holloway, James: private, Company H; age: 19; enrolled at Taylorsville, 7 May 1864; discharged at Kingston, 23 Jul 1864 for disability (reason not given).

Hamberd, Adam P.: private, Company E; age: 27; enrolled at Greeneville, 15 Mar 1863; prisoner of war record, but blank; absent on detached service, 15 Nov 1864 through Feb 1865; discharged, 2 Aug 1865.

Hamblet, Oliver M.: private, Company M; age: 33; enrolled at Jonesborough, 27 Apr 1864; mustered in at Loudon, 7 May 1864; deserted at Kingston, 2 Sep 1864; restored to duty, 15 Mar 1865; discharged, 2 Aug 1865; file contains enlistment papers.
Hampton, Marion: private, Company G; enrolled at Strawberry Plains, 10 Apr 1864; resided in Washington County, TN.; mustered at Loudon, 7 May 1864; discharged, 2 Aug 1865; file contains enlistment papers.
Hawkins, John E.: wagoner, Company E; age: 41; enrolled at Greeneville, 15 Mar 1863; appointed wagoner, 5 Jun 1863, captured and paroled at McMinnville, 3 Oct 1863; sick in hospital at Knoxville, 8 Dec 1864; sick at Greene County, 19 May 1865; discharged, 2 Aug 1865.
Hannah, William A.: private, Company A; gained from 3rd Tennessee Volunteer Infantry, 1 Mar 1865; deserted, 25 Mar 1865; joined from desertion, 7 May 1865; request to have desertion charge expunged, denied by War Department, 10 May 1888.
Harold, Albert or Elbert: musician, Company E; age: 18; enrolled at Greeneville, 15 Mar 1863; appointed musician, 5 Jun 1863; captured and paroled at McMinnville, 3 Oct 1863; absent on parole through Feb 1864; discharged, 2 Aug 1865.
Harold, William C.: corporal, Company E; age: 24; enrolled at Greeenville, 15 Mar 1863; captured and paroled at McMinnville, 3 Oct 1863; absent through Feb 1864; sick in hospital at Kingston, 30 Oct 1864; absent on detached service, 8 Dec 1864; discharged, 2 Aug 1865.
Hardin, John: private, Company A; age: 23; enrolled at Greeneville, 2 Apr 1863; absent on detached service, Jun 1863 through Feb 1864; discharged, 2 Aug 1865.
Harmon, Caswell: corporal, Company A; enrolled at Greeneville, 27 Jan 1863; sick from enrollment through 30 Jun 1863; promoted to corporal, Apr 1864; discharged, 2 Aug 1865.
Harmon, Isaac B.: private, Company A; age: 24; enrolled at Greeneville, 22 Jan 1863; deserted at McMinnville, 29 Sep 1863; gained from desertion, 7 Aug 1864, sick in hospital at Kingston, 23 Nov 1864 through Feb 1865; sick in hospital at Knoxville, 28 May 1865; discharged, 2 Aug 1865; file contains miscellaneous papers.
Harmon, John B.: private, Company A; age: 43; enrolled at Greeneville, 22 Jan 1863; deserted at McMinnville, 29 Sep 1863; gained from desertion, 7 Aug 1864; sick in hospital at Kingston, 23 Nov 1864 through Feb 1865; sick in hospital at Knoxville, 28 May 1865; discharged, 2 Aug 1865; file contains numerous papers.
**Harmon, Kennedy B.: private, Company A; age: 38; enrolled in Greeneville, 26 Jan 1863; deserted at McMinnville, 27 Sep 1863; desertion charge removed by War Department, "was attempting

to rejoin his unit at the time of capture by Confederates at Rutledge, TN., 16 Dec 1863; sent to Andersonville, GA., 14 Feb 1864; died in prison at Andersonville, 11 Jun 1864."
Harmon, Robert L.: musician, Company A; age: 28; enrolled at Greeneville, 27 Feb 1863; appointed musician, 1 May 1863; learning music, 10 Jul 1863 through Aug 1863; deserted at McMinnville, 27 Sep 1863; returned to duty, 10 Apr 1864; drummer, Jul 1864; fifer, Aug 1864; musician, Sep 1864 through Apr 1865; discharged, 2 Aug 1865.
Harmon, Sparling B.: private; age: 39, enrolled at Greeneville, 27 Jan 1863; deserted at McMinnville, 27 Sep 1863; returned from desertion, 10 Apr 1864; discharged, 2 Aug 1865; request for desertion charge to be expunged denied by War Department, 6 Apr 1887.
Harmon, Thomas J.: private, Company A; enrolled at Greeneville, 27 Jan 1863; deserted at McMinnville, 27 Sep 1863; returned to duty, 7 Apr 1864; discharged, 2 Aug 1865.
Harmon, William R.: private, Company A; enrolled at Greeneville, 25 Jul 1863; deserted at McMinnville, 27 Sep 1863; returned to duty, 1 Feb 1864; sick in hospital at Kingston, 9 Sep 1864 through Feb 1865; discharged, 2 Aug 1865; file contains enlistment and other papers.
Harold, John: Captain, Companies A, B and F&S; age: 24; enrolled at Greeneville, 12 Aug 1862 as a private; commissioned a lieutenant and detailed to brigade quartermaster, 9 Sep 1863; captured and paroled at McMinnville, 3 Oct 1863; promoted to Captain of Company B, Oct 1864; file contains miscellaneous documents.
Harris, James B.: Corporal, Company A; age: 31; captured in Hancock or Hawkins County, TN., 15 Nov 1862; confined at Knoxville and sent to Richmond for exchange, 22 Nov 1862; paroled at City Point, VA., 30 Nov 1862; enrolled in the 4th Regiment at Rutledge, 5 Jan 1863; promoted to corporal, 1 May 1863; captured and paroled at McMinnville, 3 Oct 1863; on parole when captured at Dandridge, TN., 18 Jan 1864; sent to Richmond, 20 Jan 1864; admitted to hospital at Richmond with a gunshot wound in right hand; died in Confederate prison hospital (Ward F) in Richmond of "varioloid", 28 Feb 1864.
Harris, Permenius L.: private, Company A; age: 25; enrolled at Rutledge, 5 Jan 1863; resided in Hawkins County; born: Pikeville, VA.; sick in hospital at Louisville, enrollment through 30 Jun 1863; captured ant paroled at McMinnville, 3 Oct 1863; absent until Feb 1864; discharged, 2 Aug 1865; file contains furlough request.
Harrison, Alexander: private, Company F; age: 45; enrolled at Greeneville, 1 Jul 1863; sick in hospital in Kingston, 1 Jul 1864 through Feb 1865; sick in hospital at Knoxville, 28 May 1865; discharged, 16 Jun 1865; file contains enlistment papers.

Soldiers of the Regiment   87

Harrison, David M.: private, Company C; age: 35; enrolled at Greeneville, 10 Sep 1862; captured and paroled at McMinnville, 3 Oct 1863; absent on parole until Mar - Apr 1864; discharged, 8 Jul 1865.
Harrison, George D.: private, Company D; age: 18; enrolled at Greeneville, 22 Jul 1863; captured and paroled at McMinnville, 3 Oct 1863; absent without leave, 22 Dec 1864; discharged, 2 Aug 1865; file contains enlistment papers.
Harrison, Henry M.: private, Company G; age: 18; enrolled at Greeneville, 5 Nov 1862; sick in hospital from muster in through 30 Jun 1863; captured and paroled at McMinnville, 3 Oct 1863; absent on parole through Feb 1864; discharged, 2 Aug 1865.
Harrold, Jesse E.: private, Company E; age: 21; father: Andrew Harrold; captured in Lee County, TN. (?), 27 Jul 1863; confined at Richmond, 28 Aug 1863 through Mar 1865; sent to Cox's Wharf, VA., 10 Mar 1865; paroled at Camp Chase, OH., 21 Mar 1865; sent to Tripler General Hospital, Columbus, OH, with "typho-malarial fever"; records show discharge from hospital, 25 May 1865; file contains numerous papers.
Hart, Thomas C.: musician, Company B; age: 26; enrolled at Elizabethton, 26 Dec 1862; promoted to musician, 5 Jun 1863; captured and paroled at McMinnville, 3 Oct 1863; sick in hospital at Knoxville, Jan - Feb 1865 through May 1865; discharged, 20 May 1865.
Hartley, James: private, Company B; age: 32; enrolled at Elizabethton, 13 Aug 1862; sick in hospital in Nashville, May - Jun 1863; captured and paroled at McMinnville, 3 Oct 1863; absent on parole through Feb 1865; reported missing in action, Feb 1865; War Department record shows: "he was mustered in Company F, 3rd North Carolina Mounted Infantry as 1st lieutenant, 14 Mar 1864; desertion charge by 4th Regiment, removed", 4 Nov 1902; file contains numerous papers.
Hartman, Enoch: sergeant, Company E; age: 29; enrolled at Greeneville, 23 Apr 1863; sick in hospital, 15 - 30 Jun 1863; captured and paroled at McMinnville, 3 Oct 1863; promoted to sergeant, 1 Aug 1864; discharged, 2 Aug 1865.
Haun, George W.: corporal, Company D; age: 26; enrolled at Dandridge, 1 Mar 1863; captured and paroled at McMinnville, 3 Oct 1863; promoted to corporal, 1 Jan 1865; discharged, 2 Aug 1865.
Hawkins, James: private, Company C; age: 28 ; enrolled at Greeneville, 15 Nov 1862; captured and paroled at McMinnville, 3 Oct 1863; absent on parole until Feb 1864; deserted at Kingston, 25 Aug 1864; dropped as deserted, 31 Aug 1864; restored to duty per Presidential proclamation, 7 May 1865; discharged, 2 Aug 1865.
Hayes, Jacob M. Sr.: private, Company C; age: 40; enrolled at Greeneville, 6 Apr 1863; discharged, 2 Aug 1865.

4th Tennessee Volunteer Infantry Regiment (USA)

Hayes, William R.: private, Company E; age: 19; enrolled at Greeneville, 15 Mar 1863; discharged, 19 Jun 1865.
Haney, Samuel C.: private, Company E; age: 38; enrolled at Greeneville, 15 Nov 1861; sick in hospital in Nashville from muster until discharge from service on 18 Aug 1863; discharged for unspecified disability.
Hays, Jacob: private, Company G; age: 40; enrolled at Greeneville, 6 Apr 1863; sick in hospital from muster until May 1863; deserted at Louisville, Ky., May (date not stated) 1863.
Hays, Nathan: private, Company G; age: 24; enrolled at Greeneville, 3 Jan 1863; sick in hospital from muster until May 1863; deserted at Louisville, Ky., May (date not stated) 1863.
Hays, Robert: private, Company G; age: 29; enrolled at Greeneville, 6 Apr 1863; sick in hospital from muster until May 1863; deserted at Louisville, May 1863; War Department Note: "was on recruiting duty May through 20 Sep 1863; captured at Jonesborough, confined at Richmond, 4 Oct 1863, paroled at City Point, Va., 28 Dec 1863, reported at Camp Parole, MD, 29 Dec 1863, sent to Camp Chase, OH., 11 Jan 1864, sent to provost marshal, Columbus, OH., 18 May 1864, charged with desertion for failing to report, returned to service, 29 Apr 1865, desertion charge no longer stands but can not be expunged." (War Department note, 14 Jan 1887)
Hendrix, Eli C.: corporal, Company E, age: 31; enrolled at Greeneville, 6 Apr 1863; appointed corporal, 24 Apr 1863; reported absent without leave, 15 Dec 1864; discharged, 2 Aug 1865.
Henegar, John H.: private, Company C; transferred from 3rd Tennessee Volunteer Infantry Regiment, 1 Mar 1865; discharged, 2 Aug 1865.
Henry, William: private, Company A; age: 21; enrolled at Greeneville, 8 Jan 1863; captured and paroled at McMinnville, 3 Oct 1863; absent on parole until Oct 1864; discharged, 2 Aug 1865.
Herrold, Joseph E.: captured in Lee County, TN. (?), 23 Jul 1863; brought from Salisbury, NC., confined at Richmond, 28 Aug 1863 through Mar 1865; sent to Cox's Wharf, VA., 10 Mar 1865; paroled at Camp Parole, Annapolis, MD, 25 Mar 1865; sent to Tripler General Hospital, Columbus, OH, with "typho-malarial fever"; records show he died 7 Apr 1865; father: Andrew Harrold; file contains numerous papers.
Hice, Robert: private, Company G; enrolled at Jonesborough, 1 Mar 1864; deserted at Knoxville, 17 Apr 1864.
Hickey, Edom: private, Company A; age: 18; enrolled at Newport, TN., 2 Jan 1863; received $25 bounty; mustered in at Nashville, 7 Aug 1863; captured and paroled at McMinnville, 3 Oct 1863; killed by the enemy at Newport, Cocke County, TN., 24 Dec 1863.

Hickey, John: private, Company A; age: 23; enrolled at Newport, 25 Jan 1863; captured and paroled at McMinnville, 3 Oct 1863; absent on parole until Feb 1864; deserted at Loudon, 24 May 1864.
Hickey, Levi M.: sergeant, Company B; enrolled at Elizabethton, 26 Dec 1862; promoted to corporal, 5 Jul 1863; captured and paroled at McMinnville, 3 Oct 1863; promoted to sergeant, 2 Nov 1864; discharged, 2 Aug 1865.
Hinkle, Ezra: private, Company F; received at Jonesborough by transferred from 3rd Tennessee Volunteer Infantry Regiment, 28 Apr 1865; discharged, 2 Aug 1865.
Hickman, William: private, Company A; age: 32; transferred from 3rd Tennessee Volunteer Infantry Regiment, 1 Mar 1865; discharged, 2 Aug 1865.
Hines, John W.: 1st lieutenant, Adjutant; transferred from Company B; 59th Regiment, Ohio Volunteer Infantry, 17 Jun 1864; enrolled at Kingston, 18 Jun 1864; resigned, 24 Apr 1865 cited surgeon's certificate of disability "hypertrophy of heart and general debility."
Hinkle, John: corporal, Company G; age: 19 enrolled at Greeneville, 27 Jan 1864; promoted to corporal, 1 Mar 1864; discharged, 2 Aug 1865.
Hinkle, Josiah: private, Company G; age: 22; enrolled at Greeneville, 27 Jan 1864; discharged, 2 Aug 1865.
Hockeday, Larkin L.: private, Company G; age: 38; enrolled at Taylorsville, 25 Aug 1862; captured and paroled at McMinnville, 3 Oct 1863; absent on parole through Feb 1864; absent without leave, 18 Feb 1865; dropped as a deserted at Mosier's Mill, TN., 31 Mar 1865; returned to duty by Presidential proclamation, 30 Apr 1865; discharged, 8 Jul 1865; file contains enlistment papers.
Hodge, Francis: private, Company B; age: 22; enrolled at Jonesborough, Ill., 24 Nov 1862; admitted to hospital in Louisville, 12 Jan 1863; died of measles, 7 Apr 1863; file contains casualty sheet.
Hodge, Isaac: private, Company G; age: 21; enrolled at Elizabethton, 15 Feb 1864; mustered in at Strawberry Plains, 31 Mar 1864; sick in hospital at Kingston, 7 Sep 1864 through Dec 1864; War Department note in file: "deserted Company G, 14th Kentucky Cavalry - notation of 24 Apr 1886 is canceled." discharged, 2 Aug 1865.
Hodge, James: private, Company B; age: 23; enrolled at Jonesborough, 24 Nov 1862; received $25 enlistment bonus; sick in hospital, 15 - 30 Jun 1863; sick in Nashville, Jul - Aug 1863; sick in hospital at Knoxville, 8 Mar 1864 through Jun 1864; absent on furlough, 22 Sep 1864; sick in hospital at Kingston, 31 Oct 1864 through May 1865; discharged with disability, 19 May 1865.
Hodge, Littleton: private, Company H; enrolled at Taylorsville, 1 Jan 1865; deserted at Jonesborough, 9 May 1865; War Department note:

4th Tennessee Volunteer Infantry Regiment (USA)

"application to remove desertion charge denied", 6 Oct 1890; file contains enlistment papers.
Hodge, Militon: private, Company B; age: 21; enrolled at Elizabethton, 1 Oct 1862; deserted at Louisville, 19 Feb 1863.
Hodge, Ephram F.: private, Company C; gained from transfer from 3rd Tennessee Infantry Regiment, 1 Mar 1865; discharged, 2 Aug 1865.
Hodge, Joseph R.: private, Company B; gained from transfer from 3rd Tennessee Infantry Regiment, 1 Mar 1865; discharged, 2 Aug 1865.
Holder, Henderson: private, Company D; age: 20; enrolled at Rutledge, 15 Apr 1862; discharged, 8 Jul 1865.
Holdman, John: private, Company D; age: 41; enrolled at Nashville, 11 Jul 1863; captured and paroled at McMinnville, 3 Oct 1863; absent on parole through Feb 1864; discharged, 2 Aug 1865; file contains enlistment papers.
Holly, Jacob: corporal, Company F; enrolled at Greeneville, 30 Jan 1863; appointed corporal, 15 Jun 1863; captured and paroled at McMinnville, 3 Oct 1863; discharged, 2 Aug 1865.
Holt, Bradley: private, Company F; age: 22; enrolled at Greeneville, 20 Jan 1863; prisoner of war record in file - not filled in; discharged, 2 Aug 1865; file contains enlistment papers.
Holt, Isaac: private, Company F; age: 24; mustered in at Knoxville, 2 Mar 1865; resided in Greene County; deserted at Panther Springs, TN., 30 Apr 1865; restored to duty by Presidential proclamation, 8 May 1865; deserted at Jonesborough, 24 Jun 1865; file contains enlistment papers.
Holt, James: musician, Company F; age: 32; enrolled at Greeneville, 15 Apr 1863; received $25 bounty; appointed musician, 15 Jun 1863; captured and paroled at McMinnville, 3 Oct 1863; absent on parole through Feb 1864; discharged, 2 Aug 1865.
Holtsinger, Geroge W.: Captain, Company F; age: 26; enrolled as a private at Greeneville, 26 Jan 1863; appeared on Confederate prisoner of war rolls at Louisville, 15 Apr 1863 through 16 May 1863; appointed sergeant by order of Colonel Stover, 16 Aug 1863; commissioned 1st lieutenant to replace Lt. Farnsworth, 12 Jun 1864; sick at Kingston, 23 Nov 1864; commissioned captain to replace Captain Davis, 19 Feb 1865; sick at Greeneville, 5 Mar 1865; physicians statement: "suffered typhoid fever and hepatitis"; discharged, date not clear; file contains numerous papers.
Hopkins, James: corporal, Company H; age: 25; enrolled at Kingston, 14 Jun 1864; resident of Washington County, TN., promoted to corporal, 28 Apr 1865; discharged, 2 Aug 1865; file contains enlistment papers.

Soldiers of the Regiment 91

Horton, James M.: private, Company C; age: 37; enrolled at Loudon, 7 Apr 1864; resident of Polk County, NC.; born: Spartainburg, SC.; sick in hospital at Kingston, 4 Jun 1864 through Apr 1865; discharged, 2 Aug 1865; file contains enlistment papers.
House, James F.: private, Company G; age: 18; enrolled at Greeneville, 5 Nov 1862; captured and paroled at McMinnville, 3 Oct 1863; absent on parole through Feb 1864; discharged, 2 Aug 1865.
House, William C.: private, Company C; age: 22; enrolled at Jonesborough, 6 Apr 1863; died in hospital at Nashville with fever, 15 Jun 1863; buried in College Hill Cemetery; file contains enlistment papers.
Housley, Robert W.: private, Company B; enrolled at Greeneville, 1 Jan 1862; born: Carter County; enrollment through Jun 1864, on detached service to participate in a "special raid" in East Tennessee with Colonel Kirk; prisoner of war record - but blank; discharged at Knoxville, 7 Jul 1865; file contains enlistment papers and other documents.
Houston, Elbert S.: private, Company B; age: 39; enrolled at Jonesborough, 24 Nov 1862; discharged, 2 Aug 1865.
Houston, James: private, Company F; age: 23; enrolled at Greeneville, 15 Apr 1863; sick in hospital, muster in to 30 Jun 1863; died at Nashville of "rubeola", 4 Jul 1864; buried, City Cemetery.
Houston, James M.: sergeant, Company B; enrolled at Greeneville, 24 Nov 1863; sick in hospital 15 - 30 Jun 1863; captured and paroled at McMinnville, 3 Oct 1863; promoted to corporal, 1 Aug 1864; promoted to sergeant, 20 May 1865.
Howard, David L.: private, Company H; age: 18; enrolled at Kingston, 4 Jul 1864; resided in Elizabethton; born: Grainger County; discharged, 2 Aug 1865.
Howard, Hamilton: private, Company B; age: 20; enrolled at Taylorsville, 8 Dec 1862; discharged, 2 Aug 1865; file contains enlistment papers.
Howard, John T.: private, Company H; age: 19; enrolled at Kingston, 29 Jun 1864; discharged, 2 Aug 1865.
Howell, William: private, Company H; age: 18; enrolled at Greeneville, 1 Feb 1865; resident of Buncomb County, NC., discharged, 2 Aug 1865; file contains enlistment papers.
Huddle, Charles W.: private, Company G; age: 18; enrolled at Taylorsville, 12 Apr 1865; resident of Wythe County, VA., discharged, 2 Aug 1865; file contains enlistment papers.
Huff, Jonas: corporal, Company F; age: 18; enrolled at Greeneville, 5 Apr 1863; received $25 bounty; captured and paroled, 4 Oct 1863; promoted to corporal, 3 Feb 1865; discharged, 2 Aug 1865.

Huff, Joseph: private, Company G; age: 19; enrolled at Greeneville, 5 Nov 1862; sick from muster to 30 Jun 1863; died in Nashville, 30 Jun 1863; cause of death unknown; file contains casualty sheet.
Huff, Thomas: private, Company G; age: 18; enrolled at Greeneville, 5 Nov 1862; killed in battle at McMinnville, 3 Oct 1863; file contains casualty sheet.
Hull, David M.: private, Company F; age: 19; enrolled at Greeneville, 16 Apr 1863; received $25 enlistment bounty; captured and paroled at McMinnville, 4 Oct 1863; sick at Kingston, 27 Oct 1864 through Feb 1865; discharged, 2 Aug 1865.
Hurley, Ruben: private, Company F; age: 18; enrolled at McKee County, KY., 25 Jan 1863; sick in hospital at Louisville, 15 -30 Jun 1863; captured and paroled at McMinnville, 3 Oct 1863; discharged, 2 Aug 1865.
Hutton, John N.: private, Company B; age: 23; enrolled at Robinson, Ill., 1 Apr 1863; captured and paroled at McMinnville, 3 Oct 1863; discharged, 2 Aug 1865.
Hutton, Thomas S.: corporal, Company B; age: 20; enrolled at Roinson, Ill., 1 Apr 1863; promoted to corporal, 29 Apr 1864; requested 20 day furlough to visit family living in Blount County, Jul 1865; discharged, 2 Aug 1865; file contains enlistment; papers.
Hyder, Andrew J. F.: private, Company B; age: 18; enrolled at Elizabethton, 1 Feb 1864; discharged, 2 Aug 1865; file contains enlistment papers.
Hull, Isaac B.: corporal, Company A; age: 20; enrolled at Greeneville, 1 Oct 1863; appointed corporal, 1 Apr 1864; discharged, 2 Aug 1865.
Humphreys, David E.: private, Company B; enrolled at Elizabethton, 26 Dec 1862; captured in Wise County, VA., 31 Dec 1862; paroled at City Point, VA., 18 Mar 1863; captured and paroled at McMinnville, 3 Oct 1863; absent on parole until Aug 1864; discharged, 2 Aug 1865.
Humphreys, James,: corporal, Company B; enrolled at Elizabethton, 26 Dec 1862; promoted to corporal, 5 Jun 1863; captured and paroled at McMinnville, 3 Oct 1865; absent on parole until Apr 1864; reduced to private for being on parole too long; on detached service, Nov 1864 through Feb 1865; discharged, 2 Aug 1865.
Hyder, John W.: private, Company B; age: 32; enrolled at Strawberry Plains, 29 Mar 1864; resided at Elizabethton; mustered at Loudon, 7 May 1864; discharged, 2 Aug 1865; file contains enlistment papers.
Hyder, Joseph: private, Company B; age: 24; enrolled at Elizabethton, 30 Sep 1862; discharged at Louisville for disability

Soldiers of the Regiment

(chronic pneumonia), 25 Jun 1863; file contains disability discharge papers.
Hyder, Lawson F.: sergeant, Company B; age: 19; enrolled at Elizabethton, 15 Apr 1863; promoted to sergeant, Jun 1863; captured and paroled at McMinnville, 3 Oct 1863; discharged, 2 Aug 1865.
Hyder, Nathaniel K.: private, Company H; age: 23; enrolled at Greeneville, 31 May 1863; prisoner of war record - blank; reported at Mosier's Mill, 14 Feb 1865; deserted at Mosier's Mill, 18 Mar 1865.
Ingram, Edmond: private, Company H; age: 18; enrolled at (?), 7 May 1864; died in the hospital at Kingston, 2 Jul 1864; file contains casualty sheet.
Inklebarger, Calvin: private, Company H; gained as transfer from the 3rd Tennessee Infantry Regiment, 1 Mar 1865; note in the file: "deserted, 2 Aug 1863; returned to duty, 20 Nov 1863", discharged, 2 Aug 1865.
Inman, John: private, Company D; age: 21; enrolled at Dandridge, 1 Feb 1863; mustered in at Strawberry Plains, 31 Mar 1864; sick in the hospital at Kingston, 28 Apr 1864 through Feb 1865; discharged 2 Aug 1865; file contains enlistment papers.
Innman, William: private, Company D; age: 22; enrolled at Newport, 20 Nov 1862; received $25 bounty; sick, 15 - 30 Jun 1863; captured and paroled at McMinnville, 3 Oct 1863; discharged, 2 Aug 1865.
Ira, James: private, Company H; enrolled at Kingston, 1 Sep 1864; deserted at Kingston, 12 Sep 1864.
Isely, Martin R.: private, Company F; age: 31; enrolled at Greeneville, 3 May 1863; received $25 bounty; died of typhoid fever in the hospital at Louisville, 6 Aug 1863; numerous papers in file.
Jackson, Richard R.: private, Company F; age 18; enrolled at Greeenville, 6 Apr 1863; received $25 bounty; sick in hospital at Louisville, 15 - 30 Jun 1863; captured and paroled at McMinnville, 3 Oct 1863; on detached service in Kentucky, Jun 1863 - Apr 1864; on detached service in Asheville, NC., Mar - Jun 1865.
Jackson, William W.: private, Company C; gained as a transfer from the 3rd Tennessee Infantry Regiment, 1 Mar 1865; sick in the hospital at Knoxville, Mar - Jun 1865; discharge not furnished on muster out of service.
Jane, W. Alexander: corporal, Company G; age: 18; enrolled at Greeneville, 5 Jan 1863; prisoner of war record - not filled in; promoted to corporal, 1 Mar 1864; discharged, 2 Aug 1865.
Jane, Francis M.: private, Company G; age: 16; enrolled at Greeneville, 14 Sep 1863; mustered in at Strawberry Plains, 31 Mar 1864; discharged, 2 Aug 1865.

Jane, George: private, Company G; age: 18; enrolled at Greeneville, 1 Oct 1863; mustered in at Strawberry Plains, 20 Mar 1864; on picket duty, Aug 1864; sick in Kingston, 25 Nov through Dec 1864; guarding bridge, May 1865; discharged, 2 Aug 1865.
Jane, Joseph F.: private, Company G; age: 24; enrolled at Greeneville, 15 Nov 1861; captured and paroled at McMinnville, 3 Oct 1863; sick in the hospital at Knoxville, 9 Mar 1864 through Apr 1864; mustered out, 7 Jul 1865.
Jane, Thomas W.: sergeant, Company E; age: 26; enrolled at Greeneville, 15 Nov 1861; promoted to sergeant, 26 May 1863; captured and paroled at McMinnville, 3 Oct 1863; discharged, 8 Jul 1865.
Jenes, William: private, Company G; age: 24; gained as a transfer from the 3rd Tennessee Infantry Regiment, 1 Mar 1865; discharged, 2 Aug 1865.
Jennings, Elijah: corporal, Company E; age: 28; enrolled at Greeneville, 15 Nov 1861; promoted to corporal, 26 May 1863; captured and paroled at McMinnville, 3 Oct 1863; discharged, 2 Aug 1865.
Jennings, George: private, Company E; age: 24; enrolled at Greeneville, 15 Nov 1861; captured and paroled at McMinnville, 3 Oct 1863; sick at home in Greene County with fever and not able to muster out with the Regiment; file contains commanders statement, 26 Mar 1866.
Jennings, Stephen C.: private, Company E; age: 23; enrolled at Greeneville, 15 Nov 1861; captured and paroled at McMinnville, 3 Oct 1863; sick in hospital at Nashville, 13 Aug through 22 Aug 1863, discharged, 8 Jul 1865; file contains medical record.
Johnson, George W.: private, Company A; age: 18; enrolled at Greeneville, 1 Aug 1863; mustered at Loudon, 7 May 1864; discharged, 2 Aug 1865; file contains enlistment papers.
Johnson, William L.: private, Company F; age: 28; enrolled at Greeneville, 15 Apr 1863; received $25 bonus; captured and paroled at McMinnville, 3 Oct 1863; died in the hospital at Knoxville of fever, 28 Apr 1864; file contains numerous documents.
Johnston, George W.: private, Company A; age: 50; enrolled at Greeneville, 15 Oct 1863; prisoner of war record shows that he was confined in East Tennessee, 24 Nov 1862; sick at Kingston, 30 Aug 1864 through Dec 1864; sick at Knoxville, 31 Mar 1865; mustered out at Knoxville, 29 May 1865; file contains enlistment papers.
Jones, George: private, Company D; age: 25; enrolled at Newport, 24 Jan 1863; resided in Cocke County; mustered in at Strawberry Plains, 31 Mar 1864; sick in hospital at Kingston, 25 Nov 1864; discharged, 2 Aug 1865; file contains enlistment papers.

Soldiers of the Regiment

Jones, Henry D.: private, Company F; age: 45; enrolled at Greeneville, 15 Nov 1861; resided in Carter County; captured and paroled at McMinnville, 3 Oct 1863; carried on rolls as "absent on parole" through Feb 1865; record shows that he was again captured at Markinsville, Tennessee, 8 Feb 1864; confined at Richmond, 17 Feb 1864; sent to Andersonville, GA., 18 Feb 1864; died of diarrhea, date not stated; file contains enlistment papers, casualty sheet.

Jones, James C.: sergeant, Company D; age: 25; enrolled at Rogersville, 13 Apr 1862; promoted to sergeant, 1 Jun 1863; captured and paroled at McMinnville, 3 Oct 1863; absent on parole through Feb 1864; discharged, 2 Aug 1865.

Jones, Samuel A.: corporal, Company C; age: 18; enrolled at Flat Creek, Tennessee, 6 Nov 1863; resided in Greene County; promoted to corporal, 1 Aug 1864; discharged, 2 Aug 1865; file contains enlistment papers.

Jones, Samuel J.: sergeant, Company D; enrolled at Rutledge, 6 Jan 1863; promoted to corporal, 19 Feb 1863; captured and paroled at McMinnville, 3 Oct 1863; missing in action until 21 Mar 1864 when he rejoined his unit at Strawberry Plains; guarding coal mine, 1 Oct 1864; discharged, 2 Aug 1865.

Jones, William P.: 1st Lieutenant, Company D; age: 22; enrolled at Rutledge as a private, 14 Apr 1863; sick in hospital, 30 Jan 1864; promoted to sergeant, 17 Apr 1864; commissioned 1st Lieutenant, 5 Jun 1865 at Jonesborough; discharged, 2 Aug 1865; file contains numerous papers.

Justice, Henry D.: private, Company D; age: 27; enrolled at Greeneville, 17 Mar 1863; captured and paroled at McMinnville, 3 Oct 1863; absent on parole through Feb 1864; absent without leave, 25 May 1864; returned to duty 13 Apr 1865; restored to duty by Presidential proclamation; discharged, 2 Aug 1865; War Department note: desertion charge expunged, 28 Apr 1887.

Karbaugh, Samuel: private, Company D; age: 18; enrolled at Greeneville, 30 Jan 1863; captured and paroled at McMinnville, 3 Oct 1863; discharged, 2 Aug 1865.

Karbough, Thomas F.: private, Company D; age: 19; enrolled at Greeneville, 30 Jan 1863; captured and paroled at McMinnville, 3 Oct 1863; discharged, 2 Aug 1865.

Karbaugh, William P.: private, Company D; age: 23; enrolled at Greeneville, 30 Jan 1863; captured and paroled at McMinnville, 3 Oct 1863; carried as missing in action until 18 Jan 1864; gained from missing in action at Knoxville, Apr 1864; picket duty, Apr 1864; provost guard, Jun 1864; guarding coal mine, Oct 1864; patient in the hospital at Nashville, Jan - Feb 1865; discharged, 2 Aug 1865.

Kelley, Allen J.: private, Company F; age: 18; enrolled at Mossy Creek, Tennessee, 26 Mar 1865; deserted at Jonesborough, 19 May 1865.
Kelly, Joseph C.: private, Company D; age: 18; enrolled at Newport, 1 Oct 1863; mustered at Strawberry Plains, 31 Mar 1864; deserted at Kingston, 20 Jul 1864; returned to duty, 27 Sep 1864; discharged, 2 Aug 1865; file contains court martial record.
Kesterson, Patric H.: private, company F; age: 23; enrolled at Greeneville, 1 Mar 1863; received $25 enlistment bonus; absent without leave, 15 - 30 Jun 1863; reported as deserter at Nashville (date not known, records captured).
Keys, Elbert W.: private, Company C; age: 20; enrolled at Jonesborough, 25 Dec 1862; sick in hospital, 15 - 30 Jun 1863; prisoner of war record - not filled in; discharged, 2 Aug 1865.
Keys, John: private, Company G; age: 20; enrolled at Jonesborough, 12 Sep 1862; captured in Lee County, VA., 18 Apr 1863; paroled at Camp Chase, Ohio, 26 May 1863; deserted at Nashville, Jun 1863.
Killgore, Jacob M.: private, Company G; age: 21; enrolled at Greeneville, 5 Apr 1863; appointed musician, 1 Jun 1863; discharged, 2 Aug 1863.
King, Andrew J.: private, Company C; transferred from 3rd Tennessee Infantry Regiment, 1 Mar 1865; War Department note (28 Aug 1897) shows that he enrolled 20 Nov 1862, was a resident of Anderson County; received a 20 day furlough, Jul 1865; discharged 2 Aug 1865.
King, John T.: private, Company B; age: 21; enrolled at Greeneville, 12 Aug 1862; sick in hospital, 15 - 30 Jun 1863; captured and paroled at McMinnville, 3 Oct 1863; discharged, 2 Aug 1865.
Kirk, George W.: private, Company G; enrolled at Jonesborough, 11 Aug 1863; reported absent without leave from muster through 30 Jun 1863; transferred to 2nd North Carolina Regiment, Mar 1864; War Department note (23 Oct 1895): "enrolled 15 Jun 1863, discharged 30 Jun 1863 by reason of his muster into service on that date as a Captain in Company D, 5th East Tennessee (subsequently 8th Tennessee) Cavalry."
Kirksey, Elijah: private, Company D; age: 18; enrolled at Dandridge, 17 Dec 1863; mustered at Strawberry Plains, 31 Mar 1864; resident of Jefferson County; absent without leave, 30 Jul through 30 Aug 1864; sick in hospital at Kingston, 25 Nov 1864 through Feb 1865; discharged, 2 Aug 1865; file contains enlistment papers.
Kite, Aaron D.: private, Company B and F; age: 22; enrolled at Elizabethton, Jan 1862; mustered at Knoxville, 1 Jan 1864; absent without leave, 30 Jun 1863 through Feb 1864; reported as a deserter, Aug 1864.

Soldiers of the Regiment 97

Kite, Alfred C.: private, Company B; age: 21; enrolled at Elizabethton, 1 Jan 1862; died at Nashville, Mar 1864; file contains casualty sheet.
Kite, Daniel C.: private, Company H; age: 18; enrolled at Elizabethton, 4 Jun 1864; discharged, 2 Aug 1864.
Kite, William B.: corporal, Company B; age: 22; enrolled at Greeneville, 9 Dec 1862; promoted to corporal, 5 Jun 1863; captured and paroled at McMinnville, 3 Oct 1863; deserted at Kingston, 31 Jul 1864; returned to duty, 14 Oct 1864; court martialed; file contains miscellaneous papers.
Knight, Wesley: private, Company D; age: 24; enrolled at Dandridge, 2 Jan 1863; captured and paroled at McMinnville, 3 Oct 1863; absent on parole until Mar 1864; deserted at Kingston, 20 Jun 1864; returned to duty, 13 Apr 1865; restored to duty by Presidential proclamation; War Department note (3 Oct 1887): "desertion charge can not be expunged."
Lacy, Perry: private, Company D; enrolled 17 Feb 1865 at Rutledge, absent without leave, 20 Feb 1865; deserted at Mosier's Mill, 13 Mar 1865; dropped as a deserted, 31 Mar 1865.
Lambert, John G.: private, Company A; age: 18; received as a transfer from the 3rd Tennessee Volunteer Infantry Regiment; resident of Blount County; sick in hospital at Knoxville, 25 Mar 1865; returned to duty; 22 Jul 1865; discharged, 2 Aug 1865.
Lane, Alexander: private, Company C; age: 20; enrolled at Greeneville, 6 Apr 1863; captured and paroled at McMinnville, 3 Oct 1863; absent through Feb 1864; discharged, 2 Aug 1865; pension case 531939, 4 Feb 1886.
Lane, James M.: private, Company E; age: 18; enrolled at Greeneville, 15 Mar 1863; died in the hospital at Nashville of "congestive chills", 16 Jul 1863; file contains casualty sheet.
Lane, Richard S.: captain; age: 26; enrolled at Louisville, 29 May 1863; mustered at Dandridge as 1st lieutenant, Nov 1862; promoted to captain, 31 May 1865; discharged, 2 Aug 1865; file contains numerous documents.
Lane, William: private, Company C; age: 18; enrolled at Greeneville, 15 Mar 1863; sick in hospital, 15 - 30 Jun 1863; captured and paroled at McMinnville, 3 Oct 1863; absent through Feb 1864; discharged, 2 Aug 1865; pension case 543543.
Lawson, John: private, Company F; age: 18; enrolled at Greeneville, 15 Apr 1863; died at Louisville hospital # 15, 8 Jun 1863; file contains death records.
Lawson, Gaines: major, Company D; age: 21; enrolled as a private at Rogersville, 21 Dec 1862; promoted to sergeant, 15 Apr 1863; captured and paroled at McMinnville, 3 Oct 1863; promoted to captain to replace Captain Reeves (who was promoted), 1 Apr 1864;

promoted to major, 31 May 1865; discharged, 2 Aug 1865; received Medal of Honor for gallantry in action at McMinnville, 11 Jun 1895; file contains numerous papers.
Lawson, James M.: private, Company F; age: 19; enrolled at Strawberry Plains, 1 Jan 1864; resided in Greene County; mustered in at Loudon, 7 May 1864; discharged, 2 Aug 1865.
Leal, Peter: private, Company H; enrolled at Kingston, 4 Jul 1864; absent without leave, 22 Dec 1864; discharged, 2 Aug 1865.
Leathco, William J.: private; age: 21; enrolled at Taylorsville, 8 Apr 1865; resided in Washington County, VA., discharged, 2 Aug 1865; file contains enlistment papers.
Lee, Jordan P.: private, Company E; enrolled at Jefferson, NC., 17 Sep 1862; captured and paroled at McMinnville, 3 Oct 1863; in arrest in guard house during the period Jul - Aug 1864; discharged, 8 Jul 1865; pension case 610287.
Linebaugh, Daniel: sergeant, Company A; enrolled at Greeneville, 11 Aug 1862; promoted to sergeant, 13 Feb 1863; captured and paroled at McMinnville, 3 Oct 1863; absent on parole through Feb 1864; sick in hospital at Kingston, 7 Sep 1864 through Feb 1865; mustered out at Knoxville, 29 May 1865.
Lemons, William O.: private, Company E; age: 18; enrolled at Strawberry Plains, 1 Aug 1863; resident of Greene County; mustered in at Loudon, 7 May 1865; discharged, 2 Aug 1865; file contains enlistment papers.
Lewis, George S.: private, Company C; age: 18; enrolled at Greeneville, 6 Apr 1863; captured and paroled at McMinnville, 3 Oct 1863; on furlough sick at Newmarket, TN., 10 Apr 1864 through Jul 1865; discharged, 2 Aug 1865.
Lewis, Thomas: private, Company C; age: 18; gained as a transfer from the 3rd Tennessee Volunteer Infantry, 1 Mar 1865; discharged, 2 Aug 1865.
Lewis, William M.: 1st Sergeant, Company H; gained as a private through transfer from the 3rd Tennessee Volunteer, Infantry, 1 Mar 1865; file contains court martial papers for desertion, 6 Nov 1863 through 4 Feb 1865; found not guilty of desertion, file contains numerous papers.
Lineback, John: private, Company B; age: 18; enrolled at Boone, NC., 12 Aug 1862; sick in hospital at Nashville, died (cause illegible), 26 Jul 1863; file contains casualty sheet.
Linder, William M.: private, Company G; age: 19; enrolled at Jonesborough, 5 Jun 1863; sick in hospital from muster through Jul 1863; died of pneumonia at Nashville, 3 Jul 1863.
Linebough, John: private, Company F; age: 32; enrolled at Greeneville, 15 Apr 1863; sick in hospital, 15 - 30 Jun 1863; captured and paroled at McMinnville, 3 Oct 1863; absent on parole through Feb

1864; sick in hospital, 25 Aug 1864; sick in hospital at Knoxville, 10 Feb 1865; discharged with disability (disease of chest), May 1865; pension case; file contains enlistment records.
Lipp, David W.: private, Company H; enrolled at Carter County, 15 Jun 1864; deserted at Knoxville (date not shown).
Lintz, Martin L.: private, Company F; age: 39; enrolled at Greeneville, 15 Apr 1865; received $25 bounty; appointed wagoner, 1 Jun 1864; reduced from wagoner, 1 Jul 1864; discharged, 2 Aug 1865.
Littrell, James A.: private, Company F; age: 19; enrolled at Greeneville, 15 Apr 1863; received $25 bounty; died at Nashville General Hospital #19 of typhoid fever, 9 Sep 1963; file contains casualty records.
Lloyd, Tennessee: private, Company B; age: 18; enrolled at Loudon, 1 Apr 1864; born: Johnson County; resides: Elizabethton; discharged, 2 Aug 1865.
Locke, Matthew F.: assistant surgeon; age: 27; enrolled at Taylorsville as a private in Company B, 25 Aug 1862; mustered at Nashville, 6 Apr 1863; captured and paroled at McMinnville, 3 Oct 1863; absent without leave, 1 Dec 1863; resigned from service resulting from court martial for absent without leave, 1 Apr 1864.
Logan, David L.: corporal, Company C; age: 20; enrolled at Greeneville, 6 Apr 1863; captured and paroled at McMinnville, 3 Oct 1863; re-captured in Hawkins County, 9 Feb 1864; confined at Richmond, 17 Feb 1864; sent to Andersonville but left in the hospital at Augusta, Ga., sick with pneumonia; died, 2 Apr 1864.
Long, John N.: private, Company A; age: 24; enrolled at Rogersville, 27 Jan 1863; sick in hospital from enrollment through Jun 1863; captured and paroled at McMinnville, 3 Oct 1863; discharged, 2 Aug 1865; pension case.
Long, Joseph: private, Company H; gained as transfer from 3rd Regiment Tennessee Infantry, show as a deserter in Apr 1865 in error; discharged, 2 Aug 1865.
Long, William A.: private, Company A & G; enrolled at Rutledge, 5 Jan 1863; captured and paroled at McMinnville, 3 Oct 1863; deserted at Kingston, 30 Jun 1864; returned to duty, 13 Feb 1865; War Department note in file (12 Jan 1887), desertion charge expunged from record.
Love, David: private, Company H; enrolled at Strawberry Plains, 2 May 1864; deserted at Knoxville, 11 May 1864.
Love, John A.: private, Company A; age: 23; enrolled at Greeneville, 13 Dec 1862; died in the hospital at Nashville of typhoid fever, 18 Jul 1863; file contains death records.
Love, Luther M.: corporal, Company G; age: 34; enrolled at Greeneville, 5 May 1863; captured and paroled at McMinnville, 3 Oct

1863; promoted to corporal, 1 Mar 1864; file contains enlistment papers and indication of pension case.
Lovel, John H.: private, Company D; age: 18; enrolled at Mosiers Mill, 28 Feb 1865; born: Cocke County; War Department note in file: "absent without leave from 8th Regiment Tennessee Infantry, near New Cumberland River, Kentucky until, 8 Apr 1864, returned to unit at Bulls Gap, court martial, guilty"; discharged, 2 Aug 1865; file contains enlistment papers.
Lovett, Charles A.: private, Company G; age: 33; enrolled at Jonesborough, 5 Jan 1863; mustered in 30 Jun 1863; captured and paroled at McMinnville, 3 Oct 1863; sick in hospital at Kingston, 7 Sep 1864 to Dec 1864; War Department note in file, "man actually enrolled, 5 May 1863"; note dated: 2 Aug 1899; discharged, 2 Aug 1865; indication of pension.
Lowery, James A.: private, Company D; age: 29; enrolled at Greeneville, 30 Jan 1863; captured and paroled at McMinnville, 3 Oct 1863; discharged, 2 Aug 1865; pension case.
Lowry, Samuel: private, Companies D & F; age: 18; enrolled at Dandridge, 1 Jan 1864; mustered at Knoxville, 8 Feb 1864; born: Greene County; residence, Jefferson County; transferred from company D to Company F, 30 Apr 1864; absent without leave, 8 Apr 1864; changed to desertion, 31 Aug 1864.
Loyd, James: private, Company H; age: 18; enrolled at Kingston, 4 Jul 1864; born: Hamilton County; residence: Morgan County; discharged, 2 Aug 1865.
Lusk, Landon H.P.: first lieutenant, Company F & H; age; 25; enrolled as a private at Carter County, 24 Mar 1863; received $25 bonus; promoted to hospital steward, 1 Jul 1863; on recruiting duty, May 1864; promoted to first lieutenant, 24 Jun 1865; prisoner of war record shows that he was discharged from a Confederate prison at Louisville, 16 Apr 1863; file contains oath of office.
Luster, Amos H.: private, Company A; age: 28; enrolled in Greeneville, 6 Apr 1863; captured and paroled at McMinnville, 3 Oct 1863; absent on detached duty in Kingston, Nov 1864 through Feb 1865.
Luster, James: corporal, Company A; age: 37; enrolled at Greeneville, 6 Apr 1863; deserted in McMinnville, 27 Sep 1863; returned to duty, 10 Apr 1864; promoted to corporal, 1 Aug 1864; discharged, 2 Aug 1865.
Lynch, John A.: private, Company D; age: 27; enrolled at Dandridge, 1 Mar 1863; sick, 15 - 30 Jun 1863; born in Hawkins County; captured and paroled in McMinnville, 3 Oct 1863; gained at Knoxville from missing in action, 2 Feb 1864; discharged, 2 Aug 1865; pension case # 568168.

Lynn, William: private, Company D; age: 19; enrolled at Rutledge, 15 Aug 1863; resident of Grainger County; mustered at Strawberry Plains, 31 Mar 1864; in arrest, 13 Aug 1864 for being absent without leave; died of typhoid fever in hospital near Dandridge, 23 Jan 1865; file contains death records.
Malcom, Samuel A.: private, Company F & B; age: 21; enrolled at Greeneville, 30 Jul 1862; captured at McMinnville, 3 Oct 1863; sent to Richmond, 1 Jan 1864; sent to Andersonville, Ga., 14 Mar 1864; died of diarrhea; file contains enlistment records and death records.
Malone, Andrew: private, Company A; age: 20; enrolled at Greeneville, 26 Feb 1863; mustered at Strawberry Plains, 31 Mar 1864; absent without leave from Loudon, 10 Jun 1864; dropped from rolls, 31 Aug 1864; restored to duty, 27 Mar 1865; discharged, 2 Aug 1865; prisoner of war record shows he deserted from U.S. Army at Tazewell or Knoxville, 4 Sep 1862 and was committed to jail in Knoxville, 13 Sep 1862; War Department note (14 Jun 1884): "desertion charge no longer stands".
Malone, Daniel C.: private, Company A; age: 40; enrolled at Greeneville, 5 Mar 1864; mustered into service at Strawberry Plains, 31 Mar 1864; absent without leave, 24 Dec 1864; shown back on duty, Jan through Aug 1865; discharged, 2 Aug 1865.
Malone, John H.: private, Company A; age: 23; enrolled in Greene County, 26 Feb 1863; mustered into service at Strawberry Plains, 31 Mar 1864; deserted, 23 Jul 1864 at Kingston; restored to duty, 30 Mar 1865 by Presidential proclamation; War Department note (5 Jul 1884): "desertion charge removed by Act of Congress, 5 Jul 1884; discharged from service, 2 Aug 1865.
Malone, Joseph: private, Company A; age: 30; enrolled at Greeneville, 12 Apr 1863; sick in hospital from enrollment until his death on 2 Jul 1863; died in the General Hospital at Nashville of chronic diarrhea; file contains numerous papers.
Malone, Smith H.: private, Company A; age: 25; enrolled at Greeneville, 11 Feb 1863; captured and paroled at McMinnville, 3 Oct 1863; on parole when captured by the enemy in Greene County, 20 Nov 1863; confined at Richmond, 27 Nov 1863; admitted to Hospital #21 at Richmond, 21 Dec 1863; died of "variola", 3 Jan 1864.
Maloney, John Q.: private, Company A; age: 37; enrolled at Greeneville, 27 Jan 1863; captured and paroled at McMinnville, 3 Oct 1863; absent through Feb 1864; absent without leave, 8 Oct 1864; restored to duty, 27 Mar 1865 by Presidential proclamation; discharged, 2 Aug 1865; War Department note (12 Oct 1885): "desertion charge removed"; file contains enlistment papers.

Mancior, George B.: private, Company G; age: 37; enrolled at Greeneville, 15 Nov 1861; sick in hospital, 15 - 30 Jun 1863; captured and paroled at McMinnville, 3 Oct 1863; sick in hospital at Knoxville, 24 May 1865; mustered out of service at Knoxville, 19 Jun 1865; pension case.

Manning, James: private, Company C; age: 32; gained as a transfer from the 3rd Regiment Tennessee Infantry, 1 Mar 1865; resident of Anderson County; file shows: he was appointed corporal, 12 Feb 1862; sick in the hospital in Knoxville, 12 Feb 1862; deserted, 10 Aug 1862; restored to duty from desertion, 29 Jan 1864; he was in prison (editorial note: not specified where or why, [probably for desertion]), 5 Mar 1864 through 1 May 1864.

Markland, Nathaniel J.: private, Company H; age: 24; enrolled at Elizabethton, 13 Aug 1863; mustered in at Kingston, 23 Jul 1864; deserted at Kingston, 13 Aug 1864.

Markland, P. B. (or Phillip): private, Company H; enrolled at Elizabethton, 15 Jun 1864; deserted at Knoxville, 20 Jun 1864.

Morley, Andrew A.: private, Company F; age: 32; enrolled at Taylorsville, 1 Oct 1862; received $25 bounty; captured and paroled at McMinnville, 4 Oct 1863; killed while on parole, 2 Dec 1863 (place not identified).

Marsh, Mosby: private, Company C; age: 28; gained as a transfer from the 3rd Tennessee Infantry Regiment; was a prisoner from 5 Mar 1864 until 1 Jun 1864; sick in the hospital, 14 Jun 1865; discharge not furnished.

Marshall, Houston: corporal, Company D; age: 26; enrolled in Rogersville, 13 Oct 1862; captured and paroled at McMinnville, 3 Oct 1863; promoted to corporal, 17 Apr 1864; discharged, 2 Aug 1865; pension case.

Marshall, Jospeh: private, Company D; age: 21; enrolled at Rogersville, 12 Oct 1862; sick, 15 - 30 Jun 1863; captured and paroled at McMinnville, absent on parole through Feb 1864; discharged, 2 Aug 1865; possible pension case.

Marshall, Tipton: sergeant, Company D; age: 24; enrolled at Rogersville, 14 Apr 1863; captured and paroled at McMinnville, 3 Oct 1863; promoted to sergeant, 3 Feb 1864; discharged, 8 Jul 1865; pension case.

Matheson, James F.: private, Company D; age: 18; enrolled at Taylorsville, 1 Sep 1863; mustered in at Loudon, 7 May 1864; discharged, 2 Aug 1865; file contains enlistment papers.

Mathis, Calvin A.: private, Company C; age: 19; enrolled at Jonesborough, 5 Apr 1863; captured and paroled at McMinnville, 3 Oct 1863; discharged, 2 Aug 1865; pension case.

Mattesberger, Phillip H.: private, Company C; age: 18; enrolled at Flat Creek, Greene County, 6 Nov 1863; mustered in at Loudon, 7

Soldiers of the Regiment 103

May 1864; deserted at Jonesborough, 26 May 1864; returned to duty, 5 May 1865; restored to duty by Presidential proclamation, 10 Mar 1865; prisoner of war record - blank; file contains enlistment papers.
McAn, Anslum L.: private, Company H; age: 19; enrolled at Kingston, 19 Sep 1864; deserted at Kingston, 21 Sep 1864.
McCarny, Robert C.: private, Company H; gained as a transfer from the 3rd Tennessee Infantry, 1 Mar 1865; sick in hospital at Knoxville since 6 Jun 1865; discharged at completion of term of service, 23 Jun 1865.
McCloud, William: private, Company H; age: 18; enrolled at Elizabethton, 15 Jun 1864; mustered in at Kingston, 23 Jul 1864; deserted at Kingston, 15 Aug 1864; returned to duty, 1 Dec 1864; restored to duty by order of Brigadier General Ammons.
Masoner, James H.: second lieutenant, Company G; age: 37; enrolled at Greeneville, 5 Mar 1863; commissioned at Louisville, 22 May 1863; captured and paroled at McMinnville, 3 Oct 1863; sick at Knoxville, 21 Jun 1863; resigned for physical disability, 12 Jul 1864; file contains surgeon's certificate and letter of resignation.
Masoner, John W.: corporal, Company G; age: 18; enrolled at Greeneville, 5 May 1863; promoted to corporal, 1 Jun 1863; captured and paroled at McMinnville, 3 Oct 1863; killed by the enemy while on parole in Greene County, 6 Jan 1864; file contains casualty records.
Matherly, Alexander: private, Company B; age: 30; enrolled at Elizabethton, 3 Aug 1863; mustered at Strawberry Plains, 31 Mar 1864; sick in hospital in Knoxville, 30 Jun 1863; charged with desertion at Nashville, 19 Apr 1864. War Department note: "desertion charge removed, he was in the General Hospital in Chattanooga, 14 May 1864, died of diarrhea, 8 Jul 1864"; file contains casualty sheet.
Matherly, James: private, Company B; age: 45; enrolled at Elizabethton, 1 Aug 1863; mustered in at Strawberry Plains, 31 Mar 1864; deserted at Kingston, 17 Aug 1864; War Department note: "the enlistment and muster in is canceled, he was on detached service from Company A, 13th Tennessee Cavalry from Jan 1864 through 12 Aug 1864".
Matheson, Daniel G.: corporal, Company B; age: 19; enrolled at Taylorsville, 8 Dec 1862; promoted to corporal, 5 Jun 1863; captured and paroled at McMinnville, 3 Oct 1863; reduced to ranks, 3 Oct 1864; in hospital in Knoxville, 21 Mar 1865; discharged, 2 Jun 1865; file contains enlistment papers; pension case.
McCampbell, Alexander: private, Companies B and G; age: 29; captured and paroled at McMinnville, 3 Oct 1863; absent through Feb 1864; transferred to Company B, 1 Jul 1863, discharged, 2 Aug 1865.

4th Tennessee Volunteer Infantry Regiment (USA)

McClung, Patrick A.: private, Company A; age: 19; enrolled at Maryville, 27 May 1863; deserted at Louisville, Ky., ? May 1863.

McConnel, James C.: private, Company B; age: 32; enrolled at Maryville, 1 Apr 1863; sick in Kingston, 27 Nov 1864 through Feb 1865; discharged, 2 Aug 1865.

McConnel, John: private, Company C; age: 22; enrolled at Greeneville, 6 Apr 1863; captured and paroled at McMinnville, 3 Oct 1863; absent on parole through Feb 1864; deserted at Kingston, 23 Jul 1864; restored to duty from desertion, 12 Feb 1865; War Department note (17 Oct 1888) in file that the desertion charge no longer stands; possible pension case; note in file indicates that he was captured by the enemy while on parole.

McConnell, Joseph H.: private, Company C; transferred from the 3rd Tennessee Infantry, 1 Mar 1865; discharged, 2 Aug 1865.

McCooley, Frank: private, Company H; age: 24; enrolled at Kingston, 20 Jul 1864; born: Philadelphia, Pa.; deserted at Kingston, 28 Sep 1864.

McCoy, George A.: private, Company A; age: 23; enrolled at Greeneville, 13 Dec 1862; captured and paroled at McMinnville, 3 Oct 1863; reported absent on parole; died in Cocke County while on parole (date not stated); War Department note (3 Jun 1867); "discharged"; pension case # 640751 (Widow's pension ?)

McCoy, James W.: private, Company E; age: 25; enrolled at Greeneville, 15 Nov 1861; sick in hospital, 15 - 30 Jun 1863; captured and paroled at McMinnville, 3 Oct 1863; reported in hospital in Nashville, 26 Feb 1864; absent without leave, 22 Dec 1864; discharged, 8 Jul 1865; pension case.

McDarmon, Uriah H.: private, Company H; age: 29; enrolled at Elizabethton, 6 Apr 1864; mustered in at Loudon, 7 May 1864; absent without leave, 2 Dec 1864; later reported as deserting at Knoxville, 2 Dec 1864; file contains enlistment papers.

McGhee, John A.: private, Company A; age: 36; gained as a transfer from the 3rd Tennessee Infantry, 1 Mar 1865; discharged, 2 Aug 1865.

McGinnes, George: private, Company A; age: 18; enrolled at Jonesborough, 12 Feb 1865, mustered in at Knoxville, 2 Mar 1865; deserted, 30 Jul 1865; file contains enlistment papers.

McKinney, Pleasant: private, Company H; age: 30; enrolled at Kingston, 14 Jul 1864; resident of Wilkes County, NC.; born in Jefferson County, TN.; discharged, 2 Aug 1865.

McKinney, Ransom: private, Company H; age: 18; enrolled at Kingston, 14 Jul 1864; resident of Roane County; born in Morgan County; sick at Kingston, Nov 1864; reported sick at Knoxville, 1 Mar 1865; discharged, 2 Aug 1865.

Soldiers of the Regiment 105

McKinney, William: private, Company H; age: 18; enrolled at Morristown, 15 Feb 1865; resident of Carter County; sick in hospital at Knoxville with measles, 18 Mar 1865; deserted, 2 Apr 1865; returned to duty, 10 May 1865; War Department note (4 Sep 1888), "desertion charge no longer stands"; file contains enlistment papers.

McClaughlin, Nelson: private, Company G; age: 37; enrolled at Jonesborough, 25 Sep 1862; discharged to accept at commission as second lieutenant in the 8th Tennessee Cavalry, 30 Sep 1862; file contains numerous documents.

McManes, George W.: private, Company H; age: 29; enrolled at Jonesborough, 9 Apr 1865; born and resided in Harrison County, Ga.; discharged, 2 Aug 1865; file contains enlistment papers.

McNease, Abner: private, Company C; age: 37; enrolled at Greeneville, 6 Apr 1863; died of fever at a private home in Nashville, 10 Aug 1863.

McNease, Henry: private, Company C; age: 21; enrolled at Greeneville, 6 Apr 1863; captured and paroled at McMinnville, 3 Oct 1863; absent on parole until Dec 1864; discharged, 2 Aug 1865.

McNease, James B.: private, Company C; age: 36; enrolled at Greeneville, 6 Apr 1863; sick in hospital, 15 - 30 Jun 1863; captured and paroled at McMinnville, 3 Oct 1863; absent on parole until Apr 1864; deserted at Kingston, 23 Jul 1864; restored to duty, 5 Feb 1865; discharged, 2 Aug 1865; file contains court martial papers for desertion.

McQuown, John R.: private, Company B; age: 18; enrolled at Taylorsville, 12 Feb 1865; mustered at Knoxville, 2 Mar 1865; discharged, 2 Aug 1865; file contains enlistment papers.

Milan, John W.: private, Company H; age: 21; enrolled at Jonesborough, 27 Apr 1864; born in Wilkes County, NC., resident of Louisville, Ky.; mustered in at Kingston, 23 Jul 1864; deserted at Kingston, 22 Sep 1864; received a dishonorable discharge; War Department note (11 Mar 1903) "dishonorable discharge charge void, final record is that of desertion."; file contains copy of discharge.

Mercer, Charles: private, Company A; age: 19; enrolled in Greene County, 27 Jan 1863; mustered in at Strawberry Plains, 31 Mar 1864; discharged, 2 Aug 1865; file contains enlistment papers.

Mercer, David W.: sergeant, Company A; age: 28; enrolled at Greene County, 27 Jan 1863; mustered in at Strawberry Plains, 31 Mar 1864; appointed corporal, 1 Apr 1864; promoted to sergeant, 1 Aug 1864; discharged, 2 Aug 1864.

Mercer, Joseph F.: corporal, Company E; age: 19; enrolled at Greeneville, 19 Nov 1862; appointed corporal, 26 May 1863; prisoner of war record - but blank; reduced in rank, 24 Sep 1864; discharged, 8 Jul 1865; possible pension case.

Mercer, Thomas L.: sergeant, Company A; age: 20; enrolled at Greeneville, 12 Aug 1862; captured at Cumberland Gap on the way to join the 4th Regiment, 16 Aug 1862; confined at Castle Thunder, Richmond, 10 Dec. 1862; released at Richmond, 28 Feb. 1863; arrived within Union lines, 5 Mar 1863; promoted to 5th Sergeant from corporal, 29 Aug 1863; promoted to 4th sergeant, 1 Apr. 1864; promoted to 3rd sergeant, 1 Aug 1864; discharged to accept a commission as second lieutenant; 24 Jun. 1865; file contains numerous papers.
Mercer, Elijah M.: sergeant; age: 19; enrolled at Knoxville, 25 May 1864; resident of Johnson County; born in Coldwell County, NC.; mustered in at Kingston, 23 Jul. 1864; promoted to sergeant, 23 Jul. 1864; discharged, 2 Aug 1865; file contains 10 day furlough to visit his home in Sevierville.
Michaels, David: private, Company H; enrolled at Taylorsville, 7 Apr. 1865; absent without leave, 4 Jun. 1865.
Middleton, Tarlton A.: first lieutenant: Companies G & B; age: 24; enrolled at Jonesborough as a private in Company G, 5 Mar 1863; promoted to first lieutenant in Company B; resigned for the good of the service, 27 Sep. 1864; court martial record shows: "conduct unbecoming an officer and gentleman: drunk and disorderly, drinking and playing cards with enlisted men, called Major Reeves a "damned fool".
Miller, Allen: private, Company G; age: 36; enrolled at Greeneville, 5 May 1863; captured and paroled at McMinnville, 3 Oct. 1863; sick in hospital at Knoxville, 28 Apr. 1864; died in the hospital at Knoxville of typhoid and pneumonia, 30 Apr. 1864; file contains casualty sheet.
Miller, Jeremiah B.: private, Company B; enrolled at Elizabethton, 7 Mar 1863; absent on detached service, ordered to report to Colonel John K. Miller, Commander 13th Tennessee Volunteer Cavalry, Jun. 1863; [editorial note: he was the brother of Colonel Miller]; discharged from the 4th Regiment, 26 Mar 1864; blank prisoner of war record in file.
Miller, John: corporal, Company H; age: 35; enrolled at Strawberry Plains, 5 Aug 1863; resident of Johnson County; mustered in at Loudon, 7 May 1864; promoted to corporal, 23 Jul. 1864; sick in hospital at Kingston, Sep. and Oct. 1864; died in the hospital at Kingston of smallpox, 9 Nov. 1864; file contains enlistment papers and casualty sheet.
Miller, John T.: corporal, Company H; age: 18; enrolled at Boone, NC., 6 Dec. 1863; resided in Carter County; born in Gordon County, Ga.; mustered in at Kingston, 23 Jul. 1864; promoted to corporal, 28 Apr. 1865; discharged, 2 Aug 1865.

Soldiers of the Regiment 107

Miller, Lawson: private, Company H; age: 18; enrolled in Elizabethton, 21 Sep. 1863; born in Johnson County; mustered in at Loudon, 7 May 1864; discharged, 2 Aug 1865; file contains enlistment papers.
Miller, Robert S.: sergeant, Company E; age: 19; enrolled at Greeneville, 6 Apr. 1863; appointed sergeant from private, 26 May 1863; captured and paroled at McMinnville, 3 Oct. 1863; discharged, 2 Aug 1865.
Miller, William R.: rank not stated, Company A, record shows enrollment at Elizabethton, 21 Jan. 1863; certificate of disability discharge stating "loss of right leg from wounds received in combat action, discharged at Chattanooga, 18 Aug 1866"; War Department note (1 Dec. 1920), "upon testimony received allegation of service and discharge was fraudulent. This man was not in the service of the United States as a member of the organization."; file contains numerous documents.
Milton, Joel: private, Company H; enrolled in Jonesborough, 29 Apr. 1864; deserted at Kingston, 22 Sep. 1864; born in Wilkes County, NC., resided in Gordon County, Ga.; received a dishonorable discharge, 11 Mar 1867; War Department note (21 Jun. 1894), "Commanding General action, Department of Tennessee, is without authority and the dishonorable discharge is void, final record is that of desertion."; file contains numerous documents.
Mitchell, James: private, Company G; age: 21; enrolled at Greeneville, 22 Nov. 1862; mustered in at Nashville, 15 Jun. 1863; sick in the hospital at Nashville, 15 - 30 Jun. 1863; captured and paroled at McMinnville, 3 Oct. 1863; reported absent on parole through Dec. 1864; killed by guerrillas in Jefferson County, TN., while on parole, 4 Dec. 1864; pension case; miscellaneous documents in the file.
Mitchell, James: private, Company E; age: 23; enrolled at Greeneville, 6 Apr. 1863; captured and paroled at McMinnville, 3 Oct. 1863; absent on parole through Feb. 1864; sick in the hospital in Kingston, 25 Nov. 1864 through Jan. 1865; discharged, 2 Aug 1865; pension case.
Mitchell, William: sergeant, Company E; age: 19; enrolled at Greeneville, 12 Oct. 1863; mustered in at Knoxville, 8 Feb. 1864; promoted to sergeant, 25 Aug 1864; discharged, 2 Aug 1865.
Montgomery, William T.: private, Company F; age: 27; enrolled at Greeneville, 31 May 1863; received $25 bounty; captured and paroled at McMinnville, 3 Oct. 1863; reported absent through Mar 1865; reported missing in action, Mar 1865; prisoner of war record shows he was re-captured at Cumberland Gap, while on parole, 27 Feb. 1864 and sent to Richmond, 9 Mar 1864, died at

Andersonville Prison in Georgia of diarrhea, 29 Jul. 1864; file contains casualty report.
Moore, George W.: private, Company D; age: 24; enrolled at Newport, 18 Jan. 1863; captured and paroled at McMinnville, 3 Oct. 1863; absent on parole until 13 Mar 1864; sick at Mossy Creek since 9 Apr. 1864; shown as a corporal on muster roll 30 Jun. - 29 Feb. 64; reduced in rank, 1 Jan. 1865; discharged, 2 Aug 1865; file contains numerous documents; pension case.
Moore, John A.: private, Company F; age: 26; enrolled at Greeneville, 20 Mar 1863; captured and paroled at McMinnville, 3 Oct. 1863; absent on parole through Feb. 1865; reported missing in action, Mar 1865; gained from missing in action, 31 May 1865; discharged, 2 Aug 1865; pension case.
Moore, John L.: corporal, Company E; age: 19; enrolled at Greeneville, 15 Mar 1863; reported sick in the hospital, 15 - 30 Jun. 1863; appointed corporal, 10 Oct. 1864; discharged, 2 Aug 1865.
Moore, Joseph H.: private, Company E; age: 20; enrolled at Greeneville, 15 Mar 1863; reported sick in the hospital, 15 - 30 Jun. 1863; captured and paroled at McMinnville, 3 Oct. 1863; discharged, 2 Aug 1865; pension case.
Moore, William: corporal, Company D; age: 29; enrolled at Newport, 18 Jan. 1863; promoted to corporal, 19 Feb. 1863; captured and paroled at McMinnville, 3 Oct. 1863; reduced in rank, 17 Apr. 1864; discharged, 2 Aug 1865; pension case # 600717.
Morefield, Andrew: private, Company G; age: 32; enrolled at Taylorsville, 22 Aug 1862; mustered in at Nashville, 27 Aug 1863; sick in the hospital at Kingston, 20 Sep. 1864; discharged, 8 Jul. 1865; file contains enlistment papers.
Morefield, John W.: private, Company H & G; age: 35; enrolled at Taylorsville, 7 Apr. 1865; discharged, 2 Aug 1865; file contains enlistment papers.
Morefield, William A.: private, Company G; age: 30; enrolled at Taylorsville, 22 Aug 1862; captured and paroled at McMinnville, 3 Oct. 1863; discharged, 8 Jul. 1865; file contains enlistment papers.
Morgan, John: private, Company D; age: 35; enrolled at Dandridge, 16 Jan. 1863; captured and paroled at McMinnville, 3 Oct. 1863; captured while on parole at Morristown, TN., 1 Jan. 1864; confined at Richmond, 18 Jan. 1864; admitted to hospital in Richmond, 24 Feb. 1864 through 14 Mar 1864; again, admitted to hospital, 25 Apr. 1864; paroled at City Point, VA., 30 Apr. 1864; admitted to hospital at Annapolis, Md., 12 May 1864; sent to Nashville, 15 May 1864; in arrest in Company D, 29 Aug 1864 (charges not stated); discharged, 2 Aug 1865; pension case # 103511.
Morgan, Joshua: private, Company A; age: 43; enrolled at Greeneville, 10 Jun. 1863; captured and paroled at McMinnville, 3

Soldiers of the Regiment   109

Oct. 1863; re-captured while on parole near Morristown, 1 Jan. 1864; paroled at Aikens Landing, VA., 8 May 1864; reported as hospital patient with chronic diarrhea in Camp Chase, Ohio, 21 Jul. 1864; reported to have deserted, 8 Sep. 1864; returned to duty, 10 Mar 1865; discharged, 2 Aug 1865; pension case; file contains numerous documents.
Morgan, Wiley: private, Company F; age: 23; enrolled at Greeneville, 5 Sep. 1862; received $25 bounty; captured and paroled at McMinnville, 3 Oct. 1863; discharged, 8 Jul. 1865; pension case.
Morley, William H.: private, Company G; age: 26; enrolled at Taylorsville, 22 Aug 1862; captured and paroled at McMinn-ville, 3 Oct. 1863; died in the hospital at Knoxville of "phithisis pulmonalis", 30 Jan. 1865; file contains enlistment papers and casualty report.
Morrow, John: private, Company A; age: 18; enrolled at Greeneville, 1 Apr. 1863; sick in hospital at Nashville from enrollment to 30 Jun. 1863; captured and paroled at McMinnville, 3 Oct. 1863; discharged, 2 Aug 1865; pension case.
Morrow, Samuel: corporal, Company F; age: 31; enrolled at Greeneville, 30 Mar 1863; received $25 bounty; appointed corporal, 15 Jun. 1863; captured and paroled at McMinnville, 3 Oct. 1863; died of typhoid fever in Green County while on parole, 5 Dec. 1863; file contains final statements.
Morrow, Thomas J.: private, Company A; age: 18; enrolled at Loudon, 1 Feb. 1864; mustered in at Loudon, 7 May 1864; born: Green County; discharged, 2 Aug 1865; file contains enlistment papers.
Mostly, Wiley D.: private, Company A; age: 19; born in Sullivan County; enrolled at Bulls Gap, 1 Feb. 1864; mustered in at Loudon, 7 May 1864; deserted at Loudon, 20 Aug 1864; restored to duty, 25 Nov. 1864; War Department note (6 Jul. 1885), "desertion charge removed; discharged, 2 Aug 1865; file contains enlistment papers and other documents.
Mullins, Aaron S.: corporal, Company G; age: 21; enrolled at Taylorsville, 22 Aug 1862; promoted to corporal, 1 Jul. 1864; discharged, 8 Jul. 1865; file contains enlistment papers.
Morrow, John: private, Company A; age: 18, enrolled at Greeneville, 1 Apr. 1863; sick in the hospital at Nashville from enrollment through Jun. 1863; captured and paroled at McMinnville, 3 Oct. 1863; discharged, 2 Aug 1865; pension case.
Morrow, Samuel: corporal, Company F; age: 31; enrolled at Greeneville, 30 Mar 1863; received $25 bounty; appointed corporal, 15 Jun. 1863; captured and paroled at McMinnville, 3 Oct. 1863; died in Green County of typhoid fever while on parole, 5 Dec. 1863; file contains final statements.

Morrow, Thomas J.: private, Company A; age: 18; born: Green County; enrolled at Loudon, 1 Feb. 1864; mustered in at Loudon, 7 May 1864; discharged, 2 Aug 1865; file contains enlistment papers.

Mostly, Wiley B.: private, Company A; age: 19; born: Sullivan County; enrolled at Bulls Gap, 1 Feb. 1864; deserted at Loudon, 20 Aug 1864; restored to duty, 25 Nov. 1864; War Department note (6 Jul. 1885), "desertion charge removed", discharged, 2 Aug 1865; file contains enlistment and other papers.

Mullins, Aaron A.: corporal, Company G; age: 21; enrolled at Taylorsville, 22 Aug 1862; promoted to corporal, 1 Jul. 1864; discharged, 8 Jul. 1865; file contains enlistment papers.

Munday, William R.: first lieutenant, Company G; age: 32; enrolled at a private at Jonesborough, 1 Jan. 1863; commissioned a 1st lieutenant, Company G, by Colonel Stover, 15 Jul. 1863; promoted to fill a vacancy created by the promotion of Captain West; resigned for the good of the service, 30 Jun. 1864; his resignation cites his inability to write, rendering him incompetent for service and also family hardships.

Nave, Joel: corporal, Company H; age: 18; enrolled at Elizabethton, 12 Apr. 1864; mustered in at Loudon, 7 May 1864; promoted to corporal, 23 Jul. 1864; reduced in rank by his own request, 31 Oct. 1864; sick in general hospital at Kingston, 14 Feb. 1865; died in the hospital at Knoxville of "inflammation of lungs", 7 Mar 1865; file contains casualty report.

Neace, John T.: private, Company G; age: 25; enrolled at Greeneville, 5 May 1863; captured and paroled at McMinnville, 3 Oct. 1863; on parole through Feb. 1864; reported as deserted at Knoxville, 17 Apr. 1864; returned to duty, 2 May 1865; restored to duty by Presidential proclamation; War Department note (1 Mar 1887), "desertion charge no longer stands, but not expunged"; file contains record of court martial for desertion; pension # 532615.

Nease, Adam: private, Company F; age: 29; enrolled at Greeneville, 10 Apr. 1863; received $25 bounty; captured and paroled at McMinnville, 3 Oct. 1863; absent on parole through Feb. 1864; sick in hospital at Kingston, 1 Jul. 1864 through May 1865; discharged for unspecified disability at Knoxville, 30 May 1865; pension case.

Nease, Andrew Sr.: private, Company G; age: 35; enrolled at Greeneville, 5 May 1863; captured and paroled at McMinnville, 3 Oct. 1863; absent on parole through Feb. 1864; sick in the hospital at Kingston, 7 Sep. 1864 through Apr. 1865; mustered out from hospital in Knoxville, 3 Jun. 1865; pension case.

Nease, Andrew Jr.: private, Company G; age: 18; enrolled at Greeneville, 5 May 1863; captured and paroled at McMinnville, 3 Oct. 1863; absent on parole through Feb. 1864; discharged, 2 Aug 1865; pension case.

Soldiers of the Regiment 111

Morefield, Henry: private, Company G; age: 44; enrolled at Taylorsville, 8 Apr. 1865; discharged, 2 Aug 1865; file contains enlistment papers.
Murphy, Elbert: private, Company B; age: 18; enrolled at Taylorsville, 5 Aug 1863; mustered in at Strawberry Plains, 31 Mar 1864; discharged, 2 Aug 1865.
Murphy, Elbert S.: corporal, Company G; age: 35; enrolled at Greeneville, 5 May 1863; promoted to corporal, 5 May 1863; captured and paroled at McMinnville, 3 Oct. 1863; sick in hospital at Kingston (or Knoxville), 7 Sep. 1864; mustered out from hospital, 30 May 1865.
Murphy, John: first lieutenant, Adjutant Field and Staff; mustered in at Louisville, 1 May 1863; captured and paroled at McMinnville, 3 Oct. 1863; requested 5 day furlough to go to Louisville, 13 Nov. 1863, stated that all officers of the Regiment were under arrest in Nashville; submitted resignation request, 10 May 1864; citing physical disabilities, the discharge was based on surgeons certificate naming "constitutional weakness of some time standing", 23 Apr. 1864; discharged, 12 May 1864; file contains numerous documents.
Murphy, Kemp: private, Company B; age: 22; enrolled at Taylorsville, 25 Aug 1862; captured and paroled at McMinnville, 3 Oct. 1863; discharged, 8 Jul. 1865; file contains enlistment papers; possible pension case.
Nance, Henry: private, Company H; age: 18; gained from transfer from 3rd Tennessee Volunteer Infantry Regiment, 1 May 1865; discharged, 2 Aug 1865.
Nease, John: private, Company F; age: 24; enrolled at Greeneville, 15 Apr. 1863; received $25 bounty; captured and paroled at McMinnville, 3 Oct. 1863; died in the hospital at Louisville of typhoid fever, date not stated (records captured)
Nease, Reuben: private, Company F; age: 27; enrolled at Greeneville, 10 Apr. 1863; received $25 bounty; captured and paroled at McMinnville, 3 Oct. 1863; absent on parole through Feb. 1864; sick in the hospital at Kingston, 13 Nov. 1864 through Feb. 1865; discharged, 2 Aug 1865; pension case.
Nease, William F.: private, company A; age: 22; enrolled at Greeneville, 3 Dec. 1862; sick in the hospital at Louisville from enrollment through 30 Jun. 1863; captured and paroled at McMinnville, 3 Oct. 1863; absent on parole through Feb. 1864; discharged, 2 Aug 1865; pension # 560291.
Nelson, Henry F.: private, Company E; age: 24; enrolled at Greeneville, 12 Nov. 1862; captured and paroled at McMinnville, 3 Oct. 1863; absent on parole through Feb. 1864; deserted, 17 Apr. 1865; returned to duty, 27 Apr. 1865; restored to duty by Presidential

proclamation; War Department note, "desertion no longer stands, but desertion can not be expunged from record"; pension case.
Nelson, Ira G.: private, Company G; age: 19; enrolled at Mosiers Mill, 28 Feb. 1865; mustered in at Knoxville, 2 Mar 1865; resident of Green County; discharged, 2 Aug 1865; file contains enlistment papers.
Nelson, Robert: private, Company H; age: 18; gained from transfer from 3rd Tennessee Volunteer Infantry Regiment, 1 Mar 1865; discharged, 2 Aug 1865.
Nelson, William R.: private, Company E; age: 27; enrolled at Greeneville, 15 Nov. 1862; sick in the hospital at Knoxville, 4 Apr. 1864 through Jun. 1864; mustered out, 26 Jun. 1865.
Newberry, Elias B.: private, Company E; age: 22; enrolled at Greeneville, 15 Nov. 1862; captured and paroled at McMinnville, 3 Oct. 1863; discharged, 2 May 1865; pension case.
Newberry, Henry G.: private, Company E; age: 19; enrolled at Greeneville, 17 Jan. 1862; mustered in at Knoxville, 8 Feb. 1864; absent without leave, 22 Dec. 1864; discharged, 8 Jul. 1865.
Newberry, Richard: private, Company E; age: 18; enrolled at Loudon, 1 Jan. 1864; deserted at Loudon, 13 Aug 1864.
Newberry, William S.: corporal, Company E; age: 24; enrolled at Greeneville, 15 Nov. 1861; promoted to corporal, 26 May 1863; captured and paroled at McMinnville, 3 Oct. 1863; discharged, 8 Jul. 1865.
Nichols, William B.: age: 26; enrolled at Liberty, VA., 19 Jan. 1863; sick at Louisville from muster in to 30 Jun. 1863; captured and paroled at McMinnville, 3 Oct. 1863; sick in hospital at Knoxville, 7 Sep. 1864 through May 1865; discharged from service from hospital, 19 May 1865.
Noe, William H.: private, Company H; enrolled at Kingston, 23 Jul. 1864; absent without leave, 22 Dec. 1864; absent without leave from Morristown, 13 Jan. 1865; absent, sick at home, 18 Mar 1865; discharged, 2 Aug 1865; file contains enlistment papers.
Nolen, William N.: private, Company H; age: 18; transfer from the 3rd Tennessee Infantry Regiment, 1 Mar 1865; discharged: 2 Aug 1865.
Norris, Jacob H.: private, Company H; enrolled at Taylorsville, 3 Jun. 1863; received $25 bonus; discharged to accept commission in the 12th Tennessee Cavalry, 25 Dec. 1863.
Northington, Cornelius: private, Company B; age: 19; born: Wilkes County, NC., enrolled at Taylorsville, 8 Dec. 1862; captured and paroled at McMinnville, 3 Oct. 1863; promoted to corporal, 3 Oct. 1864; promoted to sergeant, 8 Dec. 1864; reduced to private, 18 Feb. 1865; absent without leave and "running picket line" charge in file; file contains enlistment papers.

Soldiers of the Regiment   113

Northington, Hector: private, Company B; age: 23; enrolled at Taylorsville, 30 Aug 1862; captured and paroled at McMinnville, 3 Oct. 1863; during the period prior to Feb. 1864, was on detached service with Colonel Miller; discharged to accept commission in the 13th Tennessee Cavalry, 12 Apr. 1864.
Northington, Samuel E.: wagoner, Companies B and F; age: 42; enrolled at Taylorsville, 8 Dec. 1862; promoted to wagoner, 19 Feb. 1863; transferred to Company B, 29 Apr. 1864; ordered to report to Colonel Miller (13th Tennessee Cavalry) and promoted to captain, 13 Apr. 1864.
Norwood, Edward: Major/Surgeon; age: 25; enrolled in Kingston, 12 Jun. 1864; assigned to surgical hospital in Greeneville during Mar - Apr. 1864; requested 30 day leave of absence, 7 Jan. 1865; medical examination board certificate recommended leave of absence because "officer suffered hepatitis and conjunctivitis and needs a change of climate to prevent permanent disability"; later (20 Jun. 1865), requested 20 day leave of absence to visit family in Kentucky stating family illness demanding his personal attention.
Nott, Mason: private, Company A; age: 19; enrolled at Newport, 1 Oct. 1863; mustered in at Strawberry Plains, 31 Mar 1864; resident of Cocke County; deserted, 8 Apr. 1864; gained from desertion, 7 Aug 1864; died in the hospital at Greeneville of undisclosed causes, 30 May 1865.
Ogg, John C.: private, Company F; age: 20; transferred from the 3rd Regiment Tennessee Infantry, 1 Mar 1865; discharged, 2 Aug 1865.
Oliver, Elijah D.: corporal, Company H; age: 19; enrolled at Greeneville, 3 May 1864; born in Carter County; resident of Watauga County, NC.; mustered in at Kingston, 23 Jul. 1864; promoted to corporal, 1 Nov. 1864; sick in the hospital, 18 Mar through Feb. 1865; discharged, 2 Aug 1865.
Olliver, John: private, Company F; age: 18; enrolled at Rutledge, 1 Mar 1863; received $25 bounty; sick in the hospital in Louisville, 15 - 30 Jun. 1863; prisoner of war record - blank; discharged, 2 Aug 1865; records contain furlough; pension case.
Ottinger, George: private, Company G; age: 28; resident of Green County; enrolled at Newport, 5 May 1863; died of chronic diarrhea in Nashville, 9 Aug 1863.
Ottinger, Henry: private, Company A; age: 18; enrolled at Newport, 5 Apr. 1863; captured and paroled at McMinnville, 3 Oct. 1863; absent until Feb. 1864; discharged, 2 Aug 1865; pension # 712194.
Ottinger, Johnathan: corporal, Company G; age: 35; enrolled at Greeneville, 5 May 1863; promoted to corporal, 22 May 1863; captured and paroled at McMinnville, 3 Oct. 1863; reported absent on parole through Dec. 1864; discharged, 2 Aug 1865; pension case.

4th Tennessee Volunteer Infantry Regiment (USA)

Ottinger, Jonas: private, Company C; age: 25; enrolled at Newport, 6 Apr. 1863; captured and paroled at McMinnville, 3 Oct. 1863; absent on parole through Feb. 1864; discharged, 2 Aug 1865; pension # 715005 - 66346.

Ottinger, Michael: private, Company C; age: 33; enrolled at Newport, 6 Apr. 1863; captured and paroled at McMinnville, 3 Oct. 1863; absent on parole through Dec. 1864; discharged, 2 Aug 1865; pension # 727209 (92941).

Ottinger, Peter: corporal, Company A; age: 23; enrolled at Newport, 12 Aug 1862; appointed corporal, 23 Feb. 1863; captured and paroled at McMinnville, 3 Oct. 1863; sick in the hospital, 7 May 1864; detailed as a drummer at Kingston, Jul. - Aug 1864; detailed at musician, Sep. 1864 through Apr. 1865; discharged, 8 Jul. 1865; pension case.

Ottinger, Phillip H.: private, Company A; age: 26; enrolled at Newport, 13 Dec. 1862; sick in hospital from enrollment through 30 Jun. 1863; died of typhoid in general hospital at Nashville, 10 Aug 1863; file contains final statements.

Ottinger, Thomas: private, Company C; age: 21; enrolled at Newport, 5 Apr. 1863; captured and paroled at McMinnville, 3 Oct. 1863; absent on parole through Feb. 1864; discharged, 2 Aug 1865; pension case # 337292.

Overbey, William P.: private, Company A; age: 18; enrolled at Rutledge, 1 Apr. 1864; mustered in at Loudon, 7 May 1864; sick at Knoxville, 7 May 1864; deserted from convalescent camp at Knoxville, 11 Jul. 1864.

Overholce, James W.: private, Company D; age: 36; enrolled at Dandridge, 3 Jan. 1863; sick in the hospital, 15 - 30 Jun. 1863; captured and paroled at McMinnville, 3 Oct. 1863; sick in the hospital at Knoxville, 26 Apr. 1864; sick in hospital at Kingston, 18 Nov. 1864; discharged, 2 Aug 1865; pension case.

Owens, William: private, Company D; age: 18; enrolled at Dandridge, 6 Jan. 1863; sick in hospital 15 - 30 Jun. 1863; captured and paroled at McMinnville, 3 Oct. 1863; absent on parole through Feb. 1864; absent without leave, 20 Jul. - 14 Aug 1864; in arrest, 13 Aug 1864; died in the field hospital near Dandridge of typhoid fever, 24 Jan. 1865; file contains many records.

Park, William F.: musician, Company F; age: 18; enrolled at Greeneville, 6 Apr. 1863; appointed musician, 15 Jun. 1863; captured and paroled at McMinnville, 3 Oct. 1863; absent on parole through Feb. 1864; shown on the May - Jun. 1864 muster as corporal; reduced in rank, 3 Feb. 1865; musician, Oct. 1864 through Jun. 1865; discharged, 2 Aug 1865.

Parker, Elvin: private, Company G; age: 18; received as a transfer from the 3rd Infantry Regiment, 1 Mar 1865; discharged, 2 Aug 1865.

Soldiers of the Regiment 115

Parrott, Green: private, Company E; age: 18; enrolled at Greeneville, 1 Sep. 1863; mustered in at Knoxville, 8 Feb. 1864; discharged, 2 Aug 1865.
Partin, Mathew J.: private, Company A; age: 28; enrolled at Dandridge, 16 Feb. 1864; deserted at Mosier's Mill, 25 Feb. 1865.
Patterson, Edly A.: private, Company D; age: 18; enrolled at Rogersville, 15 Oct. 1863; mustered in at Loudon, 7 May 1864; discharged, 2 Aug 1865; file contains enlistment papers.
Patterson, George: quartermaster sergeant, Company G and Field and Staff; enrolled at Greeneville, 12 Jan. 1863; captured and paroled at McMinnville, 3 Oct. 1863; appeared on desertion roll, 15 Apr. through 28 Apr. 1864; promoted to quartermaster sergeant, 4 Nov. 1864; sick in hospital at Greeneville, Jun. 1865; discharged, 2 Aug 1865.
Patterson, Michael L.: Lieutenant Colonel, Field and Staff; age: 35; enrolled at Louisville, 3 Dec.. 1862; commissioned quarter-master lieutenant, 3 Dec.. 1862 by the Governor of Tennessee; promoted to major, 9 Sep. 1863; promoted to lieutenant colonel (vice Lt Col Grayson), 28 Feb. 1864; commander of 3rd Brigade, 4th Division, 12 Jun. 1864; during Jan. - Feb. 1864, sick in Officers Hospital at Knoxville; medical examiners board recommended leave of absence (4 Jan. 1864) stating "Lieutenant Colonel Patterson has one arm amputated, chronic ulcer of the other arm and chronic rheumatism, recommend a 30 day leave of absence."; resigned, 12 Mar 1865.
Patty, William: private, Company C; enrolled at Columbusville (?), 7 Apr. 1864; present for duty during Mar and Apr. 1864; no further records are in the file.
Payne, George M.: sergeant, Company C; age: 26; enrolled at Jonesborough, 6 Apr. 1863; appointed sergeant, 24 Apr. 1863; died of convulsions from inflammation of the brain in the General Hospital # 20 in Nashville, 17 Jul. 1863; buried in grave # 4897 in Nashville Cemetery; file contains final statements.
Pierce, Christian A.A.: private, Company H; age: 18; enrolled at Elizabethton, 1 Nov. 1864; mustered in at Knoxville, 2 Mar 1965; discharged, 2 Aug 1865; file contains enlistment papers.
Pearce, Nathan J.: enrolled at Elizabethton, 12 Apr. 1864; deserted at Elizabethton, 29 Apr. 1864.
Pemberton, Thomas: private, Company D; age: 19; enrolled at Rutledge, 15 Aug 1863; mustered at Strawberry Plains, 20 Mar 1864; guarding a coal mine, Oct. 1864; sick at Dandridge, 13 Jan. 1865; discharged, 2 Aug 1865; file contains enlistment papers.
Pemberton, Welcome A.: corporal, Company D; age: 21; enrolled at Rutledge, 15 Apr. 1862; promoted to corporal, 1 Jun. 1863; captured and paroled at McMinnville, 3 Oct. 1863; discharged, 8 Jul. 1865; pension case.

Penney, George W.: private, Company D; age: 26; enrolled at Newport, 20 Nov. 1862; captured and paroled at McMinnville, 3 Oct. 1863; sick in camp, Sep. - Oct. 1864; sick at Knoxville, 16 Mar 1865; discharged with disability, 26 May 1865; file contains discharge papers.
Penneybaker, Isaac S.: sergeant major, Company C; age: 29; enrolled at Harrisburg, VA., 6 Apr. 1863; captured and paroled at McMinnville, 3 Oct. 1863; died in the hospital at Camp Nelson, KY., of "purpura hemorrhagia", 19 Jan. 1864.
Peoples, David H.: private, Company F; age: 26; enrolled at Knoxville, 1 Dec. 1864; resided in Carter County; mustered in at Knoxville, 2 Mar 1865; deserted from Jonesborough, 25 Jun. 1865; returned to duty, 4 Jul. 1865; discharged, 2 Aug 1865; file contains enlistment papers.
Peters, Andrew C.: private, Company C; age: 18; enrolled at Newport, 15 Apr. 1863; captured and paroled at McMinnville, 3 Oct. 1863; absent on parole through Feb. 1864; discharged, 2 Aug 1865; pension # 727233-91720.
Peters, David F.: corporal, Company A; age: 19; enrolled at Newport, 12 Dec. 1862; appointed corporal, 1 May 1863; captured and paroled at McMinnville, 3 Oct. 1863; absent on parole through Feb. 1864; reduced in rank, 1 Apr. 1864; absent without leave, 27 May 1864; discharged, 2 Aug 1865; pension # 199841.
Peters, Frederick W.: musician, Company C; age: 40; enrolled at Greeneville, 6 Apr. 1863; appointed musician, 1 May 1863; sick in hospital, 15 - 30 Jun. 1863; captured and paroled at McMinnville, 3 Oct. 1863; absent on parole through Feb. 1864; assigned to invalid corps, Jul. 1864; absent without leave, 23 Oct. 1864; sick at Greeneville, 27 Mar 1865; discharged, 2 Aug 1865.
Peters, John: sergeant, Company C; age: 25; enrolled at Greeneville, 6 Apr. 1863; promoted to corporal, 24 Apr. 1863; captured and paroled at McMinnville, 3 Oct. 1863; promoted to 5th sergeant, 27 Nov. 1864; discharged, 2 Aug 1865; pension case.
Peters, John: musician, Company G; age: 22; enrolled at Greeneville, 5 May 1863; promoted to musician, 1 Jun. 1863; captured and paroled at McMinnville, 3 Oct. 1863; absent on parole through Feb. 1864; discharged, 2 Aug 1865; discharged, 2 Aug 1865; pension case.
Phillips, Albert: sergeant, Company F; age: 31; enrolled at Rutledge, 1 Mar 1863; received $25 bounty; sick in the hospital at Louisville, 30 Jun. 1863; appointed corporal, 1 Nov. 1864; promoted to sergeant, 3 Feb. 1865; requested 10 day furlough to go home to Grainger County (furlough in file); pension case.
Phillips, Andrew E.: sergeant, Company C; age: 22; enrolled at Greeneville, 11 Aug. 1862; captured and paroled at McMinnville, 3

Soldiers of the Regiment   117

Cot 1863; promoted from private to 3rd sergeant, 9 Sep. 1863; discharged, 8 Jul. 1865; pension case.
Phillips, Franklin: private, Company G; age: 23; enrolled at Greeneville, 6 Apr. 1863; captured and paroled at McMinnville, 3 Oct. 1863; absent on parole through Feb. 1864; discharged, 2 Aug. 1865; pension case.
Phillips, James B.: private, Company C; enrolled at Greeneville, 15 Sep. 1862; captured and paroled at McMinnville, 3 Oct. 1863; discharged, 8 Jul. 1865; pension case.
Phillips, Jesse: private, Company C; age: 31; enrolled at Jonesborough, 20 May 1863; captured and paroled at McMinnville, 3 Oct. 1863; absent on parole through Feb. 1864; on sick furlough, Jul. 1864; discharged, 2 Aug. 1865; pension case.
Phillips, John: private, Company F; age: 19; enrolled at Rutledge, 1 Jan. 1863; sick in hospital, 15 - 30 Jun. 1863; captured and paroled at McMinnville, 3 Oct. 1863; sick in hospital at Kingston, 8 Sep. 1864; discharged, 2 Aug. 1865; pension # 415007.
Phillips, John C.: corporal, Company C; enrolled at Greeneville, 6 Apr. 1863; captured and paroled at McMinnville, 3 Oct. 1863; sick at Kingston, 25 Nov. 1864 through Feb. 1865; discharged, 2 Aug. 1865; pension # 586805.
Phillips, Johnathan: private, Company F; age: 18; enrolled at Rutledge, 29 Mar 1863; died at Louisville of typhoid fever, 12 May 1863; never appeared on muster roll.
Pickering, Enos: private, Company G; age: 24; enrolled at Greeneville, 15 May 1853; sick in hospital from muster-in to 30 Jun. 1863; captured and paroled at McMinnville, 3 Oct. 1863; dropped from roll as missing in action, Apr. 1865; re-captured in Greene County, 9 Feb. 1864; sent to Andersonville, GA.; admitted to hospital at Andersonville, 22 Oct. 1864; died of "scorbutus" at Andersonville, 22 Oct. 1864.
Pickering, John: private, Company C; age: 21; enrolled at Greeneville, 15 Nov. 1861; sick in hospital at Nashville, Jul. 1863; captured and paroled at McMinnville, 3 Oct. 1863; absent on parole through Feb. 1864; pension # 557876.
Pickering, Levi: captain, Companies D and E; age: 38; previously served as a private in Company K, 1st Tennessee Cavalry; enrolled at Louisville, 9 Apr. 1863; commissioned 1st Lieutenant by Governor Johnson, 9 Apr. 1863; promoted to Captain by order of General Burnside, 29 Apr. 1863; captured and paroled at McMinnville, 3 Oct. 1863; sick in the hospital at Knoxville, 21 Mar 1864; discharged, 2 Aug. 1865; pension case.
Pierce, Andrew: private, Company G; age: 35; enrolled at Greeneville, 25 Nov. 1862; mustered in, 30 Jun. 1863; reported absent without leave, deserted at Louisville, May 1863.

Pierce, Isaac N.: private, Company C; age: 25; enrolled at Greeneville, 15 Mar 1863; sick in hospital, 15 - 30 Jun. 1863; killed in battle at Sparta, TN., 30 Nov. 1863; according to Major Patterson, he left Nashville about 1 Nov. 1863 and was with the 1st Tennessee Cavalry; casualty sheet shows that his clothing issue had been captured at McMinnville, 3 Oct. 1863; file contains final statements.
Pierce, James D.: corporal, Company H; age: 23; enrolled at Elizabethton, 1 Nov. 1864; mustered in at Knoxville, 2 Mar 1865; promoted to corporal, 28 Apr. 1865; discharged, 2 Aug. 1865; file contains enlistment papers.
Pierce, John L.: private, Company E; age: 18; born: Greene County; enrolled at Strawberry Plains, 1 Sep. 1863; mustered in at Loudon, 7 May 1864; discharged, 2 Aug. 1865; file contains enlistment papers.
Pierce, John T.: second lieutenant; Company B and H; age: 32; born: Carter County; enrolled as a private in Company B at Strawberry Plains, 1 Oct. 1863; detached on recruiting duty from muster-in through Oct. 1864; promoted to 2nd lieutenant, Company H, 31 May 1865; mustered in Company H, 5 Jun. 1865; discharged, 2 Aug. 1865.
Pierce, Pulaski L.: private, Company G; age: 19; enrolled at Greeneville, 14 Sep. 1863; mustered in at Loudon, 7 May 1864;; discharged, 2 Aug. 1865; file contains enlistment papers.
Pierce, Robert S.: corporal, Company B; age: 27; born: Carter County; enrolled at Strawberry Plains, 1 Oct. 1863; mustered-in at Kingston, 1 Oct. 1863; promoted to corporal, 2 Nov. 1864; discharged, 2 Aug. 1865.
Pierce, Samuel D.: private, Company H; age: 18; enrolled at Elizabethton, 1 Apr. 1864; mustered at Loudon, 7 May 1864; discharged, 2 Aug. 1865; file contains enlistment papers.
Pierson, John T.: private, Company D; age: 26; enrolled at Knoxville, 1 Feb. 1863; absent without leave, 20 Aug. 1863; captured and paroled at McMinnville, 3 Oct. 1863; gained from missing in action at Knoxville, Jan. 1864; sick in the hospital at Knoxville, 8 Mar 1864; guarding Lenoir Station, Apr. 1864; absent without leave, 1 May 1864; under arrest by Captain Lawson, Jun. 1864; discharged, 2 Aug. 1865; pension case # 87777.
Pine, John: private, Company B; age: 18; enrolled at Knoxville, 1 Mar 1863; shown present for duty from muster-in through discharge, discharged, 2 Aug. 1865.
Piper, Charles W.: first lieutenant, Company C; age: 19; enrolled at Greeneville, 6 Apr. 1863; appointed 2nd sergeant, 24 Apr. 1863; promoted to 1st Lieutenant, 9 Sep. 1863 by order of Colonel Stover to fill vacancy created by the promotion of Lt. Newton Hacker; captured and paroled at McMinnville, 3 Oct. 1863; absent on detached service, 21 Feb. 1864; appointed commander Company G, 14 Aug. 1864;

appointed acting Regimental Quartermaster, 12 Jun. 1865; discharged, 2 Aug. 1865; pension case.
Pleasant, William H.: private, Company B: age: 20; enrolled at Taylorsville, 22 Aug. 1862; mustered in at Nashville, 27 Aug. 1863; prisoner of war record does not indicate that he was captured and paroled at McMinnville; discharged at Knoxville, 7 Jul. 1865; pension case.
Poe, William: private, Company H; age: 17; enrolled at Taylorsville, 10 Apr. 1865; resident of Ashe County, NC.; discharged, 2 Aug. 1865; file contains enlistment papers.
Pollard, Humphrey: private, Company D; age: 23; enrolled at Dandridge, 29 Jan. 1863; sick from muster-in through 30 Jun. 1863; died at Cumberland Hospital, Nashville of typhoid fever, 10 Sep. 1863; file contains final statements.
Porter, George L.: private, Company A; age: 29; enrolled at Greene County, 1 Oct. 1863; mustered-in at Strawberry Plains, 31 Mar 1864; sick in general hospital at Knoxville, Feb. 1864 through Apr. 1864; sick at Kingston, 7 Sep. 1864 through Feb. 1865; discharged, 2 Aug. 1865.
Potter, Andrew: private, (company not indicated); age: 21; enrolled at Taylorsville, 22 Aug. 1862; shown on muster roll at Nashville, 27 Aug. 1863 and not shown on subsequent muster rolls; War Department note (5 Apr. 1890): "application for honorable discharge denied"; file contains enlistment papers.
Potter, Reuben: private, Company H; age: 18; enrolled at Elizabethton, 15 Jun. 1864; resided in Blountville, Sullivan County; born: Watauga County, NC.; deserted at Kingston, 18 Sep. 1864; returned to duty by order of Brigadier General Ammens, 5 Dec. 1864; discharged, 2 Aug. 1865; War Department note (3 Jan. 1887): "desertion charge does not stand, see also Company I, 13th Tennessee Cavalry"; note: file indicates that he enlisted in the 4th Regiment while a deserter from the 13th Regiment Tennessee Cavalry.
Powers, William: private: Company H; age: 25; enrolled (place not identified), 1 Feb. 1865; deserted at Greeneville, 25 Mar 1865.
Presley, Andrew: private, Company A; age: 34; enrolled at Greeneville, 27 Jan. 1863; captured and paroled at McMinnville, 3 Oct. 1863; absent on parole through Feb. 1864; deserted at Kingston, 23 Jul. 1864; restored to duty, 13 Feb. 1865; War Department note: "desertion charge no longer stands but can not be expunged"; discharged, 2 Aug. 1865; possible pension case.
Presley, John: private, Company A; age: 24; enrolled at Greeneville, 27 Jan. 1863; discharged, 2 Aug. 1865; War Department note (1 Jun. 1889): "application for certificate in lieu of lost discharge, certificate forwarded".

4th Tennessee Volunteer Infantry Regiment (USA)

Price, Jasper N.: private, Company G; age: 19; enrolled at Greeneville, 5 May 1863; sick from muster-in through 30 Jun. 1863; discharged, 2 Aug. 1865.
Price, John E.: corporal, Company F; age: 21; enrolled at Jonesborough, 14 Nov 1862; captured and paroled at McMinnville, 3 Oct 1863; promoted to corporal, 1 Jul 1864; discharged, 2 Aug 1865.
Price, Marcus F.: private, Company H; gained from a transfer from the 3rd Tennessee Infantry Regiment, 1 Mar 1865; discharged, 2 Aug 1865.
Proctor, Joseph K.: private, Company G; age: 30; enrolled at Greeneville, 20 Jan 1863; reported absent without leave from muster-in through 30 Jun 1863; deserted at Louisville, Apr 1863; record also shows: absent sick in hospital, Jul 1863; absent on recruiting service in East Tennessee, Aug 1863 and deserted at Nashville, Aug 1863.
Rader, George H.: private, Company F; age: 18; enrolled at Greeneville, 6 Apr 1863; captured and paroled at McMinnville, 3 Oct 1863; discharged, 2 Aug 1865.
Rader, Isaac F.: private, Company F; age; 18; enrolled at Greeneville, 15 Apr 1863; received $25 bonus; captured and paroled at McMinnville, 3 Oct 1863; absent on parole through Feb 1864; discharged, 2 Aug 1865; pension case.
Rader, Peter R.: corporal, Company F; age: 43; enrolled at Greeneville, 15 Apr 1863; appointed corporal, 15 Jun 1863; missing in action at Mosier's Mill, 1 Feb 1865; prisoner of war record shows: captured at Morristown, TN., 4 Feb 1865; confined at Lynchburg, VA., 3 Mar 1865; paroled, 26 Mar 1865; sent to Camp Chase, OH., 29 Mar 1865; discharged, 2 Aug 1865.
Rader, Powell: corporal, Company A; age: 18; enrolled at Greeneville, 13 Dec 1862; sick in hospital from enrollment through 30 Jun 1863; promoted to corporal, 1 May 1863; discharged with disability, 23 Dec 1863 at Louisville.
Ragsdill, John W.: corporal, Company A; age: 33; enrolled at Greeneville, 12 Feb 1863; promoted to corporal, 1 May 1863; deserted at Kingston, 23 Jul 1863; returned to duty, 1 May 1865; discharged, 2 Aug 1865; War Department note (14 Nov 1901): "individual deserted Company K, 1st Regiment Tennessee Cavalry, 2 Sep 1862 and enrolled in the 4th Regiment Tennessee Infantry, a violation of 50th Article of War".
Ragsdill, William: corporal, Company A; age: 36; enrolled at Greeneville, 12 Aug 1862; appointed corporal, 1 May 1863; captured and paroled at McMinnville, 3 Oct 1863; absent on parole through Feb 1864; reduced to ranks, 1 Apr 1864; deserted at Kingston, 23 Jul 1864; restored to duty, 1 May 1865; discharged, 2 Aug 1865; War Department note (15 May 1893): "his return to 4th Regiment under provision of proclamation of 11 Mar 1865, serves as a pardon for

deserting the 1st Cavalry"; prisoner of war record: "recaptured at Bulls Gap, 7 Dec 1864; confined at Richmond, 14 Dec 1864; paroled, 5 Feb 1865; sent to Camp Chase, OH., 16 Feb 1865"; possible pension case.
Rambo, James F.: corporal, Companies B and F; age: 25; enrolled at Taylorsville, 12 Aug 1862; captured and paroled at McMinnville, 3 Oct 1863; absent on parole through Feb 1864; transferred to Company F, 29 Apr 1864; promoted to corporal, 1 Apr 1865; discharged, 8 Jul 1865; file contains enlistment papers, possible pension case.
Rambo, William H.: private, Company B; age: 22; enrolled at Taylorsville, 25 Aug 1862; wounded in action at McMinnville, 3 Oct 1863; captured and paroled at McMinnville, 3 Oct 1863; discharged, 8 Jul 1865; file contains enlistment papers, pension case.
Randles, John B.: private, Company C; age: 23; gained as a transfer from the 3rd Tennessee Infantry Regiment, 1 Mar 1865; discharged, 2 Aug 1865.
Rankins, John C.: private, Company H; age: 21; gained as a transfer from the 3rd Tennessee Infantry Regiment, 1 Mar 1865; discharged, 2 Aug 1865.
Rash, Linza R.: private, Company H; age: 18; enrolled at Elizabethton, 1 Jun 1864; deserted at Strawberry Plains, 10 Jun 1864; file contains enlistment papers.
Ray, Emanuel M.: private, Company D; age not given; enrolled at Rutledge, 20 Feb 1863; mustered in at Strawberry Plains, 31 Mar 1864; promoted to corporal, 29 Apr 1864; deserted at Kingston, 20 Jul 1864; returned to duty and restored without trial, 24 Nov 1864; deserted again, 24 Dec 1864; War Department note (14 Apr 1887): "the charges of desertion, 23 and 24 Dec 1864 and (?) Feb are removed. He was absent without leave from 23 Dec 1864 to 3 Jan 1865 when he was killed by the enemy."
Ray, Joseph: private, Company G; age: 19; gained as a transfer from the 3rd Regiment Tennessee Infantry, 1 May 1865; discharged, 2 Aug 1865.
Ray, William N.: private, Company H; age: 27; gained as a transfer from Company K, 3rd Regiment Tennessee Infantry, 1 Mar 1865; sick in the hospital at Knoxville, 1 Mar 1865; discharged, 26 Jun. 1865.
Reagan, James M.: sergeant, Company C; gained as a transfer from the 3rd Tennessee Infantry, 1 Mar 1865; promoted to 5th sergeant, 8 Jul. 1865; resident of Knox County; file contains 20 day furlough request, 8 Jul. 1865; discharged, 2 Aug. 1865.
Reaser, William B.: sergeant, Company C; enrolled at Greeneville, 26 Nov. 1862; promoted to corporal, 22 May 1863; captured and paroled at McMinnville, 3 Oct. 1863; promoted to 3rd sergeant, 1 Jul. 1864; sick in the hospital at Kingston, 24 Nov. 1864 through Feb. 1865; pension case # 335810.

4th Tennessee Volunteer Infantry Regiment (USA)

Rector, John: private, Company F; age: 24; enrolled at Greeneville, 6 Apr. 1863; received $25 bonus; captured and paroled at McMinnville, 3 Oct. 1863; discharged, 2 Aug. 1865; pension case.

Reecer, Archibald: corporal, Company G; age: 18; enrolled at Greeneville, 20 Sep. 1862; sick from muster-in through 30 Jun. 1863; captured and paroled at McMinnville, 3 Oct. 1863; absent on parole through Feb. 1864; promoted to corporal, 1 Jul. 1864; discharged, 7 Jul. 1865; pension case # 565173.

Reed, William: private, Companies F & D; age: 18; enrolled at Newport, 18 Jan. 1863; received $25 bonus; transferred to Company D, 25 Aug. 1863; captured and paroled at McMinnville, 3 Oct. 1863; deserted at Kingston, 20 Jul. 1864; restored to duty from desertion, 13 Jan. 1865; War Department note (31 May 1889): desertion charge no longer stands, record of desertion can not be expunged; pension case.

Reeser, Daniel M.: private, Company C; age: 18; enrolled at Jonesborough, 1 Oct. 1863; mustered-in at Strawberry Plains, 31 Mar 1864; sent to Knoxville to be mustered out, 25 May 1865; in the hospital in Knoxville, 27 May 1865; returned to duty from hospital, 21 Jul. 1865; discharged, 2 Aug. 1865.

Reesor, Arnold M.: private, Company C; age: 31; enrolled at Jonesborough, 6 Apr. 1863; captured and paroled at McMinnville, 3 Oct. 1863; discharged, 2 Aug. 1865; possible pension case.

Reeves, George W.: corporal, Company F; age: 27; enrolled at Greeneville, 31 Jan. 1863; received $25 bonus; appointed corporal, 15 Jan. (?) 1863; captured and paroled at McMinnville, 3 Oct. 1863; reported absent on parole through Mar 1865; reported missing in action, Mar - Apr. muster 1865; re-captured at Markinsville, TN., 8 Feb. 1864 sent to Andersonville, 18 Feb. 1864; died of unknown cause at Andersonville, 22 Jul. 1864; file contains final statements.

Reeves, Thomas H.: Lieutenant Colonel, Company D and F&S; age: 21; enrolled at Greeneville, 15 Nov. 1861; mustered in Company F, 2nd Tennessee Volunteer Infantry, 6 Dec. 1861 as a private where he served 10 months before alleged desertion; joined Company D, 4th Regiment, 19 Feb. 1863; commissioned 1st Lieutenant by Governor Johnson; promoted to Captain by Colonel Stover, 29 May 1863; captured and paroled at McMinnville, 3 Oct. 1863; promoted to Major (vice Major Patterson), 12 Mar 1864; promoted to lieutenant colonel, 31 May 1865 (vice Lt. Col. Patterson resignation and resolving the desertion charge from the 2nd Infantry Regiment); discharged 2 Aug. 1865.

Reid, James J.: private, Company E; age: 22; enrolled at Greeneville, 23 Apr. 1863; captured and paroled at McMinnville, 3 Oct. 1863; on detached duty with Colonel Clay Clawson, Dec. 1863; sick in the

Soldiers of the Regiment

hospital at Kingston, 20 Jul. 1864 through Feb. 1865; discharged, 2 Aug. 1865.

Reid, Robert B.: private, Company E; age: 25; enrolled at Greeneville, 23 Apr. 1863; captured and paroled at McMinnville, 3 Oct. 1863; wounded and in the hospital at McMinnville, 28 Sep. 1863 through 16 Apr. 1865; suffered accidental gunshot wound inflicted by comrade resulting in fracture of right femur; received disability discharge, 16 Apr. 1865.

Remine, Flavius J.: private, Company E; age: 25; enrolled at Greeneville, 19 Dec 1862; captured and paroled at McMinnville, 3 Oct 1863; on detached service with Army, Department of Ohio, 2 Feb 1864 through Dec 1862; absent without leave, 23 Feb 1865; sick in hospital, 2 Apr 1865; discharged, 2 Aug 1865.

Remine, William C. P.: private, Company E; age: 19; enrolled at Greeneville, 1 Sep 1862; on detached service detailed to Colonel Crawford, 25 Dec 1863 through Feb 1865; deserted, 30 Apr 1865; returned to duty, 12 Jul 1865; discharged, 2 Aug 1865.

Renner, John: private, Company C; age: 33; enrolled at Greeneville, 5 Apr 1863; deserted at McMinnville, 30 Sep 1863; reported as a deserter from McMinnville, 23 Feb 1864; captured at Cedar Run, Greene County, 26 Mar 1864; sent to Richmond, 31 May 1864; admitted to Hospital 21 at Richmond, 6 May 1864; paroled at Aikens Landing, VA., 8 May 1864; sent to Camp Chase, Columbus, OH., 20 Jun 1864; left Camp Chase 22 Aug 1864; deserted, 24 Dec 1864; restored to duty, 28 Jan 1865; discharged, 2 Aug 1865; possible pension case; miscellaneous papers in file.

Renner, Moses: sergeant, Company A; age: 28; enrolled at Greeneville, 13 Dec 1862; appointed sergeant, 13 Feb 1863; captured and paroled at McMinnville, 3 Oct 1863; absent on parole through Feb 1864; reduced to ranks, 1 Apr 1864; absent without leave, 24 May 1864; reported as a deserter at Loudon, 30 May 1864; War Department note (8 Feb 1887): "application for desertion charge drop - denied".

Renner, Powell: sergeant, Company C; age: 34; enrolled at Greeneville, 5 Apr 1863; resided in Sullivan County, TN., appointed sergeant, 24 Apr 1863; captured and paroled at McMinnville, 3 Oct 1863; absent on parole through Feb 1864; discharged, 2 Aug 1865; pension case # 507440.

Richards, James: private, Company H; age: 18; enrolled at Jonesborough, 1 Apr 1865; discharged, 2 Aug 1865; file contains enlistment papers.

Richardson, David: private, Company H; age: 18; enrolled at Strawberry Plains, 29 Apr 1864; resident of Carter County; mustered in at Loudon, 7 May 1864; sick in hospital at Kingston, Sep 1864 through May 1865; sick in hospital at Knoxville, 1 Mar

1865 through 10 Apr 1865; died in the General Hospital at Knoxville, 20 Apr 1865; file contains enlistment papers and last statements; pension case # 311577.

Richardson, Elijah: private, Company H; age: 19; enrolled at Strawberry Plains, 29 Apr 1864; resided in Carter County; mustered in at Loudon, 7 May 1864; sick in hospital at Kingston, Sep 1864 through Dec 1864; discharged, 2 Aug 1865; file contains enlistment papers.

Ricker, Frederick: private, Company H; age: 29; enrolled at Greeneville, 1 Feb 1865; Resident of Greene County; born: Pulaski County, IN., mustered in at Knoxville, 2 Mar 1865; deserted at Greeneville, 25 Mar 1865; joined from deserton under Presidential Proclamation, 6 May 1865; discharged, 2 Aug 1865; War Department note (15 Mar 1886): desertion charge removed; file contains enlistment papers.

Riddle, John H.: private, Company H; enrolled at Jonesboro, 1 Apr 1865; deserted at Jonesborough, 5 May 1865.

Rider, Van B.: sergeant, Company D; age: 25; enrolled at Rogersville, 21 Dec 1862; received $25 bounty; promoted to sergeant, 1 Jun 1863; captured and paroled at McMinnville, 3 Oct 1863; died in Knoxville of typhoid and pneumonia fever, 1 Feb 1864; file contains final statements.

Renner, William H.: private, Company G; age: 23; enrolled at Newport, 31 May 1863; captured and paroled at McMinnville, 3 Oct 1863; absent on parole through Feb 1864; discharged, 2 Aug 1865; pension case # 106276.

Reynolds, John B.: private, Company A; age: 20; enrolled at Greeneville, 12 Aug 1862; captured and paroled at McMinnville, 3 Oct 1863; absent on parole through Feb 1864; absent on provost duty at Philadelphia, TN., Sep - Oct 1864; absent without leave, 24 Dec 1864; sick at Greeneville, 24 Jun 1865; discharged, 8 Jul 1865; pension case.

Reynolds, Joshua: private, Company A; age: 29; enrolled at Greeneville, 1 Aug 1862; captured and paroled at McMinnville, 3 Oct 1863; absent on parole through Feb 1864; absent without leave, 26 May 1864; reported as deserter at Loudon, Jul 1864; restored to duty under Presidential Proclamation, 27 Mar 1865; discharged, 2 Aug 1865; War Department note (12 Jan 1888): "desertion charge no longer stands but desertion can not be expunged"; pension case.

Reynolds, Joseph: private, Company A; age: 18; enrolled at Greene County, 1 Aug 1863; mustered in at Strawberry Plains, 31 Mar 1864; absent without leave, 15 Jun 1864; reported as deserter from Loudon, Jul 1864; restored to duty from desertion by Presidential Proclamation, 27 Mar 1865; discharged: 2 Aug 1865; War Department note (30 Sep 1886): "application for removal of desertion charge, denied"; War

Soldiers of the Regiment 125

Department note (7 May 1888): "desertion charge removed but can not be expunged".
Richards, George W.: private, Company H; age: 26; enrolled at Elizabethton, 21 May 1864; resident of Scott County, TN., mustered at Kingston, 21 May 1864; promoted to sergeant, 23 Jul 1864; reduced in rank, 26 Apr 1865; discharged, 2 Aug 1865; War Department note (20 Dec 1888): "application for certificate in lieu of discharge furnished"; file contains furlough, dated 25 May 1864, to visit home in Roane County.
Rightsell, William C.: private, Company D; age: 18; enrolled at Dandridge, 18 Jan 1863; captured and paroled at McMinnville, 3 Oct 1863; discharged, 2 Aug 1865; possible pension case.
Ripley, Sylvester B.: corporal, Company F; age: 18; enrolled at Greeneville, 15 Apr 1863; received $25 bounty; prisoner of war record - blank; appointed corporal, 3 Feb 1865; discharged, 2 Aug 1865; possible pension case.
Roach, Daniel L.: private, Company D; age: 18; enrolled at Rutledge, 18 Aug 1864; mustered in at Knoxville, 2 Dec 1864; discharged, 2 Aug 1865.
Roarark, Joshua: private, Company H; enrolled in Elizabethton, 10 Jun 1864; deserted at Knoxville, 16 Jun 1864.
Roarark, W.M.: private, Company H; enrolled at Taylorsville, 13 Apr 1865; deserted at Taylorsville, 15 Apr 1865.
Roberts, Charles W.: private, Company E; age: 23; enrolled at Greeneville, 23 Apr 1863; captured and paroled at McMinnville, 3 Oct 1863; discharged, 2 Aug 1865; War Department note (3 Dec 1889): "for prior service of this soldier, see records of Company I, 1st Tennessee Volunteers".
Roberts, James: private, Company D; age: 43; enrolled at Rutledge, 20 Apr 1863; mustered at Strawberry Plains, 31 Mar 1864; absent without leave, 15 Apr 1864; in arrest, 23 Jul 1864; deserted at Kingston, 3 Oct 1864; restored to duty, 26 Feb 1865; discharged, 2 Aug 1865; War Department note (23 Jan 1889): "deserted 2 Oct 1864, was arrested 20 Feb 1865 - desertion charge no longer stands but can not be expunged"; file contains court martial charge for desertion.
Roberts, Thomas: private, Company D; age: 18; enrolled at Rutledge, 15 Aug 1863; mustered in at Strawberry Plains, 31 Mar 1864; in arrest, 23 Jul 1864; absent without leave, 24 Dec 1864; discharged, 2 Aug 1865; file contains enlistment papers.
Roberts, William G.: private, Company C; enrolled at Greeneville, 6 Sep 1863; file contains no other records.
Robertson, Daniel: private, Company G: enrolled at Taylorsville, 1 Jun 1863; mustered in at Nashville, 27 Aug 1863; captured at McMinnville, 3 Oct 1863; dropped from rolls as missing in action,

Mar 1865; War Department note (25 May 1883): "captured in action at McMinnville, confined at Richmond, 15 Mar 1864; admitted to hospital at Richmond with diarrhea, 21 Mar 1864; transferred to small pox hospital, admitted to Howard Grove Hospital at Richmond, 22 Mar 1864 with "variola"; nothing further in known"; pension case.
Robertson, Nathaniel T.: private, Company C; age: 18; enrolled at Flat Creek, Greene County, 6 Sep 1863; mustered in at Loudon, 7 May 1864; captured by the enemy, 26 Aug 1864, (details not reported); sick in hospital after returning form missing in action, Sep 1864; sick at Kingston, Nov - Dec 1864 through Jan - Feb 1865; pension case # 605126.
Robertson, William D.: private, age: 19; enrolled at Taylorsville, 22 Aug 1862; captured and paroled at McMinnville, 3 Oct 1864; no other details; file contains enlistment papers.
Robinson, James C.: musician, Company C; age: 18; enrolled at Greeneville, 6 Apr 1863; appointed musician, 6 May 1863; sick in hospital, 15 - 30 Jun 1863; captured and paroled at McMinnville, 3 Oct 1863; absent on parole through Feb 1864; on detached service at Loudon, May - Jun 1864; discharged, 2 Aug 1865; pension case # 686230.
Robinson, John: private, Company B; age: 38; enrolled at Louisville, 19 Feb 1863; deserted at Louisville, 15 Mar 1863.
Robinson, John W.: private, Company C; gained as a transfer from Company D, 3rd Tennessee Infantry Regiment, 1 Mar 1865; sick in the hospital at Knoxville; held to make time good from 11 Aug 1864 through 16 Jan 1865; reported as a deserter at Jonesborough, 31 May 1865; War Department note (2 Oct 1919): "charge of desertion has not been removed but denied on grounds that service prior to 1 May 1865 was not faithful and that he was not prevented from completing his term of service by reason of disability encountered in line of duty."
Rogers, John F.: private, Company F; age: 20; enrolled at Dandridge, 10 Jan 1863; received $25 bounty; sick in the hospital, 15 - 30 Jun 1863; died at Louisville, date and cause not known.
Rogers, Jackson: private, Company D; age: 20; enrolled at Dandridge, 18 Jan 1863; captured and paroled at McMinnville, 3 Oct 1863; discharged, 2 Aug 1865; pension case.
Rogers, Jesse: private, Company D & F; age: 18; enrolled at Dandridge, 1 Oct 1863; born: Lee County, VA., resided in Grainger County, mustered in at Loudon, 7 May 1864; transferred to Company F, 30 Apr 1864; absent without leave, 3 Apr 1864; reported as a deserter, 1 Jul 1864; file contains enlistment papers.
Rogers, John: private, Company D; age and place of enlistment not given, admitted to Hospital 4 at Louisville and died of diarrhea, 20 May 1863.

Soldiers of the Regiment

Rogers, Samuel B.: private, Company B; age 22; enrolled at Shelbyville, KY., 20 Jan 1863; deserted at Louisville, 21 Feb 1863.
Rogers, James: private, Company D; age not given; enrolled at Dandridge, 10 Jan 1863; captured and paroled at McMinnville, 3 Oct 1863; discharged, 2 Aug 1865; pension case.
Roggers, William C.: sergeant, Company D; age: 24; enrolled at Jonesborough, 17 Dec 1862; promoted to sergeant, 15 Apr 1863; captured and paroled at McMinnville, 3 Oct 1863; deserted at Camp Nelson, KY., 14 Dec 1863; restored to duty from desertion, 4 Mar 1864 by order of General Schofield; discharged, 2 Aug 1865; War Department note (8 Dec 1885): "the charge of desertion is removed and he is considered absent without leave, 14 Dec 1863 through 4 Mar 1864."; pension case.
Rominger, L. A.: private, Company H; age not given; enrolled at Elizabethton, 1 Jun 1864; deserted at Strawberry Plains, 10 Jun 1864.
Rowe, Thomas Y.: private, Company B; age: 24; enrolled at Strawberry Plains, 1 Mar 1864; mustered in at Loudon, 7 May 1864; resided in Carter County; discharged, 2 Aug 1865; file contains enlistment papers.
Rush, David: second lieutenant, Company C; enrolled at Greeneville, 10 Aug 1862; promoted to 1Sgt, 24 Apr 1863; promoted to second lieutenant, 9 Sep 1863; captured and paroled at McMinnville, 3 Oct 1863; never returned to duty with the 4th Regiment; carried as absent without leave; discharged to accept appointment as Captain, 8th Tennessee Cavalry at Gallatin, TN.; War Department note (20 Jan 1891): "application for resignation as second lieutenant, Company C, 4th Regiment, rejected by War Department."; possible pension case.
Russell, John L.: private, Company H; age: 19; enrolled in Jul 1864 (place and day not shown); discharged at Kingston for disability, 23 Jul 1864; file contains discharge.
Ryan, George W.: private, Company B; age: 26; enrolled at Abingdon, VA., 12 Mar 1863; shown in the hospital in Nashville, Jul 1863; prisoner of war record - blank; absent without leave, 25 Jun 1864; reported as a deserter, Jul - Aug 1864; restored to duty from desertion, 13 Oct 1864 by Special Order #73, Headquarters, 4th Division; shown on daily duty as a blacksmith, Mar - Apr 1864; discharged in Knoxville, 7 Jul 1865; War Department note (15 Nov 1888): "deserted 25 Jun 1864, returned to duty, 13 Oct 1864; restored to duty without trial, charge of desertion no longer stands but record of desertion can not be expunged".
Salts, Robert M.: private, Company F; age: 26; enrolled at Greeneville, 30 Jan 1863; received $25 bounty; sick in the hospital in Nashville during the period, 30 Jun 1863 through Apr 1864; captured and paroled at McMinnville, 3 Oct 1863; absent without leave, 22 Dec 1864; discharged, 2 Aug 1865; pension case 454825.

4th Tennessee Volunteer Infantry Regiment (USA)

Sample, Robert R.: sergeant, Company D; age: 21; enrolled at Dandridge, 10 Jan 1863; promoted to sergeant, 1 Jun 1863; discharged, 2 Aug 1865.
Sauterfield, Martin V.: private, Company G; gained as a transfer from the 3rd Tennessee Volunteer Infantry, 1 Mar 1865; discharged, 2 Aug 1865.
Scott, James C.: musician, Company D; age: 36; enrolled at Greeneville, 1 Mar 1863; promoted to musician, 3 Jun 1863; absent without leave, 15 - 30 Jun 1863; reported as a deserter, 12 Jul 1863 at Nashville.
Scott, George: private, Company E; age: 18; enrolled at Greeneville, 1 Sep 1863; mustered at Knoxville, 8 Feb 1864; absent without leave, 22 Dec 1864; discharged, 2 Aug 1865; file contains enlistment papers.
Scott, Thomas: private, Company H; age: 42; enrolled at Elizabethton, 29 Apr 1864; born: Wilkes County, NC., mustered at Loudon, 7 May 1864; absent without leave, 30 Jun 1865; discharged, 2 Aug 1865; file contains enlistment papers.
Scott, William T. L.: private, Company H; enrolled at Elizabethton, 17 Apr 1864; mustered at Kingston, 23 Jul 1864; letter in file (dated 8 Jul 1864) showing Major Reeves authorizing him to go to East Tennessee on a recruiting mission for 30 days; letter in file from General Schofield to General Ammen showing soldier being sent back to his unit with time charged as furlough instead of recruiting duty, 11 Jul 1864; member deserted at Kingston, 25 Jul 1864.
Scrudgington, Alexander: private, Company A; enrolled at Greeneville, 7 Feb. 1863; captured and paroled at McMinnville, 3 Oct. 1863; while on parole, captured at Bulls Gap, TN., 7 Dec. 1864; confined at Richmond, 17 Dec. 1864; paroled, 5 Feb. 1865; reported in hospital at Annapolis, MD., 7 Feb. 1865; reported on company muster roll as absent without leave, Apr. 1864; reported as a deserter, 16 Apr. 1864; sick in the hospital at Knoxville, 3 Mar 1865; restored to duty from desertion, 19 Mar 1865 under Presidential proclamation; discharged, 2 Aug. 1865; War Department note (13 Oct. 1887): "application for removal of desertion charge denied"; possible pension case.
Seamore, Caswell: private, Company F; gained as a transfer from the 3rd Regiment Tennessee Infantry, 1 Mar 1865; discharged, 2 Aug. 1865.
Seaton, Benjamin F.: private, Company E; age: 22; enrolled at Greeneville, 15 Nov. 1861; captured and paroled at McMinnville, 3 Oct. 1863; discharged, 2 Aug. 1865; pension case.
Seaton, Isaac: private, Company E; age: 44; enrolled at Greeneville, 15 Nov. 1861; captured and paroled at McMinnville, 3 Oct. 1863; absent on parole through Feb. 1864; sick in the hospital at Kingston,

11 Aug. 1864; sick in the hospital at Knoxville, 28 May 1865; discharged, 20 Jun. 1865; pension case # 241837.
Seaton, James M.: corporal, Company E; age: 20; enrolled at Greeneville, 15 Nov. 1861; promoted to corporal, 26 May 1863; captured and paroled at McMinnville, 3 Oct. 1863; discharged, 8 Jul. 1865; possible pension case.
Self, Lewis F.: Lieutenant Regimental Quartermaster, Company A and Filed and Staff; enrolled at Greeneville, 25 Jul. 1863; mustered in at Strawberry Plains, 31 Mar 1864; promoted to quartermaster sergeant, 3 Dec. 1863; promoted to first lieutenant - regimental quartermaster, 5 Oct. 1864; resigned to accept appointment as Postmaster at Greeneville, 21 May 1865; resignation accepted by Major General Thomas, Commander at Nashville, 29 May 1865; file contains enlistment papers and numerous documents.
Sellers, Abram: private, companies B & F; age: 24; enrolled at Jonesborough, 26 Dec. 1862; War Department note: "prior to muster in, 31 Dec. 1862, he was captured in Wise County, VA., and imprisoned at Richmond; he was paroled at City Point, VA., (day not stated) Mar 1863; he was later reported sick in the hospital at Louisville, 6 Aug. 1863 and Transferred to the invalid corps.
Severs, William: private, Company G; gained as a transfer from the 3rd Tennessee Infantry Regiment; sick in the hospital at Knoxville, 21 Mar 1865; mustered out, 7 Jun. 1865.
Sexton, Daniel W.: private, Company G; age: 20; enrolled at Greeneville, 6 Sep. 1863; mustered in at Strawberry Plains, 31 Mar 1864; sick, Nov. - Dec. 1864; died from (illegible) fever at the field hospital at Mosier's Mill, 10 Feb. 1865; file contains final statements.**
Sexton, Henry: corporal, Company C; age: 39; enrolled at Greeneville, 16 Mar 1863; promoted to corporal, 21 Apr. 1863; died at Hospital # 2 at Nashville, 24 Jul. 1863 of typhoid fever, file contains final statements.
Sexton, James A.: private, Company C; age: 36; enrolled at Greeneville, 15 Jan. 1863; appointed wagoner, 6 May 1863; died at the hospital in McMinnville, 25 Sep. 1863 of typhoid fever; buried in McMinnville.
Sexton, Ransom: private, company C; age: 18; enrolled at Kingston, 29 May 1864; resided at Taylorsville, Johnson County; sick at Knoxville, 16 Feb. 1865; discharged, 2 Aug. 1865.
Shanks, Andrew J.: private, Company C; age: 23; enrolled at Greeneville, 6 Apr. 1863; captured and paroled at McMinnville, 3 Oct. 1863; absent on parole through Feb. 1864; discharged, 2 Aug. 1865; pension # 353049.
Shanks, James P.: private, Company C; age: 20; enrolled at Greeneville, 26 Mar 1863; captured and paroled at McMinnville, 3

Oct. 1863; absent on parole through Feb. 1864; discharged, 2 Aug. 1865; pension case.
Shaver, Aaron, A.: private, Company F; age: 32; enrolled at Rutledge, 5 Apr. 1862; died at Louisville, 21 Mar 1863 of typhoid and pneumonia, file contains casualty sheet.
Shaver, Andrew J.: private, Company D; age: 18; enrolled at Rutledge, 1 Feb. 1863; captured and paroled at McMinnville, 3 Oct. 1863; reported absent on parole through Aug. 1864; reported captured by the enemy and a prisoner of war, Sep. - Oct. 1864; reported missing in action, Jan. - Feb. 1865; died in Rebel prison at Richmond, 16 Feb. 1864; prisoner of war record shows: capture at McMinnville; confined at Richmond, 11 Jan. 1864; admitted to hospital in Richmond, 8 Feb. 1865; died of pneumonia.
Shaver, George, W.: sergeant, Company D; age: 34; enrolled at Rutledge, 1 Feb. 1863; captured and paroled at McMinnville, 3 Oct. 1863; promoted to corporal, 13 Jul. 1864; promoted to sergeant, 14 Jul. 1865; pension case.
Shaw, Thomas G.: private, Company E; age: 18; enrolled at Greeneville, 1 Sep. 1863; mustered in at Knoxville, 8 Feb. 1864; sick in hospital at Kingston, 30 Jul. 1864; discharged, 2 Aug. 1865.
Sheddan, Thomas W.: sergeant, Company B; age: 37; enrolled at Maryville, 12 Mar 1863; promoted to sergeant, 5 Jun. 1863; captured and paroled at McMinnville, 3 Oct. 1863; promoted to 1st sergeant, 8 Dec. 1864; requested 30 day furlough to go home to Blount County, 2 Jul. 1865; appointed Regimental Hospital Steward, 7 Jul. 1865; discharged, 2 Aug. 1865.
Sheddin, William E.: Hospital Steward, Company B; age: 33; enrolled at Robinson, IL., 1 Apr. 1862; captured and paroled at McMinnville, 3 Oct. 1863; absent on parole until 23 Jan. 1864; absent, sick on leave at home in Blount County, 26 Apr. 1864 through Nov. 1864; sick in hospital at Kingston, 21 Mar 1864; on duty with surgical department, Mar 1865; requested discharge to accept appointment as justice of peace and request rejected due to needs of the service in the field: discharged, 2 Aug. 1865; file contains discharge request.
Shell, Samuel: sergeant, Company B; age: 21; enrolled at Elizabethton, 11 Nov. 1863; promoted to sergeant, 11 May 1863; captured and paroled at McMinnville, 3 Oct. 1863; absent without leave, 15 Feb. 1864; deserted at Kingston, 7 Sep. 1864; returned to duty, 8 Oct. 1864; discharged, 2 Aug. 1865; War Department note (18 Nov. 1886): "he was captured at McMinnville and paroled 3 Oct. 1863; charges of desertion, 7 Sep. and 16 Sep. are removed under provisions of Act of Congress, 5 Jul. 1884; he was absent without authority 7 Sep. 1864 to 8 Oct. 1864". possible pension case.

Soldiers of the Regiment

Shelton, Nelson: private, Company E; age: 20; enrolled at Greeneville, 15 Mar 1863; captured and paroled at McMinnville, 3 Oct. 1863; absent on parole through Mar 1864; reported captured by the enemy while absent on parole Jul. - Aug. 1864; War Department note (16 Nov. 1904): "it was determined that the soldier was absent from his command without proper authority at the time of his capture on 9 Mar 1864"; prisoner of war record shows: "capture and parole at McMinnville, 3 Oct. 1863; recapture at Bears (Bays) Mountain, 9 Mar 1864; confined at Richmond, 26 Mar 1864; admitted to the hospital at Richmond, 2 Apr. 1864; sent to the small pox hospital, 25 Apr. 1864; admitted with "variola"; readmitted to Hospital # 21 at Richmond, 21 May 1864; released to duty, 21 May 1864; paroled at Varina, VA., 8 Oct. 1864; sent to Camp Chase, OH., 20 Oct. 1864; sent to provost marshall Columbus, OH, 19 Dec. 1864; sent to Regiment, 26 Dec. 1864"; discharged 2 Aug. 1865.
Shinliver, Charles: private, Company F; gained as a transfer from the 3rd Regiment Tennessee Infantry at Jonesborough, 28 Apr. 1865; sick in the hospital at Nashville, through Apr. 1865; discharged, 2 Aug. 1865.
Shoemaker, John: private, Company B; age: 27; enrolled at Greeneville, 5 Oct. 1862; sick in the hospital, 15 - 30 Jun. through Apr. 1864; transferred to the invalid corps, 15 Feb. 1864.
Shoven, W.W.: private, Company H; enrolled at Strawberry Plains, 2 May 1864; deserted at Knoxville, 10 May 1864.
Singletary, Frederick S.: first lieutenant, Company B; age: 20; enrolled as a private at Elizabethton, 16 Jul. 1862; mustered in as second lieutenant, Company B; 11 May 1863; captured and paroled at McMinnville, 3 Oct. 1863; on detached service, 16 Feb. 1864; letter in his file to General Schofield shows that he "started with Major Kirk of the 2nd NC. Volunteers and 16 other officers and men to the upper counties of the state when (on the 17th) they were suddenly attacked by a cavalry force and forced to disburse in various directions; was cut off and unable to rejoin the command, so proceeded to the Chilhowie Mountains and was compelled to remain there; finally made it to Sevier County ... etc."; in arrest, 11 Apr. 1864; requested permission to resign because of impending court martial charges, 9 May 1864; received general court martial for "conduct prejudice to good order and discipline; circulating a letter for signature criticizing Lieutenant Middleton; absent without leave, 4 Apr. 1864 through 6 Apr. 1864; conduct unbecoming an officer for writing a letter questioning authority of the Regimental Commander's order to move his company", 16 Aug. 1864; received a written public reprimand in the form of a general order from court martial; promoted to first lieutenant, Company B; 27 Oct. 1864; appointed acting Regimental Adjutant, 8 Mar 1865; requested a 20 day furlough

to attend to the needs of his family, 21 Jun. 1865; discharged, 2 Aug. 1865; file contains numerous papers.
Skyles, John W.: musician, Company E; age: 34; enrolled at Greeneville, 12 Nov. 1862; appointed musician, 5 Jun. 1863; captured and paroled at McMinnville, 3 Oct. 1863; detailed as musician with regiment, Jul. - Aug. 1864; absent without leave, 25 Aug. 1864; reported as deserted, 1 Nov. 1864; restored to duty, 29 Mar 1865 by Presidential proclamation; discharged, 2 Aug. 1865; War Department note (18 Dec. 1885): "application to remove desertion charge has been denied".
Skyles, Joshua B.: private, Company E; age: 22; enrolled at Greeneville, 22 Nov. 1862; captured and paroled at McMinnville, 3 Oct. 1863; died at the general hospital at Knoxville, 20 Feb. 1864.
Slimp, John: private, Company H; age: 18; enrolled at Jonesborough, 27 Apr. 1864; resident of Johnson County; mustered in at Loudon, 7 May 1864; deserted at Kingston, 18 Sep. 1864; file contains enlistment papers.
Slimp, William H.: private, Company H; age: 18; enrolled at Kingston, 21 May 1864; born: Johnson County; resides: Watauga County, NC., Boone; mustered in at Kingston, 23 Jul. 1864 deserted at Kingston, 18 Sep. 1864.
Stover, Pleasant: private, Company H; gained as a transfer from the 3rd Tennessee Infantry, 1 Mar 1865; deserted, 15 Mar 1865 at Knoxville; War Department note (17 Oct. 1901): "dishonorable discharge taken under misapprehension of the powers of military authorities, same is void, and final record is that of a deserter".
Smelser, George A.: private, Company F; age: 18; enrolled at Greeneville, 6 Apr. 1863; received $25 bounty; captured and paroled at McMinnville, 3 Oct. 1863; sick in the hospital at Kingston, 23 Nov. 1864 through Feb. 1865; discharged, 2 Aug. 1865.
Smith, George W.: private, Company G; age: 27; enrolled at Jonesborough, 1 Nov. 1862; sick from muster in to 30 Jun. 1863; captured and paroled at McMinnville, 3 Oct. 1863; discharged, 2 Aug. 1865; possible pension case.
Smith, Israel G.: private, Company A; age: 35; enrolled at Greeneville, 13 Dec. 1862; deserted at McMinnville, 29 Sep. 1863; restored to duty from desertion, 28 Jul. 1865; muster roll, Sep. - Oct. 1865, taken prisoner at Cedar Creek, TN., 27 Mar 1864; released on parole, 8 May 1864; War Department note (27 Mar 1864): "captured, Mar 26 or 27, 1864 in Greene County; confined at Richmond 31 Mar 1864; admitted to Hospital # 21 at Richmond, 6 May 1864; returned to quarters, 7 May 1864; reported at Camp Parole, MD., 11 May 1864; sent to Camp Chase, OH., 20 Jun. 1864; furlough for 20 days, 2 Aug. 1864; furlough, 25 Sep. 1864; reported as a deserter, 31 Dec.

1864; restored to duty without trial"; War Department note (13 Jan. 1886): "charge of desertion 24 Sep. 1863 is removed. He was absent without leave from 24 Sep. 1863 to 27 Mar 1864; the charge of desertion 21 Dec. 1864 is removed; he was absent without leave, 21 Dec. 1864 through 3 Feb. 1865, when he rejoined his company"; file contains numerous papers.
Smith, Jackson: private, Company C; age: 18; enrolled at Bulls Gap, 1 Feb. 1864; born: Greene County; mustered in at Loudon, 7 May 1864; deserted, 25 Aug. 1864 at Kingston; returned to duty, 7 May 1865; discharged, 2 Aug. 1865; War Department note (16 Jun. 1887): "man deserted 25 Aug. 1864 and returned 7 May 1865, under Presidential proclamation of 11 Mar 1865; desertion charges waived"; file contains enlistment papers.
Smeltzer, Henry D.: private, Company A; age: 19; enrolled at Sevierville, 1 Dec. 1864; born: Greene County; resided in Sevier County; mustered in at Knoxville, 2 Mar 1865; discharged, 2 Aug. 1865; file contains enlistment papers.
Smith, Alexander: private, Company C; age: 29; enrolled at Greeneville, 6 Apr. 1863; captured and paroled at McMinnville, 3 Oct. 1863; absent through Feb. 1865; reported missing in action, Mar - Apr. 1865; returned to duty from missing in action, 7 May 1865; had to make good time from 20 Aug. 1864, through 7 May 1865 by Presidential proclamation; discharged, 2 Aug. 1865.
Smith, Andrew: private, Company F; age: 19; enrolled at Rutledge, 1 Mar 1865; deserted at Greeneville, 25 Mar 1865.
Smith, Barnet W.: private, Company G; gained as a transfer from the 3rd Tennessee Infantry, 1 Mar 1865; discharged, 2 Aug. 1865.
Smith, Caleb A.: private, Company G; age: 26; enrolled at Elizabethton, 26 Dec. 1863; mustered in at Strawberry Plains, 31 Mar 1865; discharged, 2 Aug. 1865.
Smith, Elijah: **corporal, Company A; age: 21; enrolled at Greeneville, 13 Dec. 1862; captured and paroled at McMinnville, 3 Oct. 1863;** promoted to corporal, 1 Apr. 1864; promoted to 4th corporal, 1 Aug. 1864; died in the hospital at Knoxville, 25 Mar 1865 of asthma; file contains final statements.
Smith, Everet: private, Company H; age: 17; enrolled at Butler, 12 Jun. 1864; resided in Carter County; mustered in at Kingston, 22 Jul. 1864; discharged, 2 Aug. 1865; War Department note (19 Apr. 1889): "application for certificate in lieu of lost discharge, certificate furnished".
Smith, Finley M.: corporal, Company B; age: 35; enrolled at Elizabethton, 14 Jan. 1863; promoted to corporal, 5 Jun. 1863; captured and paroled at McMinnville, 3 Oct. 1863; reported absent on parole through Feb. 1864; died, per report of Bowling Curtis of Company B, at Bristol, TN., 25 Feb. 1864.

4th Tennessee Volunteer Infantry Regiment (USA)

Smith, John: private, Company A; age: 20; enrolled at Greeneville, 13 Dec. 1862; captured and paroled at McMinnville, 3 Oct. 1863; absent on parole through Feb. 1864; discharged, 2 Aug. 1865; pension # 608148.

Smith, John A.: private, Company A; age: 32; enrolled at Greeneville, 13 Dec. 1862; died in Cumberland Hospital at Nashville, 29 Aug. 1863 with gunshot wound in left lung; file contains final statements.

Smith, John P.: second lieutenant, Company B; age: 18; enrolled at Taylorsville, 2 Jun. 1863; sick in the hospital at Knoxville, 27 Apr. 1864; promoted to 4th corporal, 19 May 1864; promoted to sergeant, 10 Sep. 1864; promoted to second lieutenant to fill Lieutenant Singletary's vacancy, 28 Oct. 1864; requested 20 day furlough, 25 Jun. 1865, at Jonesborough to attend to urgent personal business in Johnson County, discharged, 2 Aug. 1865; file contains enlistment papers and other documents.

Smith, John W.: private, Company H; age not stated, enrolled at Elizabethton; 2 Jan. 1865; deserted at Jonesborough, 2 May 1865; file contains enlistment papers.

Smith, Josiah: private, Company C; age: 36; enrolled at Greeneville, 6 Apr. 1863; sick in the hospital, 15 - 30 Jun. 1863; sick in the hospital at Camp Nelson, 19 Dec. 1863; died in Wilson General Hospital, Camp Nelson, KY., of kidney infection, 27 Feb. 1864; file contains final statements.

Smith, Nathaniel: corporal, Company C; age: 44; enrolled at Greeneville, 1 Aug. 1862; appointed 2nd corporal, 24 Apr. 1863; captured and paroled at McMinnville, 3 Oct. 1863; absent on parole through Feb. 1864; reduced in rank, 14 Apr. 1864; on detached service, 14 Apr. 1864 through Apr. 1865 with Colonel Crawford, Chief of Scouts; discharged, 8 Jul. 1865; letter in file, 11 Apr. 1864, from Colonel Crawford, "Private Smith is a good scout, familiar with all roads and paths around Jonesborough, Fall Branch, Kingsport, Blountville .. good scouts are much needed".

Smith, Nathaniel J.: sergeant, Company H; age: 22; enrolled at Elizabethton, 27 Apr. 1864; mustered in at Loudon, 7 May 1864; discharged, 2 Aug. 1865; file contains enlistment papers.

Smith, Robert: private, Company A; muster roll May - Jun. 1865; shows "paroled prisoner", sent to Camp Chase, OH., 11 May 1865; may not be on rolls of Regiment.

Soloman, George A.: private, Company D; age: 18; enrolled at Rutledge, 20 Feb. 1863; mustered in at Strawberry Plains, 31 Mar 1864; deserted at Kingston, 20 Jul. 1864; restored to duty from desertion, 28 Nov. 1864; discharged, 2 Aug. 1865; War Department note (22 Sep. 1886): "charge of desertion 20 Jul. 1864 is removed, he

Soldiers of the Regiment 135

was absent without authority 20 Jul. 1864 to 28 Nov. 1864"; file contains enlistment papers.
Soloman, Jerry M.: private, Company A; age: 18; enrolled at Greeneville, 11 Feb. 1863; captured and paroled at McMinnville, 3 Oct. 1863; absent on parole through Feb. 1864; in arrest, 1 Aug. 1864; discharged, 2 Aug. 1865; pension # 638388.
Soloman, John W.: private, Company A; age: 23; enrolled at Greeneville, 11 Feb. 1863; captured and paroled at McMinnville, 3 Oct. 1863; absent on parole until 15 Mar 1864; prisoner of war note in file: "in charge of provost marshal in Morristown, 15 Mar 1864; sent to Strawberry Plains, 15 Mar 1864; discharged, 2 Aug. 1865; possible pension case.
Soloman, Pleasant W.: private: Company D; age: 20; enrolled at Rutledge, 20 Feb 1863; mustered in at Strawberry Plains, 31 Mar 1864; in arrest, 13 Jul 1864; absent without leave, 20 Jul 1864 through 14 Aug 1864; guarding coal mine, Oct 1864; discharged, 2 Aug 1865; file contains enlistment papers.
Spranger, Joseph: private, Company C; gained as a transfer from the 3rd Tennessee Infantry Regiment, 1 Mar 1865; discharged, 2 Aug 1865.
Speer, John C.: private, Companies H and B; age: 19; enrolled at Taylorsville, 22 Aug 1862; captured and paroled at McMinnville, 3 Oct 1863; transferred from Company H to Company B, 26 Aug 1863; provost guard, Oct 1864; discharged at Knoxville, 8 Jul 1865; file contains enlistment papers; pension # 627415.
Speer, William P.: private, Company B; age: 23; enrolled at Taylorsville, 22 May 1862; died in the hospital at McMinnville, 5 Oct 1863; cause of death not stated; file contains enlistment papers and final statements.
Spencer, Stephen M.: private, Company E; age: 19; enrolled at Greeneville, 5 May 1863; captured and paroled at McMinnville, 3 Oct 1863; absent without leave, 22 Dec 1864; discharged, 2 Aug 1865.
Sprinkle, George W.: sergeant, Company G; age: 35; enrolled at Jonesborough, 5 May 1863; promoted to sergeant, 1 Jun 1863; captured and paroled at McMinnville, 3 Oct 1863; reported absent without leave, 20 Jan 1864; deserted at Camp Nelson, KY., 20 Dec 1863; War Department note (15 Oct 1885): "charge of desertion, 20 Dec 1863 and absent without leave, 20 Jan 1864; are removed. He was absent, sick in the hospital at Camp Nelson, KY., from 20 Dec 1863 to 26 May 1864, discharged with disability, 22 Oct 1864".
Spurgen, Samuel P.: commissary sergeant, Company B; age: 27; enrolled at Blountville, 9 Dec 1862; appointed commissary sergeant, 10 Jan 1863; died in the hospital at Nashville of fever, 21 Aug 1863; buried in Nashville City Cemetery # 5090.

4th Tennessee Volunteer Infantry Regiment (USA)

Squibb, Jospeh M.: private, Company G; age: 21; enrolled at Greeeneville, 20 Feb 1862; absent without leave from muster in until 30 Jun 1863; transferred to the 2nd North Carolina Regiment as Captain, Oct 1863; War Department note (26 May 1888): "was on recruiting duty in East Tennessee and Western North Carolina until 1 Oct 1863 and is discharged from the 4th Regiment, 1 Oct 1863 by order of the Secretary of War; original discharge furnished 1 Jun 1888."

Stallings, Franklin: private, Company B; age: 20; enrolled in Knoxville, 8 Mar 1863; captured and paroled at McMinnville, 3 Oct 1863; discharged, 2 Aug 1863; possible pension case.

Stanfield, Samuel P.: First Sergeant, Company E; age: 21; enrolled at Greeneville, 15 Mar 1863; appointed sergeant, 15 Mar 1863; captured and paroled at McMinnville, 3 Oct 1863; promoted to 1st sergeant, 1 Jul 1864; discharged, 2 Aug 1865; possible pension case.

Stanton, William: private, Company E; age: 23; enrolled at Jonesborough, 18 Dec 1862; captured and paroled at McMinnville, 3 Oct 1863; absent on parole through Jun 1864; reported re-captured and in in prison, Jul - Aug 1864; reported missing in action, Mar - Apr 1865; died while in enemy prison, Andersonville, 6 Apr 1864; War Department note (3 Jul 1866): "died at Andersonville while a prisoner of war, 6 Apr 1864; after capture at McMinnville, sent to Richmond, 9 Feb 1864; sent to Americus, GA., 12 Mar 1864; admitted to hospital at Andersonville, 2 Apr 1864, died of "variola".

Starnes, John A.: private, Company C; age: 20; enrolled at Greeneville, 6 Apr 1863; captured and paroled at McMinnville, 3 Oct 1863; reported absent on parole through Feb 1865; reported missing in action, Mar - Apr 1865; returned to duty from missing in action, 7 May 1865; discharged, 2 Aug 1865; pension # 285807.

Starnes, John A.: private, Company G; age: 19; enrolled at Greeneville, 6 May 1863; captured and paroled at McMinnville, 3 Oct 1863; sick in hospital at Kingston, 24 Nov 1864 through Feb 1865; discharged, 2 Aug 1865.

Stephens, Michael: private, Company H; age: 18; enrolled at Brown's Branch, TN., 7 May 1864; born: Carter County; resident of Spring Bay, IL., mustered in at Kingston, 7 May 1864; deserted, 2 Apr 1865, returned to duty from desertion at Jonesborough, 10 May 1865; discharged, 2 Aug 1865; possible pension case.

Stewart, Samuel: private, Company G, age: 19; enrolled at Newport, 13 Dec 1862; name did not appear on later muster rolls.

Stonecipher, Jacob: private, Company E; age: 25; enrolled at Greeneville, 19 Jan 1863; captured and paroled at McMinnville, 3 Oct 1863; absent on parole through Feb 1864; discharged, 2 Aug 1865; possible pension case.

Stout, John L.: private, Company G; age: 18; enrolled at Taylorsville, 25 Aug 1862; mustered in at Nashville, 27 Aug 1863; captured and paroled at McMinnville, 3 Oct 1863; sick in the hospital at Kingston, 24 Nov 1864 through Feb 1865; died at the hospital in Jonesborough of measles, 1 May 1865; file contains enlistment papers and final statement.
Stout, John M.: private, Company B; age: 23; enrolled at Taylorsville, 1 Apr 1863; mustered in at Loudon, 7 May 1864; died at Kingston, 20 Sep 1864; letter in file (report of board of officers, 11 Sep 1864), "he was shot by Sergeant Powell Renner at Esquire Sevier's, near Kingston, on Sep 10 at 10 o'clock at night while stealing from a sweet potato patch."
Stover, Daniel: Colonel, age: 36; enrolled at Cincinnati, OH., 28 Feb 1862; sick in hospital in Nashville, 30 Jun 1863; resigned because of physical disability, 10 Aug 1864.
Stover, Lephus (Cephus) S.: private, Company F, age: 20; enrolled at Greeneville, 5 Dec 1862; received $25 bounty; absent without leave, 30 Jun 1883 through 29 Feb 1864; reported, deserted at Nashville, 12 Jul 1863; reported as a deserter, 12 Sep 1863; returned to duty from desertion, 12 Apr 1865; in arrest in Greeneville; War Department note (12 May 1897): "deserted 12 Sep 1863; returned to duty 12 Apr 1865 under Presidential proclamation of 11 Mar 1865; the charge of desertion no longer stands, the record that he was absent can not be expunged; a certificate of the soldier's honorable discharge to date, 2 Aug 1865, by reason of muster out was furnished, 18 Sep 1869 by the Commander of the Cumberand".
Taylor, Elijah: private, Company H; age: 29; born: Sullivan County; enrolled at Strawberry Plains, 29 Apr 1864; died in the General Hospital in Knoxville of chronic diarrhea, 19 Feb 1865; file contains enlistment papers and final statements.
Taylor, George: private, Company B and F; age: 20; enrolled in Robertson, IL., 1 Apr. 1863; sick in the hospital at Louisville, Jun. 63 through Aug. 1865; transferred to the 68th (?) in Aug. 1865.
Taylor, Isaac: private, Company B; age: 23; enrolled at Elizabethton, 26 Dec. 1862; absent without leave, 6 Jun. 1863; reported as a deserter at Nashville, 27 Aug. 1863.
Taylor, James M.: sergeant, Company B; age: 24; enrolled at Elizabethton, 8 Dec. 1862; promoted to sergeant, 11 May 1863; captured and paroled at McMinnville, 3 Oct. 1863; discharged, 2 Aug. 1865; possible pension case.
Taylor, James P.: private, Company D; age: 19; enrolled at Mosier's Mill, 28 Feb. 1865; born: Greene County; mustered in at Knoxville, 28 Feb. 1865; deserted at Blue Springs, TN., 20 Mar 1865; file contains enlistment papers.

Taylor, Johnathan: corporal, Company B; age: 18; enrolled at Elizabethton, 24 Nov. 1862; promoted to corporal, 5 Jun. 1863; captured and paroled at McMinnville, 3 Oct. 1863; reduced in rank by own request, May - Jun. 1864; deserted at Kingston, 19 Jul. 1864; restored to duty, 8 Oct. 1864; possible pension case.
Taylor, Joseph P.S.: private, Companies B & F; age: 18; enrolled at Robertson, IL., 1 Apr. 1863; resided in Blount County; sick in the hospital at Louisville, Jun. 1863 through Sep 1863; discharged at Nashville with disability ("phthisis pulmonalis"), 10 Sep 1863.
Taylor, Nathaniel R.: corporal, Company B; age: 41; enrolled at Elizabethton, 24 Nov. 1862; promoted to corporal, 5 Jun. 1863; captured and paroled at McMinnville, 3 Oct. 1863; absent on parole until Feb. 1864; reduced in rank from 4th corporal by own request during May and June 1864; discharged, 2 Aug. 1865.
Taylor, Richard: private, Company H; age not given; enrolled at Kingston, 19 Sep 1864; deserted at Kingston, 26 Sep 1864.
Taylor, Samuel: private, Company H; age: 18; enrolled at Loudon, 1 Jan. 1864; born: Carter County; resided in Rhea County; mustered in at Kingston, 1 Jun. 1864; deserted at Kingston, 15 Aug. 1864; War Department note (30 Apr. 1887): "application for removal of charges for desertion and honorable discharge denied".
Thomas, Hale B.: private, Company E; age: 23; enrolled at Greeneville, 15 Mar 1863; captured and paroled at McMinnville, 3 Oct. 1863; absent on parole until Feb. 1864; sick in the hospital at Knoxville, 28 May 1865; mustered out, 21 Jun. 1865; pension case.
Thomas, Orval B.: private, Company D; age: 24; enrolled at Dandridge, 16 Jan. 1863; discharged, 2 Aug. 1865.
Thomas, Thompson: private, age: 27; enrolled at Greeneville, 15 Jul. 1863; not shown on later muster rolls.
Thomason, James: private, Company F; file only contains prisoner of war record which was blank; pension 454825.
Thomason, Nathan: corporal, Company F; age: 19; enrolled at Greeneville, 15 Apr. 1863; received $25 bounty; appointed corporal, 1 Apr. 1865; discharged, 2 Aug. 1865.
Thomason, James: private, Company F; age: 23; enrolled at Greeneville, 5 Apr. 1863; sick in the hospital in Nashville, 15 - 30 Jun. 1863; appointed corporal, 29 Feb. 1864; promoted to sergeant, 1 Nov. 1864; reduced to ranks, 3 Feb. 1865 by Regimental Special Order; discharged, 2 Aug. 1865.
Thompson, Dutton: private, Company F; age: 26; enrolled in Greeneville, 26 Jan. 1863; absent without leave, 15 - 30 Jun. 1863; captured and paroled at McMinnville, 3 Oct. 1863; absent on parole until Feb. 1864; absent without leave at Loudon, 25 May 1864; reported as a deserted, 31 Aug. 1964; confederate (crossed out)

provost marshal record: shows he was arrested for being a straggler from his unit, 15 Mar 1864; sent to Strawberry Plains, 15 May 1864.
Tilley, Samuel H.: private, Company B; age: 24; enrolled at Taylorsville, 5 Aug. 1863; born: Stokes County, NC.; mustered in at Loudon, 7 May 1864; sick in hospital at Knoxville, 31 Mar 1865 through Jul. 1865; mustered out at Knoxville, 15 Jul. 1865; file contains enlistment papers.
Tilley, William C.: private, Company B; age: 20; enrolled at Taylorsville, 22 Aug. 1862; born: Stokes County, NC.; mustered in at Nashville, 26 Aug. 1863; transferred from Company H to Company B, Aug. 1863; driving team hauling logs, May 1864; prisoner of war record - blank; possible pension case.
Tipton, John W.: first lieutenant, Company H; age: 30; enrolled at Elizabethton, 9 Aug. 1863; was an enlisted man in the 13th Regiment Tennessee Volunteer Cavalry; mustered in to fill original vacancy; commissioned by Governor of Tennessee, 28 Jun. 1864; resigned for "the good of the service", 5 Jun. 1865; file contains numerous papers, including his resignation.
Toncray, Alexander R.: private, Company B; age: 20; enrolled at Elizabethton, 14 Apr. 1863; absent on leave, 15 - 30 Jun. 1863; Captured and paroled at McMinnville, 3 Oct. 1863; during the period, 30 Jun. 1863 through Feb. 1864 on recruiting duty; War Department note (28 Aug. 1882): "discharged, 20 Dec. 1863 for promotion to 1st Lieutenant in Company C, 10th Tennessee Cavalry".
Tramel, Merida: private, Company C; age: 33; enrolled at Greeneville, 16 Nov. 1861; captured and paroled at McMinnville, 3 Oct. 1863; absent on parole until Feb. 1864; discharged, 8 Jul. 1865; possible pension case.
Trantham, Thomas: private, Company A; age: 22; enrolled at Newport, 13 Dec. 1862; appointed 7th corporal, 1 Apr. 1864; absent without leave, 24 May 1864; reduced in rank, deserted at Loudon, 24 May 1864; returned to duty, 1 Feb. 1865; joined from desertion at Jonesborough, 14 May 1865; discharged, 2 Aug. 1865; file contains record of court marital.
Troutman, Henry H.: private, Company H; gained as a transfer from the 3rd Tennessee Infantry Regiment, 1 Mar 1865; sick in Knoxville, 6 Jun. 1865; discharged, 20 Jun. 1865.
Troutman, Jacob A.: corporal, Company H; gained as a transfer from the 3rd Infantry Regiment, 1 Mar 1865; promoted to corporal, 28 Apr. 1865; discharged, 2 Aug. 1865.
Troutman, Jacob C.: private, Company H; gained as a transfer from the 3rd Infantry Regiment, 1 Mar 1865; resident of North Carolina; sick in the hospital at Knoxville, 25 Mar 1865; War Department note (30 Mar 1869): "man discharged 8 Jul. 1865 at Brownlow General

Hospital in Knoxville where he had hospitalized for a accidental gunshot wound on 23 Mar 1865".
Troutman, James W.: private, Company H; gained as a transfer from the 3rd Tennessee Infantry, 1 Mar 1865; resident of Iredell County, NC.: sick in the hospital at Knoxville, 6 Jun. 1865; War Department note (21 Feb. 1888): "mustered out with company and paid to 1 Aug. 1865, see also Company K, 3rd Tennessee Infantry."
Troutman, William S.: private, Company H; gained as a transfer from the 3rd Tennessee Infantry, 1 Mar 1865; sick in the hospital at Knoxville, 6 Jun. 1865; discharged, 7 Aug. 1865.
Trumpeter, Frank: private, Company H; age: 31; enrolled at Kingston, 30 Jul. 1864; resided in Carter County; born: Germany; mustered in at Kingston, 20 Jul. 1864; deserted at Kingston, 28 Sep 1864.
Trusler, Samuel: private, Company H; age: 42; enrolled at Loudon, 10 Jan. 1864; born: Washington County, TN.; mustered in at Loudon, 7 May 1864; discharged, 2 Aug. 1865.
Turner, Thomas J.: private, Company B; age: 32; enrolled at Taylorsville, 22 Aug. 1862; captured and paroled at McMinnville, 3 Oct. 1863; absent on parole until 23 Jan. 1864; returned to Company in Knoxville, 23 Jan. 1864; absent without leave, 17 Apr. 1864; in arrest in Knoxville, 18 Feb. 1865; carpenter at the post, May 1864; scout, Aug. through Oct. 1864; sent to guard prisoners in Knoxville, Dec. 1864; in the military prison in Knoxville, 18 Feb. 1865; through May 1865; charged in General Court Martial (15 Jun. 1865) with larceny, disobeying orders, violation of Article 6 of War; found not guilty of first two charges; received oral reprimand in front of the Regiment; court martial stated that discipline was lax in his Company.
Tyler, Robert: corporal, Company C; age: 19; enrolled in Greeneville, 6 Apr. 1863; appointed corporal, 24 Apr. 1863; died at a private home in Nashville from relapse of measles and dysentery, 11 Jul. 1863; buried at Camp Watkins Grove in grave # 4859; pension # 310403.
Underwood, George: private, Company B; age: 39; enrolled at Knoxville, 8 Mar 1863; sick in the hospital 15 -30 Jun. 1863; captured and paroled at McMinnville, 3 Oct. 1863; discharged, 2 Aug. 1865.
Voncannon, Aaron: private, Company F; age: 31; enrolled at Taylorsville, 13 Sep 1862; received $25 bounty; captured and paroled at McMinnville, 3 Oct. 1863; absent on parole until Apr. 1864; absent without leave, 22 Dec. 1864; absent without leave, 15 Feb. 1865; on detached duty with 3rd North Carolina Infantry, Mar through Jun. 1865; appointed first lieutenant in 3rd North Carolina Infantry, 15 Jun. 1865; possible pension case.
Vanhuss, Daniel S.: corporal, Company B; age: 28; enrolled at Elizabethton, 2 Jun. 1863; promoted to 3rd corporal, 19 May 1864;

discharged, 8 Jul. 1865; file contains enlistment papers; possible pension case.
Vanhuss, John S.: private, Company F; age: 20; enrolled at Greeneville, 15 Nov. 1861; received $25 bounty; prisoner of war record - blank; discharged, 8 Jul. 1865.
Vanhuss, William: first sergeant, Company F; age: 24; enrolled at Greeneville, 15 Nov. 1861; received $25 bounty; appointed corporal, 26 Apr. 1863; promoted to 1st sergeant, 1 Apr. 1865; discharged, 8 Jul. 1865.
Vardaman, Pinckney: private, Company H; age: 20; enrolled at Taylorsville, 8 Apr. 1863; resided in Tellegada County, AL.; sick in the hospital at Greeneville, 8 Jun. 1865; discharged, 2 Aug. 1865; file contains enlistment papers.
Vaughn, James R.: private, Company F; age: 19; enrolled at Louisville on 24 Feb. 1863; no additional records are in the file.
Veach, John: private, Company B; age: 31; enrolled at Louisville, 9 Feb. 1863; deserted at Louisville, date unknown.
Vircy, Henry M.: private, Company H; age: 18; born: Rhea County; enrolled at Kingston, 11 Jul. 1864; resident of Roane County, discharged, 2 Aug. 1865.
Vowell, Clark: private, Company H; gained as a transfer from the 3rd Infantry Regiment, 1 Mar 1865; sick in the hospital at Knoxville, 6 Jun. 1865; discharged, 19 Jun. 1865.
Wagner, John A.: Captain, Company A and H; age: 26; enrolled in Greeneville, 27 Jun. 1863; appointed 3rd sergeant, 1 Apr. 1863; captured and paroled at McMinnville, 3 Oct. 1863; absent on parole until Feb. 1864; promoted to 2nd sergeant, 1 Aug. 1864; promoted to commissary sergeant, 1 Nov. 1864; promoted to Captain, Company H, 5 Jun. 1865 to fill the original vacancy; discharged, 2 Aug. 1865; file contains numerous papers.
Wagner, McCesney: private, Company C; age: 17; enrolled at Jonesborough, 6 Apr. 1863; captured and paroled at McMinnville, 3 Oct. 1863; absent on parole until Feb. 1864; discharged, 2 Aug. 1865; pension case.
Walker, Abner L.: private, Company B; age: 27; enrolled at Taylorsville, 5 Aug. 1863; mustered in at Knoxville, 3 Dec. 1864; discharged, 2 Aug. 1865.
Walker, James W.: private, Company F; age: 26; enrolled at Jonesborough, 3 Oct. 1862; received $25 bounty; shown on the muster roll, 30 Jun. 1863 through 29 Feb. 1864; absent without leave, date not known (record captured); deserted from Nashville, date unknown.
Walker, John S.: private, Company H; age not stated, enrolled at Kingston, 28 Jul. 1864; deserted at Kingston, 15 Aug. 1864.
Walker, Porter J.: private, Company D; age: 18; enrolled at Dandridge, 1 Nov. 1863; mustered in at Knoxville, 8 Feb. 1864; absent

without leave, 12 Jun. 1865; in confinement in Greeneville, 22 Jun. 1865; general court martial: "absent without leave, traveled 3 miles to Jonesborough where he forcefully took a horse from a private citizen"; discharged, 2 Aug. 1865.
Waddel, Madison G.: first sergeant, Company G; age: 20; enrolled at Greeneville, 28 Dec. 1862; promoted to corporal, 1 Jun. 1863; captured and paroled at McMinnville, 3 Oct. 1863; promoted to first sergeant, 29 May 1864; discharged, 2 Aug. 1865; pension # 448,674.
Waddle, Andrew J.: private, Company G; age: 44; enrolled at Jonesborough, 5 May 1863; captured and paroled at McMinnville, 3 Oct. 1863; reported absent on parole through Feb. 1865; reported missing in action, 1 Mar 1865; nothing further in the file.
Waddle, Augustis B.: corporal, Company G; enrolled at Greeneville, 14 Sep 1863; mustered in at Strawberry Plains, 31 Mar 1864; promoted to corporal, 1 May 1864; discharged, 2 Aug. 1865.
Waddle, Benjamin A.: private, Company E; age: 18; enrolled at Greeneville, 22 Jul. 1863; captured and paroled at McMinnville, 3 Oct. 1863; discharged, 2 Aug. 1865; file contains enlistment papers.
Waddle, Benjamin F.: corporal, Company E; age: 20; enrolled at Greeneville, 15 Nov. 1862; promoted to corporal, 26 May 1863; captured and paroled at McMinnville, 3 Oct. 1863; sick in the hospital at Kingston, 25 Nov. 1864 through Feb. 1865; reduced in rank, 30 Mar 1865; discharged, 8 Jul. 1865; possible pension case.
Waddle, Johnathan: private, Company F; age: 36; enrolled at Greeneville, 15 Nov. 1861; received $25 bounty; captured and paroled at McMinnville, 3 Oct. 1863; sick in the hospital at Knoxville, 18 Mar 1865; discharged, 7 Jul. 1865; possible pension case.
Waddle, Martin: private, Company G; age: 29; enrolled at Greeneville, 14 Sep 1863; mustered in at Strawberry Plains, 31 Mar 1864; discharged, 2 Aug. 1865.
Waddle, Stephen: corporal, Company E; age: 39; enrolled at Greeneville, 31 Jan. 1863; captured and paroled at McMinnville, 3 Oct. 1863; promoted to 8th corporal, Apr. 1865; discharged, 2 Aug. 1865; file contains enlistment papers.
Watson, Gordon: private, Company D; enrolled at Rutledge, 6 Jan. 1863; captured and paroled at McMinnville, 3 Oct. 1863; in arrest, 9 Aug. 1864; deserted at Kingston, 2 Oct. 1864; returned from desertion, 14 Jan. 1865; record of general court marital for: Absent without leave and desertion, 15 Apr. 1864 through 26 Apr. 1864; 20 Jul. through 9 Aug. 1864; 3 Oct. 1864 through 13 Jan. 1865; War Department note (23 Mar 1883): "charges of desertion removed, he was absent without leave 1 Oct. 1864 through 14 Jan. 1865"; file contains a letter written by Captain Lawson: "subject desertion at Kingston, and is now in Company A, 9th Tennessee Cavalry where he

Soldiers of the Regiment
143

has committed heinous offenses against citizens"; file contains numerous papers.

Watson, Phillip: private, Company D; age: 19; enrolled at Rutledge, 16 Jan. 1863; captured and paroled at McMinnville, 3 Oct. 1863; absent on parole until 2 Feb. 1864; in arrest, 19 Aug. 1864; sick at Kingston, 25 Nov. 1864 through Apr. 1865; discharged, 2 Aug. 1865.

Weaver, John H.: musician, Company B; age: 18; enrolled at Jonesborough, 28 Dec. 1862; promoted to musician, 5 Jun. 1863; in hospital at Louisville from muster in until Apr. 1863; in arrest, 24 Aug. 1864; sick in Knoxville, 10 Dec. 1864; discharged, 2 Aug. 1865; pension case.

Webster, William R.: private, Company F; gained as a transfer from the 3rd Tennessee Infantry Regiment, 1 Mar 1865; discharged, 2 Aug. 1865.

West, Gillespie: private, Company B; age: 32; enrolled at Maryville, 1 Sep 1863; mustered in at Knoxville, 1 Jan. 1864; absent without leave, 9 Mar 1864; reported as a deserter, 31 Aug. 1864.

Walrath, James E.: private, Company H: age: 21; enrolled at Kingston, 21 Jan. 1864; resident of Wilkes County, NC.; mustered in at Kingston, 21 Jun. 1864; absent without leave, 11 Dec. 1864; deserted at Sevierville, TN., 11 Dec. 1864.

Walter, George W.: sergeant, Company G; age: 18; enrolled at Jonesborough, 5 Nov. 1862; promoted to corporal, 1 Jun. 1863; captured and paroled at McMinnville, 3 Oct. 1863; promoted to sergeant, 1 Mar 1864; sick in the hospital at Knoxville, 27 May 1865; discharged, 19 Jun. 1865; possible pension case.

Ward, Rufus K.: private, Company F; age: 36; enrolled at Rogersville, 15 Nov. 1863; received $25 bounty; absent without leave, 15 - 30 Jun. 1863; deserted at Nashville, 12 Jun. 1863; restored to duty from deserter, Apr. 1865 under Presidential proclamation.

Ward, William: private, Company F; age: 18; enrolled at Newport, 11 Mar 1865; resident of Cocke County; discharged, 2 Aug. 1865; file contains enlistment papers.

Warren, Campbell E.: private, Company H; age not stated; enrolled at Elizabethton, 11 May 1864; deserted at Knoxville, 11 Jul. 1864; War Department note (13 May 1896): "in absence of record of muster into service, he is not regarded as having been in the military service of the U.S. in this organization - see also 13th Tennessee Cavalry"; file contains enlistment papers.

Warren, Elkany: private, Company H; age: 19; enrolled at Strawberry Plains, 29 Apr. 1864; mustered in at Loudon, 7 May 1864; born: Sullivan County; discharged, 2 Aug. 1865; file contains enlistment papers.

Warren, Samuel: sergeant, Company H; age: 18; enrolled at Elizabethton, 29 Apr. 1864; mustered in at Loudon, 7 May 1864;

born: Sullivan County; promoted to sergeant from corporal, 28 Apr. 1865; discharged, 2 Aug. 1865; file contains enlistment papers.
West, John N.: sergeant, Company D; age: 28; enrolled at Rutledge, 1 Feb. 1863; promoted to musician, 3 Jun. 1863; promoted to sergeant, 14 Jul. 1865; discharged, 2 Aug. 1865.
West, Samuel: Captain, Company G; age: 24; mustered in as a first lieutenant, 22 May 1863; commissioned Captain at Louisville to fill original vacancy, 15 Jun. 1863; captured and paroled at McMinnville, 3 Oct. 1863; reported killed by the enemy in Washington County, TN., while collecting his men."
Wester, Daniel C.: private, Company D; age: 20; enrolled at Rutledge, 28 Nov. 1862; captured and paroled at McMinnville, 3 Oct. 1863; discharged, 2 Aug. 1865; possible pension case.
Whalen, Michael: private, Company B; age: 36; enrolled at Elizabethton, 8 Dec. 1862; died in camp at Louisville, 7 Mar 1863; cause of death not stated; War Department note (14 Nov. 1903): "It has been determined by this Department that the named soldier was mustered into service, 19 Feb. 1863 at Louisville, KY."
White, Alfred: private, Company D; age: 18; enrolled at Dandridge, 17 Dec. 1863; mustered in at Strawberry Plains, 31 Mar 1864; discharged, 2 Aug. 1865.
White, David: private, Company D; age: 25; enrolled at Newport, 1 Aug. 1863; born: Fairfield, SC.; resident of Cocke County; mustered in at Strawberry Plains, 31 Mar 1864; reported on picket duty during May 1864 through Feb. 1865; discharged, 2 Aug. 1865; file contains enlistment papers.
White, Hugh: private, Company H; age: 18; enrolled at Elizabethton, 8 May 1864; born: Sullivan County; resided in South Carolina; mustered in at Kingston, 8 May 1864; discharged, 2 Aug. 1865.
White, Joseph: private, Company G; age: 27; enrolled at Greeneville, 22 Jul. 1863; mustered in at Knoxville, 7 Feb. 1864; discharged, 2 Aug. 1865.
White, Levi: private, Company D; age: 24; enrolled at Dandridge, 17 Dec. 1863; mustered in at Knoxville, 8 Feb. 1864; in arrest, 15 Aug. 1864; absent without leave, 20 Jul. through 15 Aug. 1864; discharged, 2 Aug. 1865; file contains 10 day furlough request, dated 7 Jul. 1865, to visit his home in Jefferson County.
White, Richard L.: private, Company H; age: 18; enrolled at Elizabethton, 29 Apr. 1864; born: Sullivan County; mustered in at Loudon, 7 May 1864; deserted at Kingston, 19 Jul. 1864; restored to duty by Presidential proclamation at Taylorsville, 18 Apr. 1865; discharged, 2 Aug. 1865; file contains enlistment papers.
White, Samuel: private, Company F; age: 21; enrolled at Nashville, 4 Jul. 1864; present for duty, 27 Aug. 1863 through Feb. 1865; on

Soldiers of the Regiment 145

detached service with Headquarters, 1st Brigade, 4th Division, 30 Mar 1865; discharged, 2 Aug. 1865; file contains enlistment papers.
White, William: corporal, Company G; age: 19; enrolled at Greeneville, 7 Nov. 1862; captured and paroled at McMinnville, 3 Oct. 1864; absent on parole until Feb. 1864; promoted to 8th corporal, 1 Jul. 1864; discharged, 2 Aug. 1865; pension: 551421/648943.
Whittaker, Jessie: private, Company C; age: 33; enrolled at Greeneville, 6 Apr. 1863; captured and paroled at McMinnville, 3 Oct. 1863; absent on parole until Feb. 1865; reported missing in action Mar 1865; discharged, 2 Aug. 1865.
Wice, James H.: private, Company D; age: 19; enrolled at Newport, 25 Jan. 1863; captured and paroled at McMinnville, 3 Oct. 1863; absent until 8 Mar 1864; absent without leave, 7 Dec. 1864; in hospital at Louisville, 16 Mar 1863; discharged, 2 Aug. 1865.
Wice, Simon: private, Company D; age: 45; enrolled at Newport, 25 Jan. 1863; captured and paroled at McMinnville, 3 Oct. 1863; absent on parole until Feb. 1864; deserted at Kingston, 20 Jul. 1864; restored to duty from desertion, 18 Jun. 1865; discharged, 2 Aug. 1865; War Department note (4 Nov. 1885): "charge of desertion, 20 Jul. 1864; is removed under the provisions of the Act of Congress, 5 Jul. 1884 - he was absent without leave, 20 Jul. 1864; through 13 Jan. 1865; pension # 681195.
Wicker, John M.: private, Company G; age: 20; enrolled at Greeneville, 15 Mar 1863; sick in the hospital from muster in until 30 Jun. 1863; died in New Albany, IN.: War Department note (20 Jun. 1888): "admitted to General Hospital 15 at Louisville, 24 May 1863 with measles and returned to duty, 14 Jul. 1863; admitted to Cumberland General Hospital, Nashville, 8 Sep 1863 with remittent fever; admitted to # 4 General Hospital at Louisville, 26 Sep 1863 with (illegible); he died in the General hospital at Tullahoma, TN., 6 Nov. 1863 of typhoid".
Wicker, Thomas: private, Company G; age: 18; enrolled at Greeneville, 15 Mar 1863; sick in the hospital from muster until 30 Jun. 1863; captured and paroled at McMinnville, 3 Oct. 1863; absent on parole until Feb. 1864; sick in the hospital at Kingston, 7 Sep 1864 through Feb. 1865; discharged, 2 Aug. 1865; possible pension case.
Wiemes, John A.: private, Company A; age: 23; enrolled at Loudon, 1 Sep 1863; born: Greene County; mustered in at Loudon, 7 May 1864; sick in the hospital at Kingston, 23 Nov. 1864; discharged, 2 Aug. 1865; file contains enlistment papers.
Wilhite, Jeremiah: private, Company E and F; age: 37; enrolled at Greeneville, 15 Mar 1863; transferred to Company F, 29 Apr. 1864; sick in the hospital at Knoxville, Mar and Apr. 1864; sick in the hospital at Knoxville, 1 May 1864; sick in the hospital at Knoxville, 28 May 1865; mustered out 24 Jun. 1865; letter in file: "soldier was

turned over to provost marshal at Murfreesboro, 17 Aug. 1864 for transport to the 4th Regiment".
Wilhite, Samuel S.: private, Company E and F; age: 30; enrolled at Greeneville, 5 Apr. 1863; transferred to Company F, 29 Apr. 1864; absent without leave, 18 Apr. 1864; guarding sick and wounded rebels, Jan. 1864; patient at Hospital # 19, Nashville, Sep - Oct. 1864; file contains nothing more.
Wilhite, James: private, Company F; age: 18; enrolled at Greeneville, 4 Apr. 1864; mustered in at Loudon, 7 May 1864; deserted at Loudon, 20 Jul. 1864; War Department note (11 Mar 1903): "this man deserted 20 Jul. 1864 and enlisted 3 Oct. 1864, in Company S, 13th Tennessee Cavalry, in violation of 22nd (now 50th) Article of War"; file contains enlistment papers.
Wilkerson, Richard T.: private, Company F; age: 22; enrolled at Greeneville, 1 Mar 1863; received $25 bounty; absent without leave, 15 - 30 Jun. 1863; deserted, date unknown, records captured.
Wilson, Alexander P.: second lieutenant, Company H; age: 42; enrolled as a private at Strawberry Plains, 5 Aug. 1863; born: Randolph County, NC.; mustered in at Loudon, 7 May 1864; discharged to accept commission, 11 Oct. 1864; file contains enlistment papers.
Wilson, Andrew E.: private, Company B; age: 24; enrolled at Taylorsville, 25 Aug. 1862; captured and paroled at McMinnville, 3 Oct. 1863; mustered out at Knoxville, 7 Jul. 1865.
Wilson, James M.: private, Company G; age: 23; enrolled at Greeneville, 7 Dec. 1862; sick in the hospital from muster in through 30 Jun. 1863; died at Hospital # 19 in Nashville, 7 Sep 1863 of Typhoid fever; buried in grave # 5187; file contains casualty sheet.
Wilson, Lawrence: private, Company C; age: 27; enrolled at Kingston, 1 Jul. 1864; resided at Taylorsville, Johnson County; born: Lankester, SC.; mustered in at Kingston, 1 Jun. 1864; discharged, 2 Aug. 1865.
Wilson, Madison: private, Company H; age: 18; enrolled at Greasy Cove, TN., 4 May 1864; resident of Johnson County; mustered in at Kingston, 4 May 1864; discharged, 2 Aug. 1865.
Wingler, Marion: private, Company H; age: 19; enrolled at Kingston, 1 May 1864; born: Wilkes County, NC.; Resident of Sullivan County; in the hospital at Knoxville with measles, 17 Mar 1865; note: hospital record shows him a resident of Watauga County, NC.; discharged, 2 Aug. 1865.
Winslow, Gustavous A.: second lieutenant, Company A; enrolled at Greeneville, 30 Jan. 1863; appointed 4th sergeant, 10 Apr. 1863; promoted to 5th sergeant, 29 Aug. 1863; captured and paroled at McMinnville, 3 Oct. 1863; promoted to 1st sergeant, 1 Apr. 1864;

Soldiers of the Regiment

commissioned second lieutenant, 13 Jun. 1864; in arrest, 29 Dec. 1864; resigned for the good of the service, 20 Jan. 1865.
Williams, Alfred: private, Company C; gained as a transfer from the 3rd Regiment Tennessee Infantry, 1 Mar 1865; forfeits 17 months pay and allowances and held to make good lost time; had deserted 20 Aug. 1862; discharged, 2 Aug. 1865.
Williams, Isaac: private, Company E; enrolled at Elizabethton, 24 Nov. 1862; captured and paroled at McMinnville, 3 Oct. 1863; discharged, 2 Aug. 1865.
Williams, Jacob: private; Company C; gained as a transfer from the 3rd Regiment Tennessee Infantry, 1 Mar 1865; forfeits 17 months and 20 days pay and allowances and held to make good lost time; had deserted 20 Aug. 1862; discharged, 2 Aug. 1865.
Williams, James: private, Company C; gained as a transfer from the 3rd Regiment Tennessee Infantry, 1 Mar 1865; forfeits 17 months pay and allowances and held to make good lost time; discharged, 2 Aug. 1865.
Willis, John H.: private, Company H; age: 20; enrolled at Kingston; 16 Nov. 1864; born: Washington County; mustered in at Knoxville, 3 Dec. 1864; resident of Marion County, VA.; absent without leave, 25 Feb. 1865; deserted at Moses Mill, TN., 25 Feb. 1865.
Wilson, Alexander B.: first lieutenant, Company F; age: 25; enrolled at Greeneville, 6 Apr. 1863; received $25 bounty; promoted to 1st sergeant, 26 Apr. 1863; captured and paroled at McMinnville, 3 Oct. 1863; promoted to second lieutenant, 5 Oct. 1864; commissioned first lieutenant, 13 Feb. 1865; responsible for ordnance since 19 Feb. 1865; discharged, 2 Aug. 1865; possible pension case.
Wood, Charles H.: private, Company H; age: 18; enrolled at Nelson County, KY., 19 Mar 1863; received $25 bounty; captured and paroled at McMinnville, 3 Oct. 1863; absent until Feb. 1864; deserted at Nashville, 6 Feb. 1864.
Wood, Jepitha: corporal, Company D; age: 23; enrolled at Newport, 27 Jan. 1863; promoted to 8th Corporal, 20 Jul. 1864; discharged, 2 Aug. 1865; pension # 431764.
Wood, William A.: private, Company G; age: 18; enrolled at Greeneville, 18 Feb. 1865; mustered in at Knoxville, 2 Mar 1865; discharged, 2 Aug. 1865; file contains enlistment papers.
Woolsey, John P.: private, Company C; age: 32; enrolled at Athens, TN., 24 May 1863; died in Hospital # 14 at Nashville, 25 Jun. 1863 of diarrhea; buried City Cemetery, Nashville; file contains final statements.
Woolsey, Stephen D.: private, Company G; age: 18; enrolled at Strawberry Plains, 14 Apr. 1864; resident of Greene County, mustered in at Loudon, 7 May 1864; died of pneumonia at Regimental Hospital

in Jefferson County, 24 Jan. 1865; mother: Alice Woolsey, Greene County; file contains enlistment papers.

Wyatt, James B: private, Company B and F; age: 24; enrolled at Taylorsville, 30 Aug 1862; captured and paroled at McMinnville, 3 Oct 1863; absent on parole through Mar 1865; reported missing in action, Apr 1865; transferred to Company F, 29 Apr 1864; note in file: "was absent on parole since 3 Oct 1863; was appointed Captain in the 13 Tennessee Cavalry, 2 Feb 1864; mustered in the 13th Cavalry, 15 May 1864"; Special Orders, Headquarters Army (16 Jun 1869): "mustered out of the 4th Regiment and honorably discharged 14 May 1864; mustered in Company M, 13th Cavalry".

Wykel, James D.: sergeant, Company F; age: 26; enrolled at Greeneville, 6 Apr. 1863; appointed 2nd sergeant, 26 Apr. 1863; no additional comments; discharged, 2 Aug. 1865.

Yarber, Tolbert C.; private, Company D; age: 25; enrolled at Dandridge, 3 Jan. 1863; captured and paroled at McMinnville, 3 Oct 1863; absent on parole until Feb. 1864; deserted at Kingston, 20 Jul. 1864; restored to duty from desertion, 22 Jan. 1865; discharged, 2 Aug. 1865; note in file: "man had family within rebel lines, left to take care of them, would have returned immediately but was cut off by the rebels"; pension # 723709 (85855)

Yoakley, Thomas: private, Company C; age: 38; enrolled at Greeneville, 6 Apr. 1863; captured and paroled at McMinnville, 3 Oct 1863; absent until Apr. 1864; sent to hospital at Uniontown, TN., 7 Apr. 1864; absent in the hospital until Jun. 1864; provost marshal record: "arrested as a straggler from his command 15 Mar 1864, sent to Strawberry Plains"; pension # 588938.

Musician Thomas C. Hart

Name Index

Adams, Abraham 48 Gillespie 48 James C. 48 Wiley 48
Adkins, Caloway 48 Calvin 48 Levi 48
Adkinson, William 48
Alexander, Andrew J. 48 Jeremiah 48
Allen, John M. 48 John W. 49 Lieutenant 14 15 Samuel H. 49 William C. 35 49
Altum, Spencer 49
Ambers, James 49
Amitage, Isaac A. 49
Ammen, General 26 31
Ammons, General 30
Anderson, King D. 49 Thomas 49
Arington, Willis 49
Armitage, Isaac A. 35 49
Armstrong, Alexander 49
Arney, Alfred J. 49
Arnold, Seth 49
Arowood, Samuel 49
Arrendell, William 50
Ashley, Benjamin H. 50
Aston, James M. 50
Atkinson, William E. 50
Ausborn, Daniel 50
Babb, Abner 50 Barnet 50 Charles 50 James W. 50 Martin V. 50 Samuel H. 50
Bagwell, Hiram 50
Baker, James A. 50 Robert N. 51
Baldwin, Drewry P. 51
Bales, Abner C. 51 Henry H. 51 Lewis R. 51
Balinger, William H. 51

Bandy, James P. 51
Banner, William D. 51
Barnes, Allen R. 51 Isaac N. 51 James H. 51 John L. 51 Madison M. 51
Barnett, Maridy 51
Basket, Burton S. 52
Bates, Adam 52 John 52
Baxter, Levi W. 52 Samuel H. 52 Thomas 52
Bayles, Abner B. 52
Beals, Henry H. 52
Bebusk, Elisha K. 70
Bell, Elbert 52
Bellomy, Hiram P. 52
Belt, Robert C. 52
Benjamin, J.P. 6 7
Benner, John 52 William 52
Berry, John D. 53
Bibens, John 53
Bible, Christian 53 John 53 Noah 53 Phillip 53
Bibons, John 53
Bird, Jacob N. 53 James 53
Bishop, Richard M. 53
Black, John W. 54
Blackburn, Captain 14 15 Richard W. 54 W.P. 54
Blaser, Christian 54
Blazer, Daniel 54 Eranens 54 Jacob 54 Peter 54 Phillip 54 Samuel 54 Soloman 54
Blevens, Allen 54 Dillens 55 Henry 55 James C. 55 Lune B. 55 Thomas 55 William H. 55
Boatman, Nathan A. 55
Bobb, Abner 55

4th Tennessee Volunteer Infantry Regiment (USA)

Bogart, William 55
Bohanon, John 55
Bolian, James 55
Boring, John W. 55
Boring, Thomas 55
Bowers, Henry N. 56
Bowler, William A. 56
Bowlin, Asa 56
Bowman, Andrew 56 Isaac J. 56 John 56 Joseph 56 Martin 56 Sparling 56 Thomas J. 56 William 56
Boyd, James I.R. 36 James J. 56
Boyle, General 31
Bozen, R.C 8
Brackett, A.B. 13
Bradshaw, George 56 John 56 John E. 57 William E. 57
Brandon, Craigue 57
Breiden, Augustus H. 57
Brimer, Robert 57
Brisandine, Thomas J. 57
Britt, Wilson 57
Britton, George E. 57 Theophilus 39 57 Valentine S. 58 William H. 58
Brock, John 58
Broglin, Tilman 58
Brooks, David J. 58 Marion W. 58 Stephen P. 58 Thomas 58
Brookshire, Joel 58
Brown, Bird W. 58 Elijah K. 58 Felix 59 Foster 59 Henry 59 Isaac W. 59 James D. 59 Newton D. 59 Robert 59 Theiphilus 59

Browning, Robert A. 59
Brownlow, William G. 4 5 10
Broyles, Adam F. 60 Anderson S. 60 Archibald 60 George F. 60 Isaac W. 60 King H. 60 Simeon 60 Thomas 60 Thomas N. 60 William 57
Brumly, David 60
Buck, Osborn D. 60
Buckner, Joseph/Jasper 61 Robert H. 61 Samuel 61
Bulden, Drewrey P. 61
Burgner, Joseph 61
Burlison, Benjamin 61
Burrell, William 61
Butler, West S. 61
Campbell, James M. 61 John H. 61 Meredith Y. 62 Rankins 62 Smith 62
Cannon, Joseph 62
Canon, Joseph 62
Canter, William 62
Carriger, Nicholas 62
Carroll, William C. 62
Carson, Tipton 62
Carter, James 27 28 29 31 James L. 34 62 Joseph F. 63 Landon 63 Robert C. 63 Robert J. 38 Russell B. 63 R.C. 19 William 63 Young 63
Casteel, Jeremiah 63
Cate, Elijah 64
Cavener, William 33 64
Chedester, Ezra B. 64 George 64 James H. 64
Chockley, Joseph W. 44 64
Christmas, William W. 64

Name Index

Clawson, George W. 64
Clay, John H. 64
Clem, John 64
Click, Green 42 64 Harvey D. 65 James R. 65 John L. 65 Levi D. 65 Marion F. 65 Washington 65
Cline, Alfred J 65 Charles C. 65 Peter 65
Cloyd, David 65
Colbock, Peter 65
Cole, Anderson L. 65
Collet, James M. 66
Combs, William 66
Cook, Augustus S. 66 John L. 66 John T. 66 Thomas J. 66
Cooke, James M. 66
Cooter, Phillip 66
Corcoran, Edward 66
Cotter, Mervin E. 66 William 66 William H. 66
Courtney, James 66
Cozart, John M. 64
Crabtree, Alexander B. 67 Jacob 67
Crawford, John H. 67 Martin 67 Thomas 67
Creswell, John E. 67
Cross, Joseph 67
Crosswhite, Alfred C. 67 John M. 67 Thomas J. 67 William C. 68
Crudgeion, George 68
Crum, Andrew 68 Emanuel 68 Michael L. 68
Crumley, Frederick 68 John 68 Rufus 68
Crye, Hugh 68

Curtis, Archibald 68 Bowling 68 John 68
Cutshall, James G. 69
Daniel, Isaac 69 John 69 Levi N. 69 Marcus 69
Dave, John 69
Davenport, Silas B. 69
Davidson, General 18
Davis, James 69 James A. 69 John M. 69 Phillip 69 Samuel B. 70 Thomas 42 70 Travis D. 70 William J. 70
Day, James R. 70
Dearstone, Christopher 70
Debus, Elisha K. 70
Deerstone, Isaac 70 Jacob 70
Dempsey, James 70
Dobson, James H. 70 Joseph W. 70 Robert M. 43 71
Dodd, Andrew J. 71 Joseph 71
Dogget, William A. 71
Donally, James C. 71
Donnelly, John M. 71
Doston, Samuel A. 71
Driskell, James 71
Dryman, John 71
Dunbar, George 71 George W. 71 William A. 71
Duncan, Pharo 72 W.H. 8
Dunkin, John 72
Dunkins, Joseph 72
Duvall, B.H. 8
Dyer, Taylor 72
Dykes, Abraham 72 Jasper 72 Jesse R. 72 Joseph 72
Eakin, Hugh M. 72 John W. 72
Earnest, Oliver P. 72

4th Tennessee Volunteer Infantry Regiment (USA)

Easterly, Abraham H. 73
Rufus 73
Eastridge, Joel 73
Edington, John H. 73 William 73
Edmonds, Elmore 73
Eggers, Joel 73
Eisenhour, Martin 73 Powell 73
Elder, Casper 73 William R. 74
Ellenburge, William 74
Ellis, Benjamin 74 Daniel 11 Isaac 74
Ellison, Benjamin 74
Elrod. Joseph 74
Emeret, William 74
Emmert, James C. 74
Ervin, Joseph 74
Estep, Henry C. 73 Ransom 73 William 73
Fair, George W. 74
Fanning, William 75
Fannon, William 75
Farguharson, Robert J. 32 75
Farnsworth, Joseph 43 75
Farnsworth, Lieutenant 14
Farris. John 75
Farrow. John W. 75
Faun, Adam 75
Fauver, Isaac 75
Fawver, John A. 75
Feathers, John C. 75
February, Joseph A. 33 76
Fellers, Jackson G. 76
Fields, John H. 76
Fincher., Samuel M. 76

Fletcher, Andrew J. 76 John 76
Fondren, Andrew C. 76 James 76
Ford, Alexander 76 John S. 76
Forrest, General 16
Forrester, John H. 77
Forster, James 77 William 77
Fortner, Jacob L. 77 John 77 Pleasant 77
Foster, Joseph A. 77 Samuel 77
Foust, Daniel 77 James 77
Fowler, John 77 Richard M. 78 William C. 78
Fox, John W. 78 Robert M. 78
Francis, Andrew J. 78
Frazier, Abner J. 78 Abner J. 42
French, Henry C. 78 Oliver T. 78
Fritz, Thomas 78
Fugatt, Andrew J. 79
Gaby, Henry H. 79
Galyon, Jasper R. 79
Garland, James D. 79 Mordica 79 Prior L. 79
Garner, James C. 79 John G. 79
Gass, Charles 79 David A. 79 George 79
Gaut, Judge 15
Gentry, James 79
George, William H. 79
Gfellers, Henry 80 Joseph 80 Madison 80 Thomas 80 Washington 80

Name Index

Gibson, Pleasant 80 Thomas 80 William 80
Gillsepie, Colonel 18
Gilmore, Samuel 80
Gleason, John 80
Glover, Daniel 80
Goan, William M. 80
Goddard, C. 20
Good, Hartsell 80 Nathan 81
Gosnell, Rufus 81
Gourley, William M. 81
Grace, David L. 81
Graham, Alexander 81 Emanuel 81 George J. 81 William 81 William A. 81
Grainger, General 13 14
Grant, General 10
Gray, Andrew C. 81 Isaac B. 82 John 82
Grayson, Benjamin C. 82 James W. 11 James W.M. 82 James W.M. 25 26 Lt Col 20
Green, Enoch 82
Greenlee, James L. Jr. 82 James L. Sr. 82 Mamon 82
Greenway, John H. 82
Greer, Thomas 83
Gregg, Benjamin 83 Henry 83 Samuel 83
Grider, Sidney E. 83 William M. 83
Griffin, James F. 83
Grubbs, Alexander 83 Andrew 83
Guin, Paine E. 83
Guinn, David 83 McDonald 83

Hacker, Newton 84 Newton J. 39
Hair, George S. 84
Hale, Andrew 84 George 84 James M. 84 John C. 84
Hall, Daniel 84 John T. 84 William 84
Hamberd, Adam P. 84
Hamblet, Oliver M. 85
Hampton, Marion 85
Haney, Samuel C. 88
Hannah, William A. 85
Hardin, John 85 Oliver 84
Harmon, Caswell 85 Isaac B. 85 John B. 85 Kennedy B. 85 Robert L. 86 Sparling B. 86 Thomas J. 86 William R. 86
Harold, Albert 85 Elbert 85 John 19 36 86 William C. 85
Harris, 1 2 5 James B. 86 Permenius L. 86
Harrison, Alexander 86 David M. 87 George D. 87 Henry M. 87
Harrold, Jesse E. 87
Hart, Thomas C. 87
Hartley, James 87
Hartman, Enoch 87
Hascall, Milo S. 20
Haun, George W. 87
Hawkins, James 87 John E. 85
Hayes, Jacob M. Sr. 87 William R. 88
Hays, Jacob 88 Nathan 88 Robert 88
Heath, Lieutenant 15
Hendrix, Eli C. 88
Henegar, John H. 88

4th Tennessee Volunteer Infantry Regiment (USA)

Henry, William 88
Herrold, Andrew 88 Joseph E. 88
Hice, Robert 88
Hickey, Edom 88 John 89 Levi M. 89
Hickman, William 89
Hines, John W. 33 John W. 89
Hinkle, Ezra 89 John 89 Josiah 89
Hockerday, Larkin L. 89
Hodge, Ephram F. 90 Francis 89 General 18 Isaac 89 James 89 Joseph R. 90 Littleton 89 Milton 90
Holder, Henderson 90
Holdman, John 90
Holloway, James 84
Holly, Jacob 90
Holsinger, George W. 43
Holt, Isaac 90 James 90
Holtsinger, George W. 90
Hopkins, James 90
Horton, James M. 91
House, James F. 91 William C. 91
Housley, Robert W. 91
Houston, Elbert S. 91 James 91 James M. 91
Howard, David L. 91
Howell, William 91
Huddle, Charles W. 91
Huff, Jonas 91 Joseph 92 Thomas 92
Hull, David M. 92 Isaac B. 92
Humphreys, James 92
Hurley, Ruben 92

Hutton, John N. 92 Thomas S. 92
Hyder, Andrew J.F. 92 John W. 92 Joseph 92 Lawson F. 93 Nathaniel K. 93
Ingram, Edmond 93
Inklebarger, Calvin 93
Inman, John 93
Innman, William 93
Ira, James 93
Isley, Martin R. 93
Jackson, Richard R. 93 William W. 93
Jane, Francis M. 93 George 94 Joseph F. 94 Thomas W. 94 W. Alexander 93
Jenes, William 94
Jennings, Elijah 94 George 94 Stephen C. 94
Johnson, Andrew 1 10 11 14 20 41 George W. 94 Governor 19 William L. 94
Johnston, George W. 94
Jones, George 94 Henry D. 95 James C. 95 Samuel A. 95 Samuel J. 95 William P. 95 William P. 40
Justice, Henry D. 95
Karbaugh, Samuel 95 Thomas F. 95 William P. 95
Kelley, Allen J. 96 Joseph C. 96
Kesterson, Patric H. 96
Ketchum, Frank T.D. 19
Keys, Elbert W. 96 John 96
Killgore, Jacob M. 96
King, Andrew J. 96 John T. 96
Kirk, George W. 96

Name Index

Kirksey, Elijah 96
Kite, Aaron D. 96 Alfred C. 97 Daniel C. 97 William B. 97
Knight, J.N. 29 Wesley 97
Lacy, Perry 97
Lambert, John C. 97
Lane, Alexander 97 James M. 97 Richard S. 40 97 William 97
Lawson, Gaines 32 40 97 James M. 98 John 97
Leal, Peter 98
Leathco, William J. 98
Lee, Jordan P. 98
Lemons, William O. 98
Lewis, George S. 98 Thomas 98 William M. 98
Lincoln, Abraham 27 President 10
Linder, William M. 98
Lineback, John 98
Linebaugh, Daniel 98
Linebaugh, John 98
Lintz, Martin L. 99
Lipp, David M. 99
Littrell, James A. 99
Lloyd, Tennessee 99
Locke, Matthew F. 99
Logan, David L. 99
Long, John N. 99 Joseph 99 William A. 99
Love, David 99 John A. 99 Luther M 99
Lovel, John H. 100
Lovett, Charles A. 100
Lowery, James A. 100
Lowry, Samuel 100

Loyd, James 100
Lusk, Landon H.P. 46 100
Luster, Amos H. 100
Lynch, John A. 100
Lynn, William 101
Malcom, Samuel A. 101
Malone, Andrew 101 Daniel C. 101 John H. 101 Joseph 101 Smith H. 101
Maloney, John Q. 101
Mancior, George 102
Manning, James 102
Markland, Nathaniel J. 102 Phillip 102 P.B. 102
Marsh, Mosby 102
Marshall, Joseph 102 Tipton 102
Martin, Colonel 18
Masoner, James H. 45 103 John W. 103
Matherly, Alexander 103 James 103
Matheson, Daniel G. 103 James F. 102
Mathis, Calvin A. 102
Mattesberger, Phillip H. 102
McAn, Anslum L. 103
McCampbell, Alexander 103
McCarny, Robert C. 103
McClaughlin, Nelson 105
McCloud, William 103
McClung, Patrick A. 104
McConnel, James C. 104 John 104
McConnell, Joseph H. 104
McCooley, Frank 104
McCoy, George A. 104 James W. 104

4th Tennessee Volunteer Infantry Regiment (USA)

McDarmon, Uriah H. 104
McGhee, John A. 104
McGinnes, George 104
McKinney, Pleasant 104 Ransom 104 William 105
McManes, George W. 105
McNease, Henry 105 James B. 105
McQuown, John R. 105
Mercer, Charles 105 David W. 105 Elijah M. 106 Joseph F. 105 Thomas L. 106
Michaels, David 106
Middleton, Tarlton A. 106 Tarlton A. 36
Milan, John W. 105
Miller, Allen 106 Jeremiah B. 106 John 106 John T. 106 Lawson 107 Robert S. 107 William R. 107
Milton, Colonel 31 Joel 107
Mitchell, James 107 William 107
Montgomery, William T. 107
Moore, George W. 108 John A. 108 John L. 108 Joseph H. 108 William 108
Morefield, Andrew 108 Henry 111 John W. 108 William A. 108
Morgan, George 28 John 108 Joshua 108
Morgan, Wiley 109
Morley, Andrew A. 102 William H. 109
Morrow, John 109 Samuel 109 Thomas J. 109 110

Mostly, Wiley B. 110 Wiley D. 109
Mullins, Aaron A. 110 Aaron S. 109
Munday, William R. 45 110
Murphy, Elbert 111 Elbert S. 111 John 33 111 Kemp 111
Nance, Henry 111
Nave, Joel 110
Neace, John T. 110
Nease, Adam 110 Andrew Jr. 110 Andrew Sr. 110 John 111 Reuben 111 William F. 111
Nelson, Henry F. 111 Ira G. 112 Robert 112 T.A.R. 4 5 William R. 112
Newberry, Elias B. 112 Henry G. 112 Richard 112 William S. 112
Nichols, William B. 112
Noe, William H. 112
Nolen, William N. 112
Norris, Jacob H. 112
Northington, Cornelius 112 Hector 113 Samuel F. 113
Norwood, Edward 32 113
Nott, Mason 113
Noxon, S.M. 19
Ogg, Elijah D. 113
Olliver, John 113
Ottinger, George 113 Henry 113 Johnathan 113 Jonas 114 Michael 114 Peter 114 Phillip H. 114 Thomas 114
Overbey, William P. 114
Overholce, James W. 114
Owens, William 114

Name Index

Palmer, John B. 22
Park, William F. 114
Parker, Elvin 114
Parrott, Green 115
Partin, Mathew J. 115
Patterson, Edly A. 115
  George 115 Judge 8
  Michael L. 13 16 19 21 25 26
  30 31 115
Patty, William 115
Payne, George M. 115
Pearce, Nathan J. 115
Pemberton, Thomas 115
  Welcome A. 115
Penney, George W. 116
Penneybaker, Isaac S. 116
Peoples, David H. 116
Peters, Andrew C. 116 David
  F. 116 Frederick W. 116
  John 116
Phillips, Albert 116 Andrew E.
  116 Franklin 117 James B.
  117 Jesse 117 John 117 John
  C. 117 Johnathan 117
Pickens, Colonel 8
Pickering, Enos 117 John 117
  Levi 19 41 117
Pierce, Andrew 117 Christian
  A. 115 Isaac N. 118 James
  D. 118 John L. 118 John T.
  46 118 Pulaski L. 118 Robert
  S. 118 Samuel D. 118
Pierson, John T. 118
Pine, John 118
Piper, Charles W. 45 118
Pleasant, William H. 119
Poe, William 119
Pollard, Humphrey 119

Porter, George L. 119
Potter, Andrew 119 Reuben
  119
Powers, William 119
Presley, John 119
Price, Jasper N. 120
Price, John E. 120
Price, Marcus F. 120
Proctor, Joseph K. 120
Rader, George H. 120 Isaac F.
  120 Peter R. 120 Powell 120
Ragsdill, John W. 120 William
  120
Rambo, James F. 121 William
  H. 121
Randles, John B. 121
Rankins, John C. 121
Rash, Linza R. 121
Ray, Emanuel M. 121 Joseph
  121 William N. 121
Reagan, James M. 121
Reaser, William B. 121
Rector, John 122
Reecer, Archibald 122
Reed, William 122
Reeser, Daniel M. 122
Reesor, Arnold M. 122
Reeves, George W. 122 Major
  21 Thomas H. 19 26 27 31
  40 122
Reid, James J. 122 Robert B.
  123
Remine, Flavius J. 123 William
  C.P. 123
Renner, John 123 Moses 123
  Powell 123 William H. 124
Reynolds, John B. 124 Joseph
  124 Joshua 124

Richards. George W. 125
James 123
Richardson, David 123 Elijah 124
Ricker, Frederick 124
Riddle, John H. 124
Rider, Van B. 124
Rightsell, William C. 125
Ripley, Sylvester B. 125
Roach, Daniel L. 125
Roarark, Joshua 125 W.M. 125
Roberts, Charles W. 125
James 125 Thomas 125
William G. 125
Robertson, Daniel 125
Nathaniel T. 126 William D. 126
Robinson, James C. 126 John 126 John W. 126
Rogers, Jackson 126 James 127 Jesse 126 John 126 John F. 126 Samuel B. 127
Roggers, William C. 127
Rominger, L.A. 127
Rowe, Thomas Y. 127
Rush, David 39 127
Russell, John L. 127
Ryan, George W. 127
Salts, Robert M. 127
Sample, Robert R. 128
Sauterfield, Martin V. 128
Scott, George 128 James C. 128 Thomas 128 William T.L. 128
Scudgington, Alexander 128
Seamore, Caswell 128

Seaton, Benjamin F. 128 Isaac 128 James M. 129
Self, Lewis F. 33 129
Sellers, Abram 129
Severs, William 129
Sexton, Daniel W. 129 Henry 129 James A. 129 Ransom 129
Shanks, Andrew J. 129 James P. 129
Shaver, Aaron A. 130 Andrew J. 130 George W. 130
Shaw, Thomas G. 130
Sheddan, Thomas W. 130
Sheddin, William F. 130
Shell, Samuel 130
Shelton, Nelson 131
Shinliver, Charles 131
Shoemaker, John 131
Shoven, W.W. 131
Singletary, Frederick S. 34 36 131 F.S. 19
Skyles, John W. 132 Joshua B. 132
Slimp, John 132 William H. 132
Smelser, George A. 132
Smeltzer, Henry D. 133
Smith, Alexander 133 Andrew 133 Barnet W. 133 E. Kirby 9 Elijah 133 Everet 133 Finley M. 133 George W. 132 Israel G. 132 Jackson 134 John 134 John A. 134 John P. 37 134 John W. 134 Josiah 134 Nathaniel 134 Nathaniel J. 134 Robert 134

Name Index

Soloman, George A. 134 Jerry M. 135 John W. 135 Pleasant W. 135
Speer, John C. 135 William P. 135
Spencer, Stephen M. 135
Spranger, Joseph 135
Sprinkle, George W. 135
Spurgen, Samuel P. 135
Squibb, Joseph M. 136
Stallings, Franklin 136
Stanfield, Samuel P. 136
Stanton, Edwin M. 11 12 E.M. 27 William 136
Starnes, John A. 136
Stephens, Michael 136
Stewart, Samuel 136
Stonecipher, Jacob 136
Stoneman, George 21 22
Stout, John L. 137 John M. 137
Stover, Cephus S. 137 Colonel 19 20 Daniel 3 12 23 25 28 30 31 137 Lephus 137 Pleasant 132
Sweeney, Robert E. 19 41
Tadlock, Alexander B. 32
Taylor, Elijah 137 George 137 Isaac 137 James M. 137 James P. 137 Johnathan 138 Joseph P.S. 138 Nathaniel R. 138 Samuel 138
Thomas, General 26 Hale B. 138 Orval B. 138 Thompson 138
Thomason, Dutton 138 James 138 Nathan 138

Tilley, Samuel H. 139 William C. 139
Tillson, General 22
Tipton, John W. 46 139
Toncray, Alexander R. 139
Tramel, Merida 139
Trantham, Thomas 139
Troutman, Henry H. 139 Jacob A. 139 Jacob C. 139 James W. 140 William S. 140
Trumpeter, Frank 140
Trusler, Samuel 140
Turner, Thomas J. 140
Tyler, Robert 140
Underwood, George 140
VanHuss, Daniel S. 140 John S. 141 William 141
Vardaman, Pinckney 141
Vaughan, James R. 141
Vaughn, John C. 21
Vircy, Henry M. 141
VonCannon, Aaron 140
Vowell, Clark 141
Waddel, Madison G. 142
Waddle, Andrew J. 142 Augustus B. 142 Benjamin A. 142 Benjamin F. 142 Johnathan 142 Martin 142 Stephen 142
Wagner, John A. 46 John A. 141 McCesney 141
Walker, Abner L. 141 James W. 141 John S. 141 Porter J. 141
Walrath, James E. 143
Walter, George W. 143
Ward, Rufus K. 143 William 143

Warren, Campbell E. 143
Eklany 143 Samuel 143
Watson, Gordon 142 Phillip 143
Weaver, John H. 143
Webster, William R. 143
West, Gillespie 143 John N. 144 Samuel 44 144
Wester, Daniel C. 144
Whalen, Michael 144
Wharton, General 18
Wheeler, General 16 17 18
Whicher, __ 8
White, Alfred 144 David 144 Hugh 144 Joseph 144 Levi 144 Richard L. 144 Samuel 144 William 145
Whittaker, Jessie 145
Wice, James H. 145 Simon 145
Wicker, John M. 145 Thomas 145
Wiemes, John A. 145
Wilhite, James 146 Jeremiah 145 Samuel S. 146
Wilkerson, Richard T. 146
Williams, Alfred 147 Isaac 147 Jacob 147 James 147
Willis, John H. 147
Wilson, Alexander B. 43 147 Alexander P. 146 Andrew E. 146 James M. 146 Lawerence 146 Madison 146
Wingler, Marion 146
Winslow, Gustavous A. 35 146
Wood, Charles H. 147 Colonel 6 Jepitha 147 William A. 147

Woolsey, John P. 147 Stephen D. 147
Wyatt, James B. 148
Wykel, James D. 148
Yarber, Tolbert C. 148
Yoakley, Thomas 148

www.ingramcontent.com/pod-product-compliance
Lightning Source LLC
Chambersburg PA
CBHW070702100426
42735CB00039B/2425